MAYA

MAYA

REVISED AND EXPANDED EDITION

Charles
Gallenkamp
with drawings by
Dolona
Roberts

The Riddle and Rediscovery
of a Lost Civilization

DAVID McKAY COMPANY, INC.   NEW YORK

Frontispiece: Head of a dignitary,
Yaxchilán. (After Maudslay.)

Maya

Library of Congress Cataloging in Publication Data

Gallenkamp, Charles.
  Maya, the riddle and rediscovery of a lost civilization.

  Bibliography: p.
  Includes index.
  1. Mayas—Antiquities.   2. Mexico—Antiquities.
3. Central America—Antiquities.   I. Title.
F1435.G16 1975   972'.004'97   75-30576
ISBN 0-679-50469-9

MANUFACTURED IN THE UNITED STATES OF AMERICA

Design by Bob Antler

10   9   8   7   6

For Tish

Preface

 Since the first edition of this book was
published in 1959, the study of Maya ar-
chaeology has benefited from a tremendous amount of intensive
research. Major excavations have been conducted at Tikal, Seibal,
Altar de Sacrificios, Dzibilchaltún, and several other key sites, adding
significantly to our knowledge of the subject. Information pertaining to
almost every aspect of Maya civilization—particularly its origins,
sociopolitical structure, economy, intellectual achievements, and the
possible causes behind its mysterious decline—has undergone a
sweeping reevaluation. Important ethnological and linguistic studies
involving contemporary Maya Indians were initiated, some of which
bear directly on archaeological problems; and there has been a
substantial increase in the volume of scientific literature concerning
recent investigations.

At the very least these developments made it necessary to update
portions of the original text. However, in view of my desire not only to
incorporate new data, but to amplify certain topics discussed in the

vii

previous version and expand the book's overall scope, the present work far exceeds the usual limits of a revised edition. Although the basic outline remains essentially unchanged, every chapter was enlarged and completely rewritten, three entirely new chapters have been added, and the drawings and photographs were extensively supplemented.

Because of the ever-increasing complexities of Maya archaeology, I have had to be selective—sometimes arbitrarily—in dealing with a topic of such immense potential. For this reason my fundamental approach emphasizes those discoveries, unresolved questions, and current frontiers of research which I consider to be of greatest importance and interest to the general reader. Obviously my indebtedness to the many explorers, scientists, and historians whose efforts made a synthesis of this kind possible is inestimable, and some measure of my debt is reflected in the bibliography.

In particular I want to express my gratitude to the following persons and institutions who assisted me so generously: Douglas W. Schwartz, Director of the School of American Research, Santa Fe; Robert J. Sharer, Associate Curator of the American Section, The University Museum, Philadelphia; the late E. Wyllys Andrews of the Middle American Research Institute, Tulane University, New Orleans; George H. Ewing, Director of the Museum of New Mexico, Santa Fe; Ignacio Bernal, Director of the Museo Nacional de Antropología, Mexico City; Mary Elizabeth Smith, Associate Professor of Art History, University of New Mexico, Albuquerque; Robert Wauchope, Director of the Middle American Research Institute, Tulane University, New Orleans; Stewart Peckham, Curator of the Laboratory of Anthropology, Santa Fe, and its librarian, Evelyn Ely. I am also indebted to the Helene Wurlitzer Foundation of Taos, New Mexico, and the Hillman Foundation of Pittsburgh, Pennsylvania, for financial support which aided me in carrying out field research. Special thanks are due Dolona Roberts for her enthusiastic cooperation in preparing the drawings for this book, and to my wife, Tish, for invaluable help in editing, typing, and proofreading the manuscript, as well as for her unending encouragement throughout the project.

CHARLES GALLENKAMP
Santa Fe, New Mexico

Acknowledgments

Grateful acknowledgments are made to the following for permission to use quotations, photographs, and drawings from their publications:

Archaeology: "The Mystery of the Temple of the Inscriptions," by Alberto Ruz Lhuillier; Carnegie Institution of Washington: *Bonampak, Chiapas, Mexico,* by Karl Ruppert, J. Eric Thompson, and Tatiana Proskouriakoff, and *An Album of Maya Architecture,* by Tatiana Proskouriakoff; *Explorers Journal:* "Balankanche—Throne of the Tiger Priest," by E. Wyllys Andrews; Edward H. Thompson, Andover, Massachusetts: *People of the Serpent,* by Edward H. Thompson; Middle American Research Institute, Tulane University: *The Ethno-Botany of the Maya,* by Ralph L. Roys; New York Graphic Society: *Mexico: Pre-Hispanic Paintings,* preface by Jacques Soustelle; Peabody Museum of Archaeology and Ethnology, Harvard University: *Relación de las cosas de Yucatán,* by Diego de Landa, translated and edited by Alfred M. Tozzer; Rutgers University Press: *Incidents of*

Travel in Central America, Chiapas, and Yucatan, by John Lloyd Stephens, edited by Richard L. Predmore; *The Saturday Evening Post*: "The Mystery of the Mayan Temple," by Alberto Ruz Lhuillier and J. Alden Mason; School of American Research and the University of Utah: *Florentine Codex: General History of the Things of New Spain*, by Bernardo de Sahagún, translated and edited by Arthur J.O. Anderson and Charles E. Dibble; Stanford University Press: *The Ancient Maya*, by Sylvanus G. Morley, Third Edition, revised by George W. Brainerd (Copyright 1946, 1947, and 1956 by the Board of Trustees of the Leland Stanford Junior University); University of Oklahoma Press: *Incidents of Travel in Yucatan*, by John Lloyd Stephens, edited by Victor W. von Hagen; University of Pennsylvania Museum: *The American Collections of the University Museum: The Ancient Civilizations of Middle America*, by J. Alden Mason.

Contents

MAYA

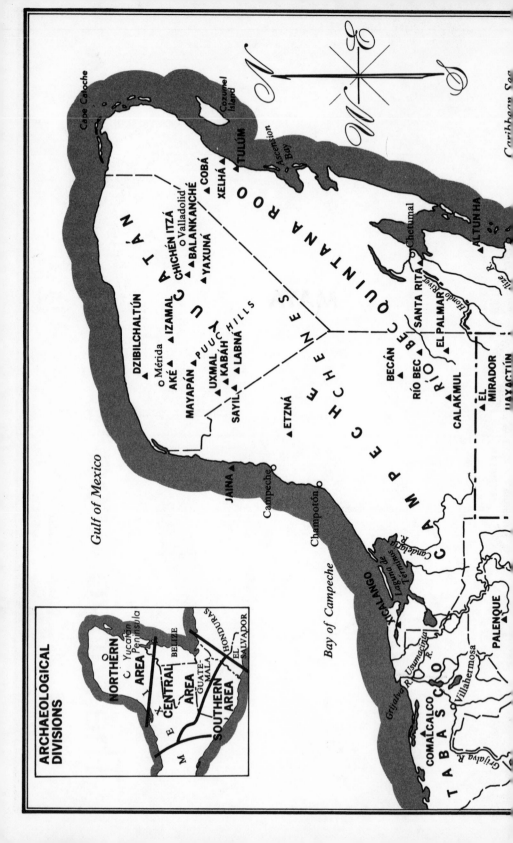

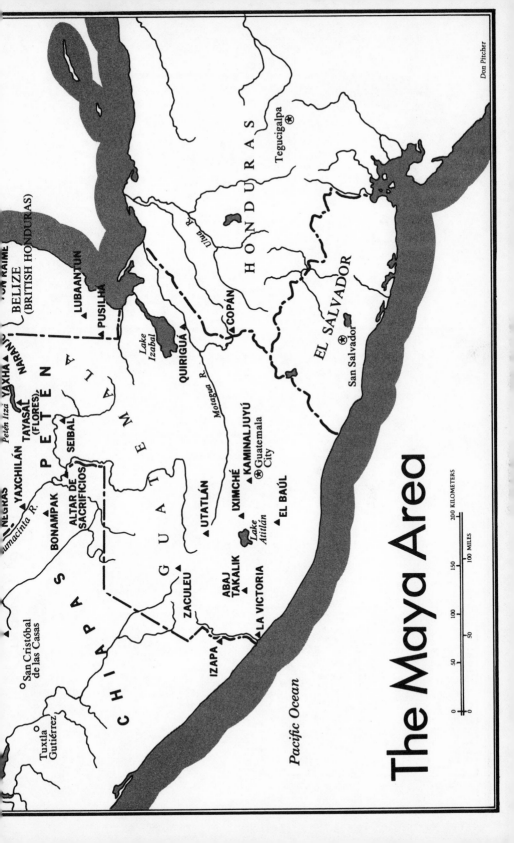

The Maya Area

Pacific Ocean

Don Pitcher

Tuxtla Gutiérrez ○
San Cristóbal de las Casas ○

C H I A P A S

IZAPA ▲
ZACULEU ▲
ABAJ TAKALIK ▲
LA VICTORIA ▲
UTATLÁN ▲
Lake Atitlán
IXIMCHÉ ▲
KAMINALJUYÚ ▲
⊛ Guatemala City
EL BAÚL ▲

NEGRAS ▲
YAXCHILÁN ▲
Usumacinta R.
BONAMPAK ▲
ALTAR DE SACRIFICIOS ▲
SEIBAL ▲

G U A T E M A L A

P E T É N

Petén Itzá
TAYASAL (FLORES) ▲
YAXHÁ ▲
NARANJO ▲

ON KAIMÉ
BELIZE (BRITISH HONDURAS)
LUBAANTÚN ▲
PUSILHÁ ▲

Lake Izabal
QUIRIGUÁ ▲
Motagua R.
COPÁN ▲

Ulúa R.
H O N D U R A S
⊛ Tegucigalpa

EL SALVADOR
⊛ San Salvador

0   50   100   150   200 KILOMETERS
0   50   100 MILES

1

DISCOVERY AND CONQUEST: THE DEATH OF A CIVILIZATION

On the map the area formerly occupied by the Maya comprises the southernmost section of the district known archaeologically as Mesoamerica, the region extending roughly from the drainages of the Lerma and Pánuco rivers in Mexico southward into Honduras and El Salvador.* Encompassing a total expanse of approximately 125,000 square miles, the Maya realm is situated entirely in a tropical zone and consists of essentially two distinct environments—lowlands and highlands—although it is frequently subdivided into three sectors designated as the Northern Lowlands, Southern Lowlands, and Highlands, or alternately as the Northern, Central, and Southern Areas.

Included in the Northern Area are the states of Yucatán, the

---

* In its generally accepted context, the term Mesoamerica (sometimes called Middle America) defines those areas of Mexico and Central America that witnessed the development of highly advanced pre-Columbian civilizations such as the Olmec, Maya, Teotihuacán, Zapotec, Toltec, and Aztec, all of which shared a number of closely related cultural traits.

upper half of Campeche, and the Territory of Quintana Roo in Mexico, which together form part of the Yucatán Peninsula—a thumb-shaped land mass projecting into the Gulf of Mexico usually referred to collectively as Yucatán. Almost imperceptibly this region joins the thickly forested wilderness of the Central Area that stretches from southern Campeche, Tabasco, and eastern Chiapas across the Department of Petén in Guatemala, Belize (British Honduras), and the western edge of Honduras. Immediately to the south lie the rugged, volcano-studded highlands of the Southern Area, embracing southeastern Chiapas, southern Guatemala, and a portion of western El Salvador.

When Spanish explorers first entered this territory early in the sixteenth century, they revealed one of the greatest geographical marvels of their age. Not only did they discover the astonishing splendors of Maya civilization, but they also opened the gateway to all of Mexico and Central America, with its tumultuous landscape, abundant natural resources, and panoply of indigenous peoples. Before them lay an entirely new world—nameless, unmarked on existing charts, and totally unsuspected.

From the outset of their explorations, the Spaniards found evidence of prosperous native kingdoms in the form of gold jewelry obtained in trade from Indians along Mexico's eastern coast. Eagerly they flocked to these shores in the belief that here at last was the legendary El Dorado, which lured a generation of their countrymen onto the unknown Western Sea and ultimately led to the colonization of Latin America. In vain they had searched for the manifestations of this glorious illusion: the golden Temple of Doboyda, the jeweled sepulchres of Zenu, the elusive passage to Cathay and the Spice Islands, and a paradise rumored to exist in the Indies "where the sands sparkled with gems, and golden pebbles as large as birds' eggs were dragged in nets out of the rivers." Now it suddenly appeared as if these desperately sought dreams were about to materialize.

Driven by the restless spirit of adventure, inspired by religious zeal, hungry for the wealth and royal favors to be gained by conquering unclaimed frontiers, the Spaniards—the knights-errant of the Age of Exploration—looked to these newly discovered lands with avid interest, unaware that their quest would soon plunge them into a prolonged death struggle with the Maya and result in the destruction of what was once the most brilliant civilization in ancient America. Nor did they suspect that this was the opening chapter in an historical event of extraordinary magnitude: the conquest of Mexico and Central America by a handful of intrepid Spanish soldiers in the face of overwhelming odds, unfamiliar terrain, and appalling hardships.

So far as we know, the earliest recorded contact with the Maya occurred during the last voyage made by Christopher Columbus to the New World in 1502. Near the island of Guanaja off the northern coast of Honduras, his ships encountered a canoe carrying Indian traders who supposedly came from a province called *Maia* or *Maiam,* the name from which the word *Maya* was subsequently derived. It is not certain whether *Maia* referred to the Yucatán Peninsula or Honduras, and because Columbus sailed east after leaving Guanaja, he never visited the country described by his native informants.

Only vague references to *Maia* as reported by Columbus appeared in contemporary records, and the existence of the Maya did not become known to the outside world until 1517, when three ships commanded by Francisco Hernández de Córdova reached Cape Catoche on the northeastern tip of Yucatán after being blown off course by a storm. Weeks later the survivors of Córdova's expedition— almost dead from wounds, thirst, and starvation—arrived in Cuba with astonishing tales of mysterious cities discovered on Yucatán's coastline and savage battles waged against hoards of Maya warriors, one of which left Córdova himself mortally wounded. Most important, they brought back ornaments looted from Maya temples—necklaces, effigies, and diadems made of copper and low-grade gold.

However inferior the quality of the gold, the Spaniards' avarice was suddenly inflamed. Immediately the governor of Cuba, Diego Valásquez, organized another expedition under the command of his nephew, Juan de Grijalva. Setting out early in April of 1518, Grijalva's ships first reconnoitered Yucatán's eastern coast between Cozumel Island and Ascensión Bay, then retraced Córdova's previous route around Cape Catoche, explored the large inlet known as Laguna de Términos, and journeyed a few miles inland along the Río de Tabasco (later renamed Río de Grijalva), which empties into the Bay of Campeche. Near the mouth of this river the Spaniards encountered a group of Maya from whom they obtained a number of gold objects in trade. Here, too, they heard rumors of the fabulously rich Aztec empire alleged by their informants to be located toward "the direction of the sunset" in a region called *Méjico*. In an effort to verify these intriguing tales, Grijalva sailed up the Mexican coast past the Tonalá, Coatzacoalcos, and Jamapa rivers as far north as the present city of Veracruz. By then the accuracy of the reports could no longer be questioned: at the entrance of the Río Jamapa the explorers met emissaries sent by the Aztec emperor Montezuma to appease them with large quantities of gold—a fatal mistake that was to cost Montezuma his empire and launch the Conquest of Mexico.

Lured by Grijalva's startling revelations, the illustrious conquistador, Hernando Cortés, marched into the heart of the Aztec realm in 1519 with soldiers, artillery, horses, and thousands of Indian allies—mostly Totonacs and Tlaxcalans, whose hatred of the Aztecs prompted them to join the Spaniards' cause—and trampled its glories to dust in one of history's most celebrated military campaigns. Within two years Cortés had defeated the Aztecs' once-feared armies, destroyed their magnificent capital of Tenochtitlán (rebuilt as Mexico City), and looted its treasuries of a fortune in gold, silver, and precious stones. Indeed, his stunning victory quickly opened the way for the tide of conquest and colonization to spread throughout the rest of Mexico and Central America, imposing a "new order" upon their vanquished peoples compounded of greed, exploitation, and the unyielding intolerance of the Spanish Inquisition.

Soon vast sections of the Maya area began to fall under the Spaniards' rapacious yoke. In 1523 Cortés sent one of his captains, Pedro de Alvarado, with a force of approximately 400 soldiers and 20,000 Indian auxiliaries, to conquer Guatemala and El Salvador, an assignment Alvarado carried out with relentless brutality. Early in 1524 an expedition led by Cristóbal de Olid was dispatched by Cortés to colonize Honduras, and although Olid was later killed in an ill-fated rebellion against Cortés, the pacification of Honduras was swiftly completed under Alvarado's direction. And in 1526 a wealthy adventurer named Francisco de Montejo received a royal decree authorizing him to undertake what became the longest and most difficult campaign of the entire Conquest—the subjugation of Yucatán.

Montejo's first colony on Yucatán's eastern coast, established in the autumn of 1527, was promptly decimated by outbreaks of disease, threats of mutiny among his soldiers, and determined native resistance, thus forcing him to withdraw temporarily to Mexico. Three years later, aided by his son, Francisco de Montejo the Younger, he invaded the peninsula from the direction of Campeche and attempted to found colonies in several different locations, including a garrison at the now famous ruined city of Chichén Itzá. Eventually these settlements were also deserted because of unrelenting hardships, constant attacks by the Maya, and the growing disillusionment of his army, leaving the elder Montejo impoverished and bitterly disappointed by his failures.

Not until 1541 did Montejo the Younger, empowered by his aging father to carry on the venture, again return to Yucatán—this time with roughly 350 well-equipped soldiers augmented by a sizable force of Indian allies recruited among a group of Maya known as the Xiu, who had unexpectedly offered their support. A series of skillfully executed military expeditions were sent to subdue those provinces which refused to yield peacefully, and within less than a year, marked by bloody fighting against often superior native armies, Montejo succeeded in conquering the entire western half of the peninsula. Next he selected an ancient town called T'ho as the site of a permanent capital, and on January 6, 1542, he founded the "Very Noble and Loyal City of Mérida." Using this as a base of operations, Montejo gradually extended his campaign into the hostile districts to the north and east, and by the end of 1546 his troops had gained control over virtually all of Yucatán.

Only one part of the Maya area still remained completely free of Spanish encroachment—the jungle-covered lowlands of northern Guatemala now comprising the Department of Petén. Even though much of this forbidding wilderness was then uninhabited, scattered groups of Maya lived elsewhere in its remote depths, the largest of which were the Itzá, whose capital of Tayasal was situated on an island in Lake Petén Itzá. Yet despite its isolation, the rapid pace of colonial expansion on the Petén's borders eventually brought the full impact of the Conquest upon the Itzá with shattering force. In 1618 two Franciscan friars, Juan de Orbita and Bartolomé de Fuensalida, attempted unsuccessfully to introduce Christianity at Tayasal. Four years later another missionary named Diego Delgado was taken captive and sacrificed by the Itzá, and when subsequent efforts at peaceful conversion failed, the governor of Yucatán, Martín de Ursúa, resolved to subdue the Itzá by military action.

Early in March of 1697, Ursúa arrived at Lake Petén Itzá with an impressive array of infantrymen, cavalry, artillery, and Indian auxiliaries. After constructing a large galley from which Tayasal could be assaulted by water, he launched an attack that quickly turned into a massacre. With their infantry crowded aboard the ship, the Spaniards approached Tayasal under a protective barrage of musket fire. Soon an advanced guard of soldiers swarmed onto the island and engaged its defenders in hand-to-hand combat, while the gunners on the boat continued firing at the terrified Indians with devastating effect. Hundreds were either killed outright or drowned as they sought to escape by swimming across the lake, and within a matter of hours the Itzá legions were hopelessly routed, enabling Ursúa and his victorious army to occupy the city.

With Tayasal's swift demise the last stronghold of sustained Maya resistance was decisively crushed, and its survivors were inexorably consigned to the ominous destiny already inflicted upon the rest of their kinspeople. Marching behind the banner of "God, Glory, and Gold," the conquistadors, equipped with awesome weapons—arquebuses, artillery, cavalry, metal armor, crossbows, and swords, none of which the Indians had seen before—had accomplished their goals with incredible efficiency. In their wake came hoards of colonists whose dreams of empire would wreak further havoc upon the Maya, reducing them to a life of persecution, servitude, and poverty. Even the remarkable legacy of their past as embodied in ruined cities and plundered works of art rapidly faded into oblivion in the pitiless struggle for survival that now ensued.

From the beginning of Spanish supremacy in Mexico and Central America, the relegation of the Indians to various forms of slavery and the confiscation of their lands became an accepted practice. Initially the principal instrument for achieving these ends was the so-called *encomienda*. Under this quasi-feudal system the conquistadors were awarded land grants together with the services of natives who became vassals of the landowners. Indians thus conscripted were transplanted

Figure from a ceramic vase, Nebaj, Guatemala.

from their villages to the estates of the *encomenderos,* where in addition to supplying labor for mining, construction projects, cultivating crops, and household duties, they were required to pay regular tributes in such products as cloth, cacao, game animals, fowl, cotton, wax, and salt.

In theory the granting of an *encomienda* imposed certain obligations on the landowner regarding the humane treatment of native workers. Yet these were frequently ignored or circumvented, and the conditions under which the Indians existed quickly became intolerable. Along with the burden of enforced labor and tributes, any expression of resistance or disloyalty toward the *encomenderos* brought severe punishment in the form of beatings, imprisonment, torture, or execution. Quite often Indians guilty of "rebellious" acts were sold into outright bondage, and the ruthless exploitation of slaves grew into a profitable business, resulting in incredible tyranny and suffering.

Due largely to agitation for reform by certain factions within the Dominican Order (led by the brilliant humanitarian Bartolomé de Las Casas), the "New Laws of the Indies" were enacted in 1542, aimed at abolishing both slavery and the *encomiendas,* neither of which was looked upon favorably by Spain's emperor, Charles V. But the outcry by colonists against these changes was so vehement that the New Laws were later modified, allowing many *encomiendas* to endure well into the eighteenth century. And despite the permanent outlawing of slavery, subtler forms of bondage survived in the Maya area until the late 1800s—namely "debt peonage" and enforced taxation whereby laborers were indentured to the landowners under false pretenses.

Even more serious than these abuses, however, was the introduction of European diseases against which the Maya had developed no natural immunity. Among the worst were smallpox, influenza, yellow fever, measles, tuberculosis, and amebic dysentery; and many researchers believe malaria and hookworm, extremely prevalent in the region today, may originally have been brought to America by slaves from Africa, where both diseases are endemic. Entire towns were repeatedly decimated by epidemics—particularly of smallpox, yellow fever, and measles—resulting in appalling fatalities throughout the area. In fact, so horrifying were the effects of European diseases upon the Maya that some authorities estimate the population of certain tribes was reduced by seventy-five to ninety percent in the century immediately after the Conquest.

Added to the other misfortunes suffered by the Maya was the systematic effort by the Spaniards to eradicate their culture. Most of their towns were forcibly abandoned and the inhabitants removed either to settlements established by the *encomenderos* or to larger centers where the tasks of administrative control and conversion to Christianity could be more easily carried out. Native concepts of government and city planning were remodeled along European lines, and the colonists sought to impose their own social, political, and economic institutions, usually with exceedingly disruptive consequences.

Simultaneously, Franciscan and Dominican friars undertook the complete obliteration of Maya religious beliefs. Important temples, shrines, and altars were pulled down or smashed. Any attempt to worship idols was strictly forbidden. No one was permitted to wear ceremonial costumes, the enactment of pagan rituals was vigorously suppressed, and steps were taken to eliminate the influence of native priests. Instruction in the Catholic faith was mandatory, and those Indians who refused to accept conversion were subjected to harsh penalties.

Although some missionaries worked devotedly to protect the natives against religious and civil abuses (often evoking widespread hostility among the *encomenderos* by their actions), Christian dogma was frequently enforced by brutal methods. Various sixteenth-century accounts document the use of torture during the interrogation of Indians suspected of idolatry. Whipping, beating, mutilation, and scalding with boiling water were commonly employed in such cases, and chronicles written around 1563 by the alcalde of Mérida, Diego Quijada, describe other types of torture used by the friars: twisting ropes around the arms and legs with sticks, the use of pulleys to stretch the joints, scorching the flesh with wax tapers, and forcing water down a victim's throat to make his stomach swell, then standing on him until "water mixed with blood" flowed from his mouth, nose, and ears.

Such acts inevitably prompted the Maya to formulate desperate plots to overthrow their oppressors. Armed uprisings constantly erupted in various parts of the region, resulting in bloody massacres of colonists and the destruction of their towns, livestock, orchards, and crops. As late as 1847 the most successful of these rebellions—the famous War of the Castes—broke out in Yucatán, and before it was finally quelled large sections of the peninsula had been overrun by native armies, most of the haciendas in their path were burned, and the city of Mérida itself was seriously threatened. Yet none of these insurrections achieved anything more than momentary success. Each time, the Maya were unable to sustain their victories, and they invariably found themselves reduced to their previous status. Irrevocably their traditions and ethnic identity continued to fade into obscurity, while the pressures aimed at blotting out the legacy of their past remained as unyielding as ever.

In Yucatán these objectives were largely initiated by one man, a religious fanatic whose curious complexity made him both a relentless enemy and a dedicated student of Maya culture. In 1549 a Franciscan friar named Diego de Landa arrived in Mérida to serve in the nearby monastery of Izamal. The spirit of the Inquisition burned brightly in the young cleric's determination to perform his duties, and he soon acquired a reputation as a missionary of extraordinary zeal. Wherever he traveled throughout Yucatán he instituted the swift destruction of all remaining vestiges of the native religion; nor did he hesitate to apply the severe measures by which he believed pagans were "cleansed," frequently resorting to the most persuasive methods of torture.

Enraged by the Indians' stubborn refusal to renounce their deeply rooted beliefs, Landa continually sought more forceful ways of eradicating their heritage. Such an opportunity arose in the town of Maní, forty miles southeast of Mérida, where he discovered a repository of ancient hieroglyphic books. Here Landa committed an act of wanton destruction that robbed future scholars of what was undoubtedly one of the most important sources of information about the Maya to survive into historic times. He ordered the manuscripts confiscated and publicly burned.

On the prescribed day—July 12, 1562—the disastrous auto-da-fé was carried out. Landa later wrote that because the books "contained nothing in which there was not to be seen superstitions and lies of the devil, we burned them all. . . ." In an instant an archaeological treasure of inestimable value lay smoldering in the embers of Landa's terrible deed.

The incident was particularly regrettable since there is considerable evidence that Maya literature had reached a remarkably high degree of development. Their books—or codices, as they are properly called—consisted of elongated strips of paper (approximately eight to nine inches wide and several yards long) made from the bark of the *copo* or wild fig tree. These were then strengthened by the application of a natural gum substance and coated with white stucco. Onto this surface scribes laboriously drew figures and hieroglyphic symbols, coloring them with vegetable and mineral paints. Each strip of paper was folded back-to-back like a screen to form pages and may have been enclosed between wooden or leather covers, making a volume not unlike a modern book in outward appearance.

Only three Maya codices of questionable authenticity are presently known to exist. The finest of these, the Dresden Codex, was discovered in Vienna in 1739 and eventually acquired by the Royal Library in Dresden, Germany. Sections of two codices were found in Spain during the 1860s, but later examination showed them to be part of the same document now designated as the Codex Tro-Cortesianus, which is preserved in the Museum of Archaeology and History in Madrid. The third manuscript, the Codex Peresianus, is in the possession of the Bibliothèque National in Paris where it accidentally came to light in 1860 in a box of discarded papers. Unfortunately, much of this codex is missing and the surviving pages are only partially legible due to their extremely decayed condition.

On April 20, 1971, another codex purportedly of Maya origin was displayed at the Grolier Club in New York. According to Michael D. Coe, a noted archaeologist and the show's organizer, this eleven-page fragment known as the Grolier Codex was part of a funerary offering found in a cave either in Yucatán or Chiapas. No information was released as to its ownership or the circumstances of its discovery, though it is rumored to belong to a private collector in Mexico. Despite a radiocarbon analysis of its paper which produced a date of A.D. 1230 (plus or minus a possible error of 130 years), several scholars have expressed reservations about its age. The renowned authority J. Eric Thompson pronounced it an outright forgery cleverly painted on ancient paper, a charge rejected by Coe, who maintains it is genuine.

Valuable though these codices are to archaeological research, they reveal nothing whatsoever about actual historical occurrences. Instead they deal entirely with astronomy, calendrics, divination, and ritualism. For example, the Dresden Codex contains data on the cycles of the planet Venus, tables for predicting solar eclipses, and divinatory almanacs. Similarly, the Codex Tro-Cortesianus is concerned with ritualism and prophecy, the Peresianus manuscript is largely devoted to ceremonies associated with various aspects of the calendar, and the Grolier Codex pertains exclusively to the influence of Venus on religious beliefs and astrology.

We can only speculate regarding other subjects the Maya treated in their codices, although several sixteenth-century Spanish chroniclers reported the existence of books involving genealogy, history, mythology, and science. What priceless records illuminating otherwise obscure facets of Maya civilization were destroyed in Landa's auto-da-fé will never be known. Quite possibly the books at Maní might have clarified many puzzling enigmas now confronting archaeologists. Surely the ravaged manuscripts would have been enormously helpful in deciphering Maya hieroglyphic writing, only a small portion of which can presently be read—mainly those texts pertaining to astronomy, calendrics, and mathematics.

Other indications of Maya literary achievements have come down to us via historical sources. After the Conquest missionaries began teaching the Indians to read and write the Spanish alphabet and use it in translating their own language. Oddly enough, it was necessary to invent only two new alphabetical symbols in order to represent all the sounds present in the Maya tongues. One of these is an *sh* phoneme designated by a Portuguese *x* and pronounced as in Uxmal (oosh-mal); the other is a *dz* or *tz* sound first indicated by an inverted *c* (ɔ) and now written as *dz* in words like Dzibilchaltún. Such instruction was originally undertaken to facilitate the propagation of Christianity, but inevitably it was used by the Maya to compile narratives intended to preserve their rapidly passing heritage.

Several of these documents have survived to convey in eloquent language the recollections of anonymous authors concerning history, folklore, and customs. From the Guatemalan highlands came a manuscript known as the *Popol Vuh*, a fragmentary record of the myths, cosmology, and religious beliefs of the Quiché Maya. Another work discovered in the same region, *The Annals of the Cakchiquels*, contains similar information about the Cakchiquel tribe and deals in considerable detail with their history up through the period of the Conquest. And an important collection of native chronicles from Yucatán was assembled in the *Books of Chilam Balam*, named after an order of "Jaguar Priests" renowned for their abilities as prophets. Sections of about fourteen of these manuscripts have turned up so far—each bearing the name of the town where it was written—and although they pertain mainly to folklore, calendrics, astrology, and medicine, three of them contain accounts of historical incidents dating from the centuries after A.D. 1000.

Some scholars believe that portions of the *Books of Chilam Balam* were translated directly from older hieroglyphic codices—an intriguing possibility in view of archaeological research which has verified certain details relating to specific cities, ruling families, and political alliances mentioned in these works. If this information was actually based on hieroglyphic texts (as opposed to oral traditions), we can appreciate even more fully the potential loss to science inflicted by Landa's burning of the codices at Maní. Assuming they could be deciphered, it is reasonable to suppose that these books might have shed light on a broad spectrum of factual events. No doubt other collections of codices also existed at the time of the Conquest which were subsequently lost or destroyed; one such group of manuscripts was reportedly in the possession of the Itzá at Tayasal as late as 1697, but no one knows what became of them after that city's downfall.

In spite of the tragic vandalism wrought by Landa's inquisitorial

Detail of Stela D at Copán showing a long-nosed god emerging from a serpent's mouth. (After Maudslay.)

fervor, his later career unexpectedly resulted in a scholarly contribution of unique importance. To better prepare himself for his ecclesiastical labors he had plunged into a thorough study of Maya culture shortly after his arrival in Yucatán. He soon became fluent in the Yucatec language and spent much of his time with members of Maya ruling families—especially the Xiu and Cocom, who were formerly among the region's most powerful dynasties—questioning them about every aspect of native life. Even during his wide-ranging crusades to remote sections of the peninsula, he diligently gathered information from local inhabitants whenever the opportunity arose. Unwittingly, Landa was to emerge from these pursuits as an eminent student of the ancient traditions he sought to abolish.

About the year 1566 he began writing a treatise on the Maya based upon his earlier studies. Landa may have undertaken the project as a guide for younger missionaries or in the hope of lessening official criticism of his brutal treatment of the Indians and the auto-da-fé at Maní. Indeed, in 1563 he had been recalled to Spain to account for his actions before the Council of the Indies only to return triumphantly ten years later after being elected Bishop of Yucatán. Whatever his purpose in writing the work, Landa's manuscript, entitled *Relación de las cosas de Yucatán*, is the most extensive ethnographic account of the area to emerge from the colonial period and has therefore been of immense value to archaeologists in reconstructing various facets of Maya civilization.

Unfortunately, the original draft of the *Relación* was eventually lost, and it was not until 1863 that a French antiquarian, Abbé Charles Étienne Brasseur de Bourbourg, discovered a copy in the Library of the Academy of History in Madrid. Some sections of the text were missing, but enough remained intact to provide detailed descriptions of ceremonies, religious beliefs, arts, social customs, warfare, and a wealth of other information. Of particular interest are Landa's notes on Maya hieroglyphic writing and calendrics, and he even attempted to devise an "alphabet" for use in reading the inscriptions. Essentially it consisted of drawings representing figures or objects which when pronounced in Yucatec sounded similar to the characters of the Spanish alphabet; for instance, one of the signs for *a* illustrated by Landa is the head of a turtle, and the Yucatec word for turtle is *ac*—a literal

phonetic approach that has proved of little practical value in understanding the complexities of Maya hieroglyphs. Nevertheless, his
contribution to our knowledge of the calendrical glyphs was tremendous, and in this regard the *Relación* has often been called the nearest
thing to a Rosetta Stone (the celebrated key to the decipherment of
Egyptian hieroglyphics) ever to come out of the Maya area.

Although Landa's *Relación* constitutes our most exhaustive early
source pertaining to Maya culture, it is by no means the only such
document in existence. Valuable ethnological data are found in a
number of accounts written by churchmen, native chroniclers, and
historians during the colonial era. Francisco Ximénez, a Dominican
friar who spent years among the Quiché, Cakchiquel, and Tzutuhil
tribes in the Guatemalan highlands, published several books dealing
with native history and customs. Eyewitness reports of the Itzá at
Tayasal are preserved in the journals of the Franciscan monk Andrés
de Avendaño, and the historical works of Juan de Villaguitierre
Soto-Mayor. Important material on the Maya of Yucatán is contained
in the writings of Gaspar Antonio Chi (a member of the Xiu family
who probably served as one of Landa's informants), Cervantes de
Salazar, Bernardo de Lizana, and Diego López de Cogolludo, whose
Historia de Yucatán (1688) is among the most useful sources.
References to the Maya also appear in various general histories of
Mexico and Central America, including those by Las Casas, Oviedo,
Gómara, Torquemada, Clavijero, and the famous chronicler of the
Conquest, Bernal Díaz del Castillo.

Especially notable was the work of Antonio de Ciudad Real, a
Franciscan friar who came to Yucatán in 1573. This remarkable
scholar-missionary quickly developed a keen interest in Maya culture
and learned to speak Yucatec so fluently that Cogolludo called him
"the greatest master of the [native tongue] this country has produced."
Aside from his linguistic studies, Ciudad Real traveled extensively in
Mexico and Central America, writing on various aspects of aboriginal
life, and his most prodigious undertaking was a dictionary of the
Yucatec language with Spanish translations known as the *Gran
diccionario o calepino de la lengua maya de Yucatán,* a project that
reportedly required forty years to complete and filled six volumes of
more than 200 pages each.

Some time later the manuscript of this monumental work disappeared without a trace, but in the 1860s Brasseur de Bourbourg purchased a dictionary matching the description of Ciudad Real's *Calepino* for four pesos in a secondhand bookshop in Mexico City. It had apparently been written in the monastery at Motul near Mérida where Ciudad Real is known to have resided for several years, and examination by the Yucatecan linguist and epigrapher Juan Martínez Hernández established that this document—known today as the Motul Dictionary—is almost certainly a part at least of Ciudad Real's long-missing *Calepino*. Now a priceless possession of the John Carter Brown Library in Providence, Rhode Island, it ranks among the most important aids to Maya research ever discovered.

Except for the efforts of these authors, we would know practically nothing about the Maya as they existed in the years before prolonged European contact radically altered their culture. Such matters held little interest for the fortune-hungry colonists who overran the country after the Conquest; their primary concern was land, cheap labor, and the expanding economic frontiers of a newly won empire, and few of them had any concern for the past achievements of pagan "devil worshipers." Nor could the Maya themselves hope to preserve more than desultory fragments of their legacy. Already most of their cities either lay in ruins or had recently been deserted, leaving them to the ravages of time and the all-pervasive jungle. With the passing of the ruling classes and native priesthood, such esoteric knowledge as astronomy, calendrics, hieroglyphic writing, and mathematics soon faded from memory. Innumerable examples of Maya art and architecture were deliberately destroyed by the Spaniards, and the suppression of the religious beliefs which had inspired these creations extinguished any further artistic expression. Worst of all, the obliteration of their civilization was so thorough, and so swiftly were alien values and concepts substituted in its place, there was no hope that future generations could ever resurrect it.

Yet the Maya had declined not only because of the onslaught of Spanish invaders, although this was certainly the decisive factor. There is unmistakable evidence that their culture was in the process of dissolution long before the conquistadors' arrival. For over a century prior to the Conquest, Yucatán was the scene of civil unrest, internecine warfare, and social decay. Earlier attempts at centralized government had broken down, and the entire peninsula was split into sixteen independent provinces ruled by chieftains who constantly fought among themselves. In Guatemala the two strongest tribes—the Quiché and Cakchiquel—had likewise joined with their respective allies in a prolonged struggle for control of the highlands. Everywhere militarism supplanted the creative endeavors of past centuries, and there was a marked disintegration in art, architecture, and intellectual pursuits. Uprisings, intrigue, and political assassinations had beset nearly all of the Maya area, touching off smoldering enmities which the Spaniards quickly exploited to their own advantage.

Like acts of punishment from the gods, a series of natural catastrophes overtook the Maya in the midst of these tribulations. Native chronicles record a severe hurricane which laid waste to vast portions of Yucatán sometime around 1464. Sixteen years later a devastating pestilence swept through the area, and in 1514 an epidemic (probably of smallpox introduced from Spanish colonies in Panama) broke out, causing its victims to suffer "great pestules which rotted their bodies with a terrible stench." According to another account, swarms of locusts ravaged Yucatán for five years until "nothing green was left, and they experienced such a famine that people fell dead on the roads."

From the *Books of Chilam Balam* a cryptic chant warned the Maya of portents heralding the end of their age:

> *Eat, eat, thou hast bread;*
> *Drink, drink, thou hast water;*
> *On that day, dust possesses the earth,*
> *On that day, a blight is on the face of the earth,*
> *On that day, a cloud arises,*
> *On that day, a mountain rises,*
> *On that day, a strong man seizes the land,*
> *On that day, things fall to ruin,*
> *On that day, the tender leaf is destroyed,*
> *On that day, the dying eyes are closed,*
> *On that day, three signs are on the tree,*
> *On that day, three generations hang there,*

On that day, the battle flag is raised,
And they are scattered afar in the forests.

History's eternal drama had again been enacted. Maya civilization—one of the most remarkable expressions of higher attainments in pre-Columbian America—was destroyed, utterly obliterated from the stage of human affairs. Everything the Maya had accomplished lay buried in their ruined cities, enshrouded in the primeval jungle out of which they were spawned centuries ago. For the living Maya only two paths of survival lay open: a pallid existence of servitude under foreign overlords, or the alternative which claimed those who sought to escape from oppression by fleeing to remote areas, to live like progeny of the Stone Age "scattered afar in the forests."

It now remained for men possessed of insatiable curiosity about the past to reclaim the Maya from permanent obscurity, men of less worldly ambitions than their Spanish predecessors—explorers, historians, and archaeologists to whom the quest for knowledge was as enticing as the lure of gold.

2

JOHN LLOYD STEPHENS:
THE CITIES COME
TO LIGHT

 In 1836 a meeting occurred in London which
was to bear profoundly upon the enigma of
the long-forgotten Maya cities. John Lloyd Stephens, an American
lawyer with a predilection for travel and antiquities, encountered the
English artist and architect, Frederick Catherwood. Although they met
by accident, the course of their lives had been conspicuously similar,
for both men had traveled extensively and were deeply immersed in
Greco-Roman, Egyptian, and Near Eastern archaeology.

Stephens was born in Shrewsbury, New Jersey, in 1805, the son
of a moderately wealthy merchant named Benjamin Stephens. He
spent his childhood in New York City where his family moved in
1806, and after graduating from Columbia University he entered
Tapping Reeve's Law School in Litchfield, Connecticut. Eventually he
joined his father's mercantile company, opened a law office on Wall
Street, and became involved in politics, but these pursuits did not
satisfy his adventurous nature and he periodically abandoned them in
order to travel.

While on an extended trip in 1835 he toured France, Italy, and Greece, visited Constantinople, and journeyed into Russia, Poland, and Austria. The next year he sailed up the Nile from Cairo to Aswân, ventured across the Sinai Peninsula to Mount Sinai and Aqaba, explored the ruined city of Petra in Arabia, and traveled to Jerusalem, the Dead Sea, Nazareth, and Beirut. At the conclusion of these journeys, Stephens published two highly successful books—*Incidents of Travel in Egypt, Arabia Petraea, and the Holy Land* (1837) and *Incidents of Travel in Greece, Turkey, Russia, and Poland* (1838)— which firmly established his reputation as a travel writer of exceptional ability.

Frederick Catherwood had long been a serious student of antiquities. After spending his youth in the London suburb of Hoxton where he was born in 1799, he worked as an architect's apprentice, studied drawing and painting, and exhibited at the Royal Academy. He later went to Italy, Sicily, and Greece to study classical architecture and sculpture, and from there he traveled widely in Egypt, making scale drawings of archaeological monuments at Memphis, Abydos, Karnak, Deir el-Bahri, Luxor, and Thebes. In 1823 Catherwood was engaged as an architectural consultant by Mehemet Ali to supervise the restoration of Cairo's mosques, and the following year he set off on a journey through Sinai, Arabia, and the Holy Land, during which he drew a detailed plan of the Mosque of Omar in Jerusalem and sketched the ruins of Jarash, Baalbek, and Palmyra.

This experience left Catherwood unusually adept at rendering skillful reproductions of sculpture, architecture, and inscriptions. Unlike the works of so many artist-travelers of the period who indulged in romantic fantasies, his drawings reflected the unerring pen and critical eye of an accomplished draftsman and scholar, and he often employed a camera lucida to insure the accuracy of minute details. The fact that Stephens was guided by the same integrity in his literary observations made their meeting a fortunate one in view of future events. Both men were destined to play singularly important roles in bringing the achievements of Maya civilization to public attention.

Soon after returning from his Near Eastern tour in 1836, Stephens read an account written by an officer in the Spanish army—a Captain Antonio del Río—describing a ruined city known as Palenque located in the rain forest of Chiapas in southern Mexico. Working with a crew of Indian laborers, del Río had partially excavated some of its buildings in 1787, but the report of his findings vanished into an archive in Madrid until 1822, when an English translation was published in London. Entitled *Description of the Ruins of an Ancient City* and illustrated with engravings by a German artist and soldier of fortune, Jean-Frédéric Waldeck, it was this work which first awakened Stephens' interest in Maya archaeology.

Several years later a friend showed Stephens a portfolio containing Waldeck's drawings of ruins in Yucatán. Waldeck—who among his many exploits is said to have studied painting under Jacques Louis David, served with Napoleon's army in Italy and Egypt, traveled extensively in Africa, and sailed with the notorious Lord Cochrane during Chile's war of independence against Spain—had only recently returned from a lengthy sojourn in Mexico. In 1838 he published a volume entitled *Voyage Pittoresque et Archéologique dans la Province d'Yucatán*, its pages filled with engravings of Maya sculpture, architecture, and inscriptions executed in a style reminiscent of Piranesi and embellished by Waldeck's vivid imagination. Figures of priests and chieftains appeared in unmistakably Phoenician dress, shattered buildings were reconstructed to resemble Egyptian and Assyrian temples, and he even depicted certain sculptured heads found among the ruins as those of elephants. Nonetheless, the exotic images of rulers and gods, ornate monuments, and intricate decorative motifs adorning structures of seemingly Herculean proportions excited Stephens' imagination.

His interest was further heightened by a series of books known as *Antiquities of Mexico*, the work of an eccentric Irish nobleman named Edward King, the viscount of Kingsborough. While studying an Aztec codex in the Bodleian Library at Oxford in 1814, Lord Kingsborough had succumbed to the lure of Mexican and Central American archaeology, and thereafter it became an ill-fated obsession. For years he relentlessly sought everything on the subject then available in European museums and archives, and between 1831 and 1848 the results of his labors appeared in nine enormous folio volumes printed on handmade paper and illustrated with etchings and lithographs of pre-Columbian sculpture, architecture, and codices. Out of the jumbled text, written partly in Latin, Greek, Hebrew, Sanskrit, and

English, loomed the author's firm conviction that the American Indians were descendants of the biblical Lost Tribes of Israel. But Kingsborough's admirable attempt to prove this theory eventually brought about his untimely demise. He died in a debtor's prison, unable to pay the staggering expense of his publications.

Other reports of ruins in Mexico and Central America soon came to Stephens' attention: a volume entitled *Antiquités Mexicaines* by a Spanish army officer named Guillelmo Dupaix; an article by a Yucatecan diplomat, Lorenzo de Zavala, containing a description of the ruins of Uxmal in Yucatán; the writings of the renowned German naturalist and explorer Alexander von Humboldt, whose famous treatise on Mexico, *Vues des Cordillères et Monuments des Peuples Indigènes de l'Amérique*, appeared in France in 1814; and an entry in the *Proceedings of the American Antiquarian Society* by Juan Galindo, an Irish-born soldier, adventurer, and civil servant then residing in Guatemala, which described a vast ruined city known as Copán hidden in the wilderness of western Honduras. Finally Stephens' curiosity was aroused beyond resistance, and early in the spring of 1839 he announced his intention to explore the jungles of Central America in an effort to obtain positive proof of the existence of these mysterious ruins.

Not surprisingly, his plan touched off a flurry of wild speculation. The public's imagination, already excited by sensational archaeological discoveries in Italy, Greece, the Near East, and Egypt, was captivated by Stephens' intriguing quest. But professional historians were openly skeptical of its merits. Most scholars viewed the American Indians as having never risen above a condition of barest savagery, and the suggestion that civilizations of the highest order had once flourished in the Western Hemisphere was wholly unacceptable in academic circles. At this time the relatively new science of archaeology had scarcely been applied in America. Few systematic excavations were being carried out anywhere in the area, and prevailing theories concerning its antiquities were largely based on studies of widely scattered museum collections or pure speculation. Many important ethnohistoric documents, such as Landa's *Relación*, still lay undiscovered in various libraries, and the eyewitness accounts of sixteenth-century Spanish explorers, who first observed the splendid achievements of the Aztecs,

Maya, and Incas before their destruction, were either ignored or discounted. It was generally agreed that the conquistadors had been blinded by grandiose illusions; their descriptions of sprawling cities, lavish temples and palaces, superb works of art, and treasures of gold, silver, and precious stones were viewed as exaggerations or outright fantasies.

The attitude of most scholars was aptly expressed by the famous Scottish historian William Robertson when he wrote in his widely read *History of America* (1777): "America was not peopled by any nation of the ancient continent, which had made considerable progress in civilization. The inhabitants of the New World were in a state of society so extremely rude as to be unacquainted with those arts which are the first essays of human ingenuity in its advance towards improvement. Even the most celebrated nations of America were strangers to many of those simple inventions which were almost coeval with society in other parts of the world, and were known in the earliest periods of civil life with which we have acquaintance."

Robertson further declared that "neither the Mexicans nor Peruvians [were] entitled to rank with those nations which merit the name civilized." Regarding the magnificent Aztec and Maya cities which had so astounded early chroniclers, he insisted they were "more fit to be the habitation of men just emerging from barbarity than the residence of a polished people. . . . Nor does the fabric of their temples and other public edifices appear to have been such as entitled them to the high praise bestowed upon them by many Spanish authors. . . . Such structures convey no high idea of progress in art and ingenuity; and one can hardly conceive that [buildings] more crude and simple could have occurred to a nation in its first efforts towards erecting any great work. . . ."

In view of this sentiment, Stephens was acutely aware that in the event his search proved successful he would need evidence to support his discoveries. No one was better qualified to provide such material than his friend Frederick Catherwood, whose superb drawings of Egyptian, Greek, and Roman antiquities had achieved considerable recognition. Eager for an opportunity to explore new areas, Catherwood (who had recently arrived in New York from England, joined an architectural firm, and opened an exhibition of huge panoramas depicting scenes from his earlier travels) promptly accepted Stephens' offer to accompany him. As their first objective they decided to seek the ancient city of Copán in Honduras.

On the eve of their departure, Stephens was awarded the post of United States ambassador to Central America, a position for which he had applied upon the sudden death of the former minister. His appointment was especially fortunate since the countries Stephens intended to visit were locked in the midst of violent internal disturbances. Rebellious armies were fighting for political control of Central America's dawning republics. Opposing factions within the contending forces were battling among themselves; attempts to preserve law and order had broken down, and the countryside teemed with marauding soldiers, bandits, and smugglers. All things considered, the situation was hardly encouraging to travelers entering upon a purely scholarly quest, though Stephens believed his diplomatic passport would afford some degree of immunity from these dangers.

In October of 1839 the explorers embarked by ship for Belize in

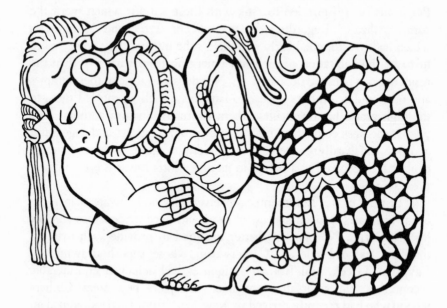

Detail of Stela D, Copán. (After Maudslay.)

British Honduras. From there they boarded a steamer which sailed due south to Punta Gorda, then up the Río Dulce to Lake Izabal, a short distance inland from the northeastern coast of Guatemala. At a small village situated on the southern edge of the lake, they hired guides and pack mules for the overland journey across a rugged barrier known as Mico Mountain into the war-torn interior of Guatemala.

Slowly they ascended the mountain's treacherous slopes toward what they hoped would be the ruins of Copán. Once engulfed by the tangled rain forest blanketing their route, Stephens had sufficient reason to question the wisdom of his undertaking. With each mile it became increasingly difficult to imagine that a civilization had ever flourished in such hostile surroundings, and they proceeded, as Stephens recalled, "with the hope rather than the expectation of finding wonders."

Of the hazards that befell them from the outset of their journey, Stephens wrote: "The ascent began precipitously and by an extraordinary passage, a narrow gulley worn by the tracks of mules and the washing of mountain torrents. It was so deep that the sides were higher than our heads, and so narrow that we could barely pass through without touching them. Our whole caravan moved singly through this muddy defile. The muleteers scattered among them and on the bank above, extricating the mules as they stuck fast, raising them as they fell, arranging their cargoes, cursing, shouting, and lashing them on; if one stopped, all behind were blocked up, unable to turn. Any sudden start pressed us against the sides of the gulley, and there was no small danger of getting a leg crushed. Emerging from this defile, we came again to deep mudholes and projecting roots of trees, which added to the difficulty of a steep ascent. . . . The woods were of impenetrable thickness and we could see nothing but the detestable path before us. . . . We were dragged through mudholes, squeezed in gulleys, knocked against trees, and tumbled over roots. Every step required care and great physical exertion, and . . . I felt that our inglorious epitaph might well read: 'tossed over the head of a mule, brained by the trunk of a mahogany tree, and buried in the mud of Mico Mountain.' "

Eventually they emerged into thickly forested highlands, crossed the Río Motagua, and ascended a volcanic plateau near Guatemala's eastern border. But scarcely had the physical rigors of their journey eased when they encountered political dangers. Upon entering the village of Camotán, a few miles from their destination, they were suddenly "arrested" by a band of soldiers, Indians, and mestizos— "ragged and ferocious-looking fellows," wrote Stephens, "armed with staves of office, swords, clubs, muskets, and machetes. . . ." When the officer in charge of the group examined Stephens' diplomatic passport, he angrily declared it invalid and ordered them held in confinement during a precarious night of negotiations. Stephens' refusal to surrender his passport, even with "two assassin scoundrels," as he described them, pointing muskets at his chest, almost brought the expedition to a disastrous end. But the matter was finally resolved as mysteriously as it began, and the next morning they were released without explanation. Hastily they departed Camotán, crossed into Honduras, and proceeded to a remote Indian settlement bearing the name of Copán, a disappointing place which Stephens reported "consisted of half a dozen miserable huts thatched with corn."

Here again the appearance of outsiders was an unwelcome event. No one knew anything about ruins such as Stephens described, but all agreed that the one person who might be of assistance was Don Gregorio, a suspicious, ill-tempered tyrant who was the self-styled *patrón* of the village. Don Gregorio received them with cold indifference. Neither gestures of friendship nor offers of money could alter his menacing disposition, but he eventually consented to help in the hope of ridding himself of unwanted visitors. He knew of an Indian who could lead them to the ruins, and they were allowed to stay overnight at his hacienda until the necessary arrangements were completed.

Early the next day Stephens and Catherwood, accompanied by their newly acquired guide, set off by mule into the fathomless jungle. In places the underbrush was so dense they were forced to travel on foot along a path cleared with machetes. Soon they reached the edge of a stream called the Río Copán, and on the opposite bank a stone wall roughly a hundred feet high and thickly overgrown with trees was clearly visible. Quickly they forged the river and climbed a weathered stairway leading to a terrace from which vestiges of other structures were barely discernible in the surrounding forest. When the explorers descended into its shadowy depths, they found themselves in the midst of wonders exceeding their wildest expectations.

Scattered about were gigantic sculptured monoliths and altars, some standing erect, others fallen over or broken, their surfaces richly carved with masks, animals, human figures, and inscriptions. Huge pyramid-shaped structures reached up through the trees, scarcely visible amid the rubble and undergrowth enveloping them. Elsewhere were the remains of stairways, platforms, buildings, and walls, all shattered by the roots of trees and vines growing between the fissured stones. Grotesque heads of jaguars, serpents, and mythical creatures had fallen from their facades—images of unknown gods in whose veneration the once magnificent temples had been erected. Obviously Copán was formerly the scene of extraordinary artistic and intellectual achievements, and wherever Stephens and Catherwood looked they saw miracles frozen in its crumbled monuments. As a traveler who had visited the site years before remarked: "The genii who attended on King Solomon seem to have been the artists."

"Who were the people who built this city?" Stephens wrote. ". . . America, say historians, was peopled by savages, but savages never reared these structures, savages never carved these stones. . . . Architecture, sculpture, and painting, all the arts which embellish life, had flourished in this overgrown forest; orators, warriors, and states-men, beauty, ambition, and glory had lived and passed away, and none knew that such things had been or could tell of their past existence. . . .

"The city was desolate. . . . It lay before us like a shattered bark in the midst of the ocean, her masts gone, her name effaced, her crew perished, and none to tell whence she came, to whom she belonged, how long on her voyage, or what caused her destruction—her lost people to be traced only by some fancied resemblance in the construction of the vessel, and, perhaps, never to be known at all. . . . All was mystery, dark, impenetrable mystery. . . ."

After setting up quarters in a native hut near the site, Stephens recruited a small group of Indian workmen from the village and soon the task of reclaiming Copán from its jungle grave was under way. But hardly had explorations begun when a serious problem of diplomacy arose, touched off by the growing resentment of Don Gregorio. Aside from his instinctive dislike of outsiders, he was angered that some of his laborers were being lured away by the high wages Stephens offered them to work at the ruins. Viewing this as an open challenge to his authority, Don Gregorio denounced Stephens and Catherwood as disruptive, suspicious, and politically dangerous; and to prove these charges he submitted the testimony of two Indians from Camotán who claimed that Stephens' party had "escaped" from imprisonment and were chased to the borders of Honduras by a detachment of soldiers under orders to kill them.

Stephens was finally able to quiet the villagers' apprehensions by exhibiting his diplomatic passport, letters of recommendation, and a note which arrived unexpectedly from the district's military commander—a General Cascara—expressing regrets over their false arrest at Camotán. Still, they found themselves in a precarious position; they were strangers in a remote country torn by civil unrest and subject to the caprices of irresponsible *politicos*. Should anyone seriously question their right to continue the exploration of Copán, they would be without legal recourse. Realizing the gravity of the situation, Stephens sought a means of insuring the completion of their project. He resolved to purchase the ruins.

The land on which they were located was owned by one Don José María Acevedo, a respected member of the village whose wife the explorers had previously treated for a severe attack of rheumatism. Eager to discuss the transaction, Stephens visited Don José's home. He emphatically denied the rumors being spread by Don Gregorio, assured him of his good intentions, and explained the reasons for his interest in the ruined city. "In short," he wrote, "in plain English, I asked him, 'What will you take for the ruins?' I think he was not more surprised than if I had asked to buy his poor old wife. . . ."

After several days of deliberation, Don José consented to sell. To him the land was useless: almost six thousand acres of rain forest littered with meaningless carved stones and mounds of rubble. And the price he was offered—fifty dollars—was irresistible. Despite last-minute delays caused by Don Gregorio's violent objections, the sale was finally completed amid a pompous display of deeds, official credentials, and witnesses. Stephens was well pleased with the arrangement; the sensation of owning an ancient city in the wilds of Honduras had an undeniable enchantment about it. Under the circumstances it was also a practical necessity, and he now resumed his archaeological quest with renewed confidence.

Equipped with machetes, measuring tapes, and a compass, Stephens and his Indian workmen undertook the tasks of investigating new sections of the ruins, surveying and mapping structures, and clearing vegetation from monuments. Meanwhile Catherwood, often ankle deep in mud and severely hampered by rain, inadequate light, and swarms of mosquitoes, painstakingly drew each important discovery.

"It is impossible to describe the interest with which I explored these ruins," recalled Stephens of his first days at the site. "The ground was entirely new; there were no guidebooks or guides; the whole was virgin soil. We could not see ten yards before us, and never knew what we should stumble upon next. At one time we stopped to cut away branches and vines, which concealed the face of a monument . . . a sculptured corner of which protruded from the earth. I leaned over with breathless anxiety while the Indians worked, and an eye, an ear, a foot, or a hand was disentombed; and when the machete rang against the chiseled stone, I pushed the Indians away and cleared out the loose earth with my hands. The beauty of the sculpture, the solemn stillness of the woods disturbed only by the scrambling of monkeys and the chattering of parrots, the desolation of the city, and the mystery that hung over it, all created an interest higher, if possible, than I had ever felt among the ruins of the Old World."

Gradually the outlines of Copán's ground plan began to emerge from the wilderness. Roughly oriented along a north–south axis, the city was located on the west bank of the Río Copán and consisted of a huge acropolis, five adjoining plazas, and several outlying districts. The principal group of buildings was situated atop the acropolis, which covered approximately twelve acres and reached 125 feet at its highest point. Near the center of this artificial mound a massive pyramid rose up in a series of terraces to a flat summit. Immediately west of this structure was a rectangular courtyard surrounded by smaller pyramids, temples, and platforms. To the east lay another plaza enclosed by terraces, stairways, and buildings heavily ornamented with sculptured friezes, including a temple (unknown at the time of Stephens' visit) with a doorway constructed in the form of a stylized serpent's mouth.

Adjacent to the northeast corner of the acropolis stood one of the most spectacular achievements of Copán's builders—the Temple of the Hieroglyphic Stairway, a terraced pyramid ascended by a flight of stairs thirty feet wide, sixty-five feet high, and consisting of sixty-three steps flanked by decorative ramps. Every stone used to construct the risers was carved with hieroglyphs, and the entire stairway was composed of almost 2,500 individual glyphs, the longest single inscription ever found in the Maya area.

Next to the Hieroglyphic Stairway was a ball court made up of an I-shaped stone floor bordered on two sides by slanting walls attached to platforms crowned with temples. North of this complex the city opened onto a broad courtyard—the Great Plaza—containing a number of stelae and altars richly carved in high relief with effigies, human figures, florid decorative motifs, and hieroglyphs. Stephens correctly assumed that these remarkable "idols" were originally erected to commemorate historical events or the passing of certain time intervals. "In workmanship," he noted, "[they are] equal to the finest Egyptian sculpture. Indeed, it would be impossible, with the best instruments of modern times, to cut stone more perfectly."

For almost two weeks Stephens and Catherwood labored to redeem Copán's secrets from the depths of the forest. Scarcely an hour passed without revealing some new cause for speculation, and Stephens' brain fairly reeled with the mysteries surrounding the ruins. "In regard to the age of this desolate city," he wrote, "I shall not at present offer any conjecture. Some idea might perhaps be formed from the accumulations of earth and the gigantic trees growing on top of the ruined structures, but it would be uncertain and unsatisfactory. Nor shall I at this moment offer any conjecture in regard to the people who built it; or to the time when or the means by which it was depopulated . . . or as to whether it fell by the sword, or famine, or pestilence. The trees which shroud it may have sprung from the blood of its slaughtered inhabitants; they may have perished howling with hunger; or pestilence, like the cholera, may have piled its streets with the dead and driven forever the feeble remnants from their homes. . . . One thing I believe: its history is graven on its monuments. No Champollion has yet brought to them the energies of his inquiring mind. Who shall read them?

> *"Chaos of ruins! who shall trace the void,*
> *O'er the dim fragments cast a lunar light,*
> *And say, 'here was or is,' where all is doubly night?"*

Having stayed at Copán longer than expected, it was decided that Stephens would travel to Guatemala City to fulfill certain diplomatic obligations while Catherwood continued working at the site. Specifically, Stephens' instructions directed him to present his credentials to representatives of Central America's federal government, close the United States legation in Guatemala City, and secure the ratification of a trade agreement. But in view of the civil turmoil then ravaging the area, it proved to be a frustrating mission. Stephens' efforts to locate anything resembling a unified government ultimately carried him from Guatemala to El Salvador, Nicaragua, and Costa Rica without success, and nowhere was he able to find any individual or group empowered to negotiate treaties. "Under the circumstances," he reported, ". . . I made a formal return to the authorities in Washington, in effect, 'after diligent search, no government found.' " Not that Stephens was unduly disturbed by this turn of events. His interest in politics had long since yielded to archaeology, and he pursued his official duties in the knowledge that once accomplished he would be free to resume his explorations. He was now intent upon seeking the city of Palenque in Chiapas.

During Stephens' absence Catherwood had discovered another ruin of major importance. Known as Quiriguá, it was located thirty miles north of Copán near the Río Motagua. Quiriguá's structures covered a relatively small area, but Catherwood was able to discern the unmistakable outlines of pyramids, stairways, and platforms, together with stone sculpture decorated with zoomorphs, human figures, and hieroglyphs.

On the basis of Catherwood's observations, Stephens concluded that Copán and Quiriguá exhibited similar characteristics and had probably been erected by the same people. "Of one thing there is no doubt," he wrote in reference to Quiriguá, "a large city once stood

there; its name lost, its history unknown. Except for a notice taken
from Mr. Catherwood's notes and inserted . . . in a Guatemalan paper
which found its way also to the [United States] and Europe, no account
of its existence has ever before been published. . . . Every traveler
from Izabal to Guatemala has passed within three hours of it; we
ourselves had done the same; and yet, there it lay, like the rock-built
city of Edom, unvisited, unsought, and utterly unknown."

By April of 1840 the explorers were launched upon their quest for
Palenque. Setting out from Guatemala City with an entourage of
Indian carriers, they journeyed westward via Antigua, Lake Atitlán,
and Quezaltenango into southern Mexico. Entering Chiapas at the
town of Comitán, they endured ten days of severe hardships caused by
drenching rains, extremely hazardous trails, and oppressive heat before
reaching Santo Domingo del Palenque—a remote village from which
the ruined city of Palenque (the Spanish word for "palisade") a few
miles to the west took its name. When they finally stumbled into Santo
Domingo's muddy streets, their only thought was to recover from what

Detail of Stela B, Copán. (After Maudslay.)

Stephens described as their "shattered condition" brought on by illness, hunger, and exhaustion.

But the idea of deserted temples, palaces, and monuments lying about in the overgrown forest soon revived their determination. And when they were led to Palenque's ruins they could scarcely contain their elation. Upon approaching the site, Stephens recalled: "We spurred up a sharp ascent of [stones], so steep the mules could barely climb it, to a terrace which, like the whole road, was so covered with trees it was impossible to make out the form. . . . We stopped at the foot of a second [terrace] when our Indians cried out *El Palacio* (The Palace), and through openings in the trees we saw the front of a large building richly ornamented with stuccoed figures on the pilasters, curious and elegant, with trees growing close against it, their branches entering the doors; in style and effect it was unique, extraordinary, and mournfully beautiful. We tied our mules . . . ascended a flight of steps forced apart and thrown down by trees, and entered the palace. For a few moments we ranged along the corridor and into the courtyard, and after the first gaze of eager curiosity was over, went back to the entrance. Standing in the doorway, we fired a *feu-de-joie* of four rounds each, using up the last charge of our firearms. But for this way of giving vent to our satisfaction we should have made the roof of the old palace ring with a hurrah."

Situated on a high artificial terrace, this imposing building—now called the Great Palace—was a massive labyrinth of vaulted rooms, narrow corridors, and subterranean chambers arranged around four inner courtyards. Near its center a square tower suggestive of an Oriental pagoda rose to a height of fifty feet above the ground level. Sculpture, bas-reliefs, and hieroglyphic inscriptions of exceptional quality embellished the palace's facades, walls, and plazas, and many of these decorations had originally been painted with brilliant colors, traces of which were still visible. The building's outer pilasters were adorned with a series of exquisite stucco reliefs representing life-sized "portraits" of ruling lords or priests bedecked in elaborate costumes. Some of them stood in rigid solemnity, holding plumed staffs and flanked by seated attendants. Others were frozen in courtly attitudes, with one foot rising slightly from the ground, their bodies bent gently forward, clasping ritual scepters in their outstretched hands.

Near the southwest corner of the Great Palace, a terraced pyramid sixty-five feet high lay buried under a thick mantle of vegetation. With Indians wielding machetes ahead of them, Stephens and Catherwood struggled up its crumbled stairway until they reached a temple whose lavish ornamentation struck them speechless. Leading into its interior were five doorways divided by pilasters decorated with stucco reliefs and panels of hieroglyphs. Its upper facade reflected a maze of sculptured designs, and crowning the roof were the remains of an openwork crest or "comb" made of stucco and cut stone. "No description and no drawing can give the moral sublimity of the spectacle," commented Stephens on first viewing this superb structure —the Temple of the Inscriptions.

Inside the building a corridor opened into three narrow vaulted chambers divided by partitions. Set in the interior walls were three limestone tablets covered with hieroglyphs finely carved in low relief. Two of these panels, flanking the entrance to the central chamber, measured eight by thirteen feet and contained 240 individual glyphs; the third tablet, imbedded in the central chamber's rear wall, was considerably smaller—slightly over three feet wide—but because of its location within the temple's inner recesses its inscriptions were almost perfectly preserved.

Everywhere lay more evidence of Palenque's former grandeur: stairways, plazas, fragments of sculpture, overgrown temples, and an underground aqueduct designed to channel a small stream—the Río Otolum—through the center of the city. East of the Great Palace stood a group of structures now bearing such descriptive names as the Temple of the Sun, Temple of the Cross, Temple of the Beau Relief, and Temple of the Foliated Cross, all of them ornamented with limestone and stucco relief sculpture of unusual refinement. Enclosing the city's northern boundary was another complex of courtyards, platforms, and temples dominated by a lofty terraced pyramid supporting a building known as the Temple of the Count, the roof of which was originally decorated with a gigantic stucco mask long since destroyed by decay.

As he had done at Copán, Stephens wandered through Palenque's ruins in utter astonishment. "Here were the remains," he wrote, "of a cultivated, polished, and peculiar people, who had passed through all the stages incident to the rise and fall of nations, had reached their golden age, and had perished, entirely unknown. The links connecting them with the human family were severed and lost; these were the only memorials of their footsteps upon earth. We lived in the ruined palace of their kings; we went up to their desolate temples and fallen altars; and wherever we moved we saw evidence of their taste, their skill in arts, their wealth and power. In the midst of desolation and ruin we looked back to the past, cleared away the gloomy forest, and fancied every building perfect, with its terraces and pyramids, its sculptured and painted ornaments, grand, lofty, and imposing. . . . We called back into life the strange people who gazed at us in sadness from the walls; pictured them, in fanciful costumes and adorned with plumes of feathers, ascending the terraces of the palace and the steps leading to the temple. . . . In the romance of the world's history, nothing ever impressed me more forcibly than the spectacle of this once great and lovely city, overturned, desolate, and lost; discovered by accident, overgrown with trees, it did not even have a name to distinguish it. Apart from everything else, it was a mourning witness to the world's mutations."

After a month at the site further exploration was made increasingly difficult by the onset of the rainy season. Every morning swollen black clouds rode in on restless winds and broke upon the forest with drenching fury. The walls of the buildings dripped with moisture, and droves of mosquitoes swarmed in their darkened vaults. For several weeks Catherwood had suffered intermittent attacks of malaria; rarely did anyone sleep longer than three or four hours a night, and then it was with "twinging apprehensions of the snakes and reptiles, lizards and scorpions which infested the ruins."

By June, Stephens and Catherwood were forced to leave Palenque. Journeying north across palmetto-studded savannas to the Usumacinta River, they proceeded by boat through Chiapas and the crocodile-infested swamps of Tabasco and Campeche to a point where the Usumacinta's waters empty into the Gulf of Campeche. From the island of Carmen at the mouth of Laguna de Términos they boarded a ship bound for Yucatán with the intention of examining the ancient city of Uxmal near Mérida.

Once again the sight that confronted them defied all expectations.

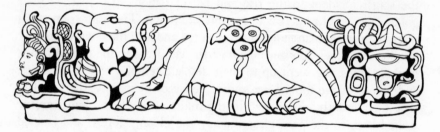

An altar decoration, Copán. (After Maudslay.)

Standing in the midst of Uxmal's ruins was an extraordinary building called the Palace of the Governors. Elevated on a high terraced platform, this structure was 320 feet long, forty feet wide, and contained twenty-four vaulted chambers. Its facade was decorated with thousands of carved stones carefully set into an intricate mosaic of geometric designs, stylized masks, and human faces. Often described as the most beautiful example of Maya architecture in existence, Stephens spoke without exaggeration when he remarked: "There is no rudeness or barbarity in its design or proportions; on the contrary, the whole wears an air of symmetry and grandeur. If it stood this day on its grand artificial terrace in Hyde Park or the Garden of the Tuileries, it would form a new order . . . not unworthy to stand side by side with the remains of Egyptian, Grecian, and Roman art."

Adjacent to the Palace of the Governors was a large cluster of mounds, pyramids, and platforms, their details obliterated by debris and underbrush. Several hundred yards to the north stood a group of four rectangular buildings enclosing a wide courtyard. Known as the Nunnery Quadrangle, each of these structures, which contained double rows of cell-like rooms, was richly ornamented with geometric mosaics, serpents, and masks. East of this complex a truncated pyramid rose to a height of eighty-four feet, with two steeply inclined stairways leading to a magnificent temple—the House of the Magician—at its summit. Visible in every direction were other mounds, ruined buildings, and outcroppings of walls, and there could be no doubt Uxmal had once been a city of major importance.

But the exploration of Uxmal was short-lived. While sketching among the ruins, Catherwood, now experiencing the symptoms of acute malaria, collapsed and was carried in delirium to a nearby hacienda.

On the thirty-first day of July, 1840, the explorers arrived back in New York, where they quickly began preparing the results of their expedition for publication. Stephens' two-volume account entitled *Incidents of Travel in Central America, Chiapas, and Yucatan*, illustrated with Catherwood's superb engravings, appeared in June of 1841. Its impact was phenomenal!

Historians read with dismay his vivid descriptions of the long-ignored ruins. Raging academic debates erupted over various theories which sought to explain their existence. Scholars reexamined the narratives of the Conquest and the accounts of early travelers, searching for new clues and interpretations; the images in Catherwood's drawings were compared with classical, Near Eastern, and Oriental antiquities in an attempt to define possible analogies, and occultists seized upon Stephens' discoveries as "proof" of their belief in lost continents and vanished races.

Amid this storm of controversy the ever curious Stephens and Catherwood, accompanied by a physician and naturalist from Boston, Dr. Samuel Cabot, Jr., embarked upon a second expedition to Yucatán in October of 1841.

Six weeks were required to complete their unfinished survey of Uxmal. Next they spent three months investigating a number of other ruins, exploring the Wells of Bolonchén (where the Maya had drawn water from a vast system of underground cisterns), and examining sections of ancient stone roads that once traversed the area. March of 1842 found them camped at Chichén Itzá, the most celebrated of Yucatán's archaeological sites. For eighteen days they wandered awe-struck through acres of impressive buildings now familiar to thousands of travelers who visit Chichén Itzá every year—among them the Temple of the Warriors, El Castillo, the Ball Court, the Temple of the Jaguars, the Observatory, and Las Monjas, some of which, Stephens declared, "may be regarded as the most important [ruins] we have met with in our entire explorations. . . ."

Early in April they sailed to Cozumel Island and explored the nearby city of Tulúm, a walled complex of pyramids, temples, and

palaces located atop a windswept cliff on the coast of Quintana Roo. En
route back to Mérida they stopped to inspect the huge mounds of
rubble marking the ruins of Dzilám, Izamal, and Aké, the last sites
visited by the explorers whose union had been responsible for
uncovering so many archaeological wonders. After seven months in the
field, Catherwood's health was again failing, and Stephens, fortified
with new evidence, was eager to plunge into the waiting caldron of
academic debate. On May 18, 1842, having "now bid farewell to
ruins," as Stephens regretfully noted, they departed from the port of
Sisal bound for New York.

Immediately upon returning, Stephens began writing another
book, *Incidents of Travel in Yucatan*, which was published early in
1843. In its preface he described the work as a record of "the most
extensive journey ever made by a stranger to [Yucatán], and . . . an
account of visits to forty-four ruined cities in which remains or vestiges
of ancient populations were found. . . . For a brief space the stillness
that reigned around them was broken, and they were again left to
solitude and silence. Time and the elements are hastening them to utter
destruction. In a few generations, great edifices, their facades covered
with sculptured ornaments, already cracked and yawning, must fall and
become mere shapeless mounds. It has been the fortune of the author to
step between them and the entire destruction to which they are
destined; and it is his hope to snatch from oblivion the perishing but
still gigantic memorials of a mysterious people."

In retrospect, John Lloyd Stephens had succeeded admirably in
laying the undeniable splendors of Maya civilization before the world.
Eventually, his explorations opened the way for scholars to begin
systematically probing these remarkable ruins, and his perceptive books
on the subject—long ago acclaimed as classics—have remained in print
and are still widely read. With ample justification Stephens has been
called "the father of Maya archaeology," and he ranks in the forefront
of that select group of gifted amateurs such as Schliemann, Botta,
Rawlinson, and Layard who contributed so enormously to our
knowledge of antiquity.

3

MYTHS
AND THEORY:
THE BIRTH
OF A SCIENCE

 By the mid-1840s the existence of ruins of advanced civilizations in Mexico and Central America could no longer be seriously challenged. But when questions arose concerning the identity of their builders, most antiquarians steadfastly retreated to the only acceptable sources of possible inspiration: Europe, Asia, the Near East, Africa—in short, any area of influence which precluded the suggestion of an indigenous development.

Ultimately the realization of the scope and achievements of these ancient civilizations added new intensity to the already heated controversy surrounding the origins of the American Indians. In a flood of articles, popular books, and scientific papers, innumerable theories were advanced to demonstrate that the Indians were descended from such widely diversified ancestry as the Assyrians, Hittites, Phoenicians, Scythians, Chinese, Hindus, Tartars, Norsemen,

Welsh, Irish, and a host of other peoples, all of whom had allegedly reached America at some unknown time in the past.

Various sixteenth-century Spanish historians concluded that the Indians were descendants of the Lost Tribes of Israel, who they believed had sailed across the Atlantic after their expulsion from Samaria by the Assyrians (as related in the Old Testament) about 721 B.C. In later years this hypothesis was expounded by William Penn, Cotton Mather, Roger Williams, and many other prominent figures, and the appearance in the 1830s of Lord Kingsborough's impressive folios, *Antiquities of Mexico*, lent an air of scholarly credence to this so-called "Jewish Theory." It received additional impetus from the Mormon Church, whose founder, Joseph Smith, incorporated the idea of Israelite migrations to America into his *Book of Mormon*. Even today the New World Archaeological Foundation, organized and financed by the Mormons, is carrying out excavations in an attempt to confirm the validity of Smith's teachings.

With the upsurge of interest in Egypt during the nineteenth century, a number of students advocated that certain pre-Columbian cultures originally stemmed from the Nile Valley. Great significance was attributed to traits associated with Egyptian antiquities which also occurred in the Western Hemisphere. For example, pyramids, temples, hieroglyphic writing, elaborate tombs, bas-relief sculpture, and sun worship were common to both regions. Mummies wrapped in woven shrouds had been excavated in Peru and Bolivia, and some of the figures depicted in Maya sculpture were vaguely suggestive of elephants. To many observers these apparent analogies constituted positive proof of former contacts between Egypt and America, either by means of ships or long-vanished land connections.

Numerous authors championed this theory with reckless abandon. Among its leading exponents was Augustus Le Plongeon, an eccentric French adventurer, self-styled physician, and amateur archaeologist who traveled extensively in Yucatán and conducted haphazard excavations at Chichén Itzá. In two wildly imaginative books, *Queen Moo and the Egyptian Sphinx* and *Sacred Mysteries Among the Maya and the Quichés: Their Relation to the Mysteries of Egypt, Greece, Chaldea, and India*, Le Plongeon compiled a staggering amount of spurious information to support his belief in direct links between Yucatán and Egypt.

Not content to let the matter rest there, he endowed the Maya with incredible technological advances (including electricity and telegraphic communications!), and even insisted that they had established colonies in the Nile Valley, Mesopotamia, and India over 11,500 years ago.

Another prominent writer on this subject was G. Elliot Smith, an Australian anatomist who became interested in Egyptology while teaching at the Cairo Medical School. Eventually Smith formulated a theory, detailed in a lengthy work entitled *Human History*, which held that the basic attributes of civilization—namely agriculture, the invention of metals, urbanization, architecture, writing, and art—had originated in the Nile Valley and subsequently spread to Europe, Asia, and America. Smith quickly found an enthusiastic disciple in the person of William J. Perry, a professor of comparative religion at the University of Manchester, whose widely read book, *The Children of the Sun*, outlined the routes by which civilized attainments had supposedly been diffused from Egypt to other parts of the world. According to the conclusions reached by Smith and Perry, these influences were ultimately transmitted to America via Southeast Asia and achieved their maximum expression in the emergence of Maya civilization.

Naturally a dilemma of such protean aspects—one involving unaccounted-for races and vanished civilizations—also encouraged the popular occult belief that the Indians were survivors of "lost continents" long since submerged beneath the sea. Exactly which of these mysterious lands they had allegedly come from was a matter of sharp disagreement, but there were three persistent choices: Atlantis, Lemuria, and Mu.

Unquestionably the most famous was Atlantis. Originally described by the Greek philosopher Plato in his dialogues *Timaeus* and *Critias*, this imaginary paradise was located in the Atlantic just west of the Straits of Gibraltar and had once been the center of a vast empire whose power extended into Europe and Asia. Dominating the island was a magnificent city filled with splendid temples, villas, and gardens, and the surrounding countryside abounded with game animals, wild fruit, herbs, and spices, all of which, wrote Plato, "that sacred island lying beneath the sun brought forth . . . in infinite abundance." Supposedly the Atlanteans had enjoyed an untroubled existence "as

42 MAYA ⊂⋑

long as the divine nature lasted in them, they were obedient to the laws, and well affectioned toward the gods." But as invariably happens when humans achieve an idyllic state, they slowly fell victim to corruption, jealousy, and greed, thus causing the angry gods to plunge the island into the ocean, never to be heard from again—or so Plato thought.

He had created Atlantis to prove a philosophical point, yet his tale continued to hold an almost mystical fascination for countless writers, antiquarians, and occultists. Such intellects as Voltaire, Montaigne, and Buffon debated the possibility of the legendary continent's existence. Even the renowned scientist-philosopher Sir Francis Bacon succumbed to its lure, drawing upon Plato's ideas to set forth his own Utopian concepts in an unfinished essay entitled *New Atlantis* (1627). No less a scholar than Brasseur de Bourbourg, the discoverer of Landa's *Relación* and the Motul Dictionary, and a highly respected student of pre-Columbian antiquities, published a curious work in 1868 known as *Quatre Lettres sur le Mexique* in which he offered a rash of outlandish theories seeking to prove that Atlantis had been the "mother culture" of all ancient civilizations, including those of Mexico and Central America. And in 1882 a lawyer from Minnesota named Ignatius Donnelly released what became the most celebrated book ever written on the subject—*Atlantis: The Antediluvian World*. Not only did Donnelly view Plato's narrative as historical fact rather than allegorical fancy, he envisioned Atlantis as the Garden of Eden, the scene of mankind's transition from savagery to civilization, and the place from which advanced culture spread to Europe, Egypt, the Orient, and America. Strangely enough, the fascination with Atlantis has endured unabated to the present day; it still figures prominently in the teachings of various occult groups, and several books have recently appeared recounting attempts to locate the fabled island by scientific methods.

Another vanished land was believed to have existed in the Indian Ocean. First suggested in the mid-nineteenth century by an English zoologist named Philip Sclater to explain the geographical distribution of lemurs, this continent—known as Lemuria—was later embellished by the vivid imagination of the noted theosophist Helena P. Blavatsky. According to her famous treatise, *The Secret Doctrine*, Lemuria was inhabited by creatures of the most bizarre description: egg-laying, hermaphroditic giants who gave rise to several "root races" from which various branches of mankind eventually evolved, including the American Indians, whose ancestors were the Fourth Root Race.

No less fantastic was the continent of Mu, supposedly located somewhere in the area of the Pacific bordered by Easter Island, Hawaii, the Ladrones, and Fiji. Numerous writers have offered varying accounts of Mu (some identify Mu and Lemuria as the same island), but its principal advocate was James Churchward, who allegedly discovered a record of Mu's history inscribed on a set of stone tablets acquired in India from a Hindu priest. In a series of books entitled *The Lost Continent of Mu*, *The Children of Mu*, and *Sacred Symbols of Mu*, Churchward conjured up an astonishing picture of a tropical paradise inhabited simultaneously by dinosaurs, an assortment of modern animals and birds, and exactly 64,000,000 humans whose technical prowess enabled them to develop a highly advanced civilization over 50,000 years ago. Unfortunately, however, Mu sank into oblivion amid earthquakes and a fiery holocaust when the "gas chambers" supporting the island unexpectedly collapsed, though by then colonists from Mu had already settled in Europe, Asia, and America.

For years the debate over the origin of the Indians raged on, seemingly without hope of resolution. New theories, usually predicated on extremely tenuous evidence, constantly appeared in print, and endless analogies were drawn between various pre-Columbian cultures and the whole panoply of Indo-European civilizations. The existence in Mexico and Central America of terraced pyramids (similar to Sumerian ziggurats), calendrical systems, mathematics, and sculptured figures with beards or Negroid features implied to many observers a connection with such peoples as the Assyrians, Phoenicians, Hittites, Babylonians, or Carthaginians. Other students viewed certain motifs in Mesoamerican art—lotus blossoms, tree-of-life designs, scrolls, dragon-like creatures, sun disks, and sea monsters—as conclusive evidence that massive migrations had reached America from India, Southeast Asia, China, or Japan. Inscriptions on a stone found near Paraíba, Brazil, in 1872 were pronounced to be a Canaanite text. Burial mounds in the Mississippi Valley yielded tablets inscribed with markings variously interpreted as Arabic, Chinese, Hebraic, Greek, Celtic, Sumerian, and Gaelic, and several monoliths supposedly bearing a Viking script turned up along the eastern coast of the United States. But regardless of how much these arguments differed in specific details, they all served the same basic purpose—to prove that America's aboriginal cultures were either founded or strongly influenced by immigrants from distant lands, a concept which is still being expounded today.*

As early as 1840, John Lloyd Stephens concluded in his book, *Incidents of Travel in Central America, Chiapas, and Yucatan*, that the ruins he had explored were those of an *indigenous* civilization, accomplishments born of an inherent genius apart from any outside influences. Categorically, he ruled out the principal sources of foreign inspiration from which Maya culture might have sprung. "I set out with the proposition that they are not Cyclopean," he wrote, "and do not resemble the works of Greek or Roman; there is nothing in Europe like them. . . ." So far as Asia was concerned, Stephens found little evidence for serious comparisons. He saw no similarity between Maya buildings and those of ancient China or Japan, and he emphasized the complete absence in Mexico and Central America of the artificially excavated caves and rock chambers typical of Buddhist and Hindu temples.

Stephens then challenged the premises on which Maya and Egyptian architecture were so often equated, particularly the occurrence of pyramids in both regions. "The pyramidal form," he observed, "is one which suggests itself to human intelligence in every country as the simplest and surest mode of erecting a high structure upon a solid foundation. It cannot be regarded as a ground for assigning

---

* Although modern archaeologists have traditionally rejected the idea of contacts between the ancient civilizations of the Old World and America, they have recently begun to reexamine this problem in the light of new evidence—especially a number of remarkably parallel culture traits which appear to indicate that certain pre-Columbian peoples may have experienced limited contacts with groups from Europe, the Near East, and Asia. For a detailed discussion of this question, see the following publications: Carroll L. Riley, J. Charles Kelley, Campbell W. Pennington, and Robert L. Rands, editors, *Man Across the Sea* (Austin: University of Texas Press, 1971); Cyrus H. Gordon, *Before Columbus* (New York: Crown Publishers, 1971); Gordon F. Ekholm, "Transpacific Contacts," in *Prehistoric Man in the New World*, edited by Jesse D. Jennings and Edward Norbeck (Chicago: University of Chicago Press, 1964); David H. Kelley, "Eurasian Evidence and the Mayan Calendar Correlation Problem," in *Mesoamerican Archaeology: New Approaches*, edited by Norman Hammond (Austin: University of Texas Press, 1974); Emilio Estrada and Betty J. Meggers, "A Complex of Traits of Probable Transpacific Origin on the Coast of Ecuador," *American Anthropologist*, Vol. 63 (1961); Robert Heine-Geldern, "The Problem of Transpacific Influences," in *Handbook of Middle American Indians*, Vol. 4, edited by Gordon F. Ekholm and Gordon R. Willey (Austin: University of Texas Press, 1966).

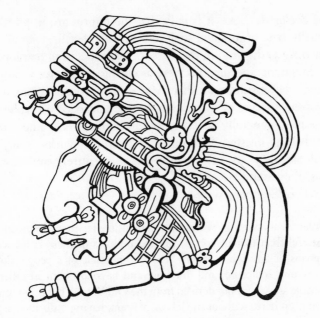

Head of an elite figure, Yaxchilán. (After Maudslay.)

a common origin to all people among whom structures of that character are found unless the similarity is preserved in its most striking features." Egyptian pyramids, he pointed out, were characteristically uniform in design and intended solely as burial places; by contrast those in America varied greatly in form and were constructed primarily to support temples or shrines on their summits.

With regard to other types of structures, Stephens noted that massive columns, "a distinguishing feature of Egyptian architecture," were absent in Maya ruins. Nor did they exhibit the *dromos* (avenue of approach), the *pronaos* (porch or vestibule), or the *adytum* (inner sanctum) usually found in Egyptian temples. He cited marked differences in comparative methods of construction and decorative embellishment, and the relatively small stones used by the Maya were, in Stephens' words, "scarcely worthy of being laid in the walls of an Egyptian temple." Furthermore, he conceded only the most superficial resemblances between the sculpture of the two areas. "If there be any at all," he declared, ". . . it is only that the figures are in profile, and this is equally true of all good sculpture in bas-relief."

Exploding as they did in the midst of overwhelming opinion to the contrary, Stephens' speculations were as daring as they were prophetic. In refuting the assumption that Maya civilization stemmed from Indo-European sources of inspiration, he had advanced a revolutionary hypothesis now generally accepted by archaeologists. "The works of these people," he insisted, "are different from the works of any other known people; they are of a new order, and entirely and absolutely anomalous: they stand alone."

Elsewhere Stephens wrote:

Unless I am wrong, we have a conclusion far more interesting and wonderful than that of connecting the builders of these cities with the Egyptians or any other people. It is the spectacle of a people skilled in architecture, sculpture, and drawing, and beyond doubt in other more perishable arts . . . not derived from the Old World, but originating and growing up here, without models or masters, having a distinct, separate, independent existence: like the plants and fruits of the soil, indigenous.

I am inclined to think that there are not sufficient grounds for the belief in the great antiquity . . . ascribed to these ruins; that they are not the work of a people who have passed away and whose history has become unknown. Opposed as is my idea to all previous speculations, I am inclined to think that they were constructed by the races who occupied the country at the time of the invasion by the Spaniards, or of some not very distant progenitors.

It perhaps destroys much of the interest that hangs over these ruins to assign to them a modern date; but we live in an age whose spirit is to discard phantasms and arrive at truth, and the interest lost in one particular is supplied in another scarcely inferior; for, the nearer we can bring the builders of these cities to our own times, the greater is our chance of knowing all. Throughout the country the convents are rich in manuscripts and documents written by the early fathers, caciques, and Indians, who very soon acquired the knowledge of Spanish and the art of writing. These have never been examined with the slightest reference to this subject; and I cannot help thinking that some precious memorial is now mouldering in the library of a neighboring convent, which would determine the history of some one of these ruined cities; moreover, I cannot help believing that the tablets of hieroglyphs will yet be read. No strong curiosity has hitherto been directed to them. . . . For centuries the hieroglyphics of Egypt were inscrutable, and, though not perhaps in our day, I feel persuaded that a key surer than that of the Rosetta Stone will be discovered. And if only three centuries have elapsed since any one of these unknown cities was inhabited, the race of the inhabitants is not extinct. Their descendants are still in the land, scattered, perhaps, and retired, like our own Indians, into wildernesses which have never yet been penetrated by a white man. . . .

In 1881 a former officer in the British foreign service, Alfred P. Maudslay, embarked on a campaign of wide-ranging explorations that signaled the birth of Maya research as a science. During the course of seven expeditions covering a period of thirteen years, Maudslay traveled throughout the region, mapping sites, surveying buildings, and making plaster casts of monuments and inscriptions. He also compiled

Figure from a ceramic vase, Chamá, Guatemala.

48 MAYA

a superb photographic record of Maya antiquities, which were included together with accurate drawings and a descriptive text in his five-volume contribution to a monumental work on the natural history of the area entitled *Biologia Centrali-Americana*, published in London between 1889 and 1902. With this study Maudslay set a standard of scholarship seldom equalled in the annals of archaeology, and even today it remains an indispensable reference.

Soon after Maudslay began his explorations, various scientific institutions entered the field of Maya research. By 1892 the Peabody Museum of Archaeology and Ethnology at Harvard University had inaugurated a series of expeditions, conducted by an Austrian explorer-photographer named Teobert Maler, to survey remote sites in Yucatán, the Petén, and the drainage of the Usumacinta River. In 1914 the Carnegie Institution of Washington undertook an ambitious program of study, eventually leading to excavations at Uaxactún, Copán, Chichén Itzá, Kaminaljuyú, Mayapán, and several other major ruins. Significant projects were later carried out by the British Museum, the University of Berlin, the Field Museum of Natural History in Chicago, and more recently by the University of Pennsylvania, the Middle American Research Institute at Tulane University, and the Instituto Nacional de Antropología y Historia in Mexico.

With the advent of systematic excavations, the silent realm of earth which had enveloped the ruins for centuries was finally penetrated. Gradually it became possible to trace stylistic developments in art and architecture, to define chronological sequences, and to classify the enormous quantities of pottery unearthed by archaeologists, which provided a highly sensitive indicator of cultural change, outside influences, and technological advances. Simultaneously, naturalists studied the region's geology, climate, flora, and fauna to determine the effects of environment on the evolution of Maya civilization, while ethnologists and linguists worked among contemporary Maya tribes, examining their culture for possible links with the past. Equally important was the evaluation of ethnohistoric documents in the form of early Spanish chronicles, colonial records, and native manuscripts, especially where associations could be made between these sources and specific archaeological questions.

One of the principal tasks facing scholars was the decipherment of Maya hieroglyphic writing and the correlation of their calendar with our own. Explorations have revealed a bewildering profusion of hieroglyphic texts inscribed on ceramics, monuments, tablets, ornaments, and on the walls, lintels, doorjambs, columns, and stairways of ruined structures. Obviously no comprehensive insight into Maya civilization could be achieved without some knowledge of the content of these inscriptions, but this problem has proved extremely difficult to resolve. Epigraphers quickly recognized the system of writing used by the Maya as both unique in pre-Columbian America and totally unrelated to Indo-European scripts, leaving them with no precedents to follow in deciphering it. Only through painstaking efforts on the part of many students using a variety of approaches has any progress at all been made toward this end—and that has been disappointingly limited.

Although Landa had failed in his attempt to formulate an alphabet for reading the inscriptions, his *Relación* contained drawings of the hieroglyphs representing the days and months of the calendar, their Yucatec names, and information on the divisions of the 365-day solar year. He had further noted that the Maya recorded twenty-year periods called *katuns* and sketched a diagram to show how they were calculated. In making these observations Landa provided the cornerstone on which future efforts to interpret the hieroglyphs rested, but this material remained unknown until Brasseur de Bourbourg discovered the manuscript of the *Relación* in 1863.

Not long thereafter a number of scholars began challenging the problem of glyphic decipherment with unrelenting zeal. Among the most prominent early contributors to the development of Maya epigraphy were Ernst Förstemann, Charles P. Bowditch, Joseph T. Goodman (the newspaper editor who gave Mark Twain his first job writing for the *Territorial Enterprise* in Virginia City, Nevada), J. E. Teeple, William Gates, Eduard Seler, and Hermann Beyer, each of whom made significant advances in both theoretical studies and the reading of individual glyphs. In recent years the leading figures in this field have been the late Sylvanus G. Morley, recognized as the foremost Mayanist of his day, and the English archaeologist J. Eric Thompson, whose prolific writings have added tremendously to our overall knowledge of the subject. In fact, Thompson's exhaustive work, *Maya Hieroglyphic Writing: An Introduction*, is the most comprehensive reference currently available, and in 1972 he published the first complete translation of the Dresden Codex.

During the past two decades the study of Maya hieroglyphics has entered an intensive new phase. In 1952 a Russian scientist, Yuri Knorozov, began reporting on the results of his efforts to apply computer technology to the problem of decipherment. Using a revolutionary approach, he translated a number of glyphs by analyzing elements that in his opinion represent consonant–vowel patterns and offer a key to reading the inscriptions phonetically. Admittedly, Knorozov's conclusions are extremely controversial, but his methods have awakened a serious interest in the question of phoneticism in Maya writing and some students feel they hold enormous promise. Along with other experimental concepts of which Knorozov's work is but one example, a massive effort is now under way to assemble as much new information as possible as a basis for future research. To accomplish this, a far-reaching program—the Maya Hieroglyphic Inscription Study—was launched in 1968 under the direction of a Scottish explorer named Ian Graham. Jointly sponsored by the Guttman Foundation of New York and the Peabody Museum, Graham's project, which is expected to require at least fifteen years to complete, is aimed at seeking out and recording previously unknown inscriptions throughout the area.

Notwithstanding the unending efforts of dedicated scholars, the decipherment of Maya writing remains a singularly elusive goal. Granted that most of the inscriptions involving calendrics, astronomy, and mathematics can now be easily read, only a small portion of those glyphs presumably dealing with such matters as history, religion, or mythology are presently understood. Specialists do not even agree on the exact function of many glyphic elements or to what extent they are ideographic, syllabic, or phonetic. Nor can they fully explain the relationship of ancient inscriptions to the various Maya languages spoken in historic times.

Such problems result from structural complexities inherent in the hieroglyphs themselves. Basically, the inscriptions are intended to be read in double columns from left to right and top to bottom. Each individual glyph is composed of a combination of symbols, including a main or central element together with variable affixes. The latter serve to modify the meaning of the central element (often in curiously subtle ways), and they appear as prefixes attached above or to the left of the central element, as postfixes occurring below it or to the right, or in some cases as infixes incorporated into the central element itself. Glyphic components are frequently quite abstract and difficult to recognize, and there are a distressingly large number of possible combinations of central elements and affixes. In his *Catalog of Maya Hieroglyphs*, J. Eric Thompson lists a total of 492 probable main elements and 370 affixes, and elsewhere he notes an example of a particular central element occurring with eighty separate arrangements of affixes.

Many glyphs had two distinct forms which were interchangeable —a "normal" form represented by abstract or symbolic signs and a "head variant" form derived from the heads of deities, humans, animals, birds, and mythological creatures. Apparently the choice of a specific glyph form, its dimensions and stylistic traits, or the exact position of affixes in relation to main elements was largely determined by aesthetic considerations. Marked differences existed between the type of glyphs seen in the codices and those inscribed on sculpture and ceramics, and there is considerable evidence that the hieroglyphs underwent some degree of evolution in the sense that new glyphs frequently appeared and older ones either changed in design or ceased to be used.

Despite slow progress in hieroglyphic decipherment, efforts to correlate the Maya and Gregorian calendars have been considerably more successful. Early attempts to solve this question rested primarily upon cross-checking native dates as recorded in post-Conquest documents for which we have precise Gregorian equivalents. For instance, the *Books of Chilam Balam* contain information on the twenty-year *katun* period coinciding with the founding of Mérida by the Spaniards on January 6, 1542. In his *Relación*, Landa cited an example of a date in an ancient system called the Calendar Round probably corresponding to July 26, 1553, and several other chronicles give indications of the *katuns* in which important events of the Conquest took place. Working backward from these historically known occurrences, it was theoretically possible to reconstruct Maya calendrics alongside our own time scale.

But the matter was not that simple. By the sixteenth century the so-called "Long Count" calendar formerly used by the Maya (see Chapter 5), which recorded a series of continuous time segments beginning from a fixed starting point in the distant past, had been replaced by an abbreviated system known as the "Short Count" or *u kahlay katunob* (literally "count of the *katuns*"). With this method only repeating cycles of thirteen *katuns* were computed, and since a *katun* was actually composed of 19.71 years (due to the fact that a 360-day year was employed in these calculations), the *u kahlay katunob* consisted of 13 × 19.71 years, or the equivalent of 256¼ years in the Gregorian calendar. Unfortunately, Short Count dates tell us nothing except the day on which a particular *katun* ended, and the knowledge of exactly where each *katun* fitted into the overall scheme of Long Count chronology—information clearly understood by the Maya—has since been lost. In effect, these *katun* cycles appear to "float" in time; they are accurate within isolated spans of 256¼ years, while giving no indication of their relation to longer periods—as if, for instance, we knew the years and decades referred to by specific dates, but not the centuries or millennia. Hence numerous uncertainties surrounding the correct order of the *katuns* mentioned in post-Conquest sources have made the problem of correlation exceedingly complex.

Of the various methods proposed for equating the Maya and Gregorian calendars, two have been most commonly used in recent years. One was devised by the late Herbert J. Spinden, an outstanding student of Maya art who subsequently turned his attention to hieroglyphic writing and calendrics. An alternate system was first suggested by Joseph T. Goodman and later modified by Juan Martínez Hernández and J. Eric Thompson. According to Spinden's calculations, all dates in the Maya calendar are 260 years earlier than those of the Goodman-Martínez-Thompson chronology, and the relative accuracy of these correlations has long been the subject of a heated controversy.

A major breakthrough in resolving this debate resulted from the use of radiocarbon dating, a technique developed in 1947 by a physicist at the University of Chicago named Willard F. Libby. This ingenious means of determining the age of organic matter is based on the fact that the atmosphere contains among its other elements a radioactive substance designated as Carbon 14. It is formed by the action of cosmic radiation upon nitrogen, and it accumulates within most living organisms in direct proportion to the quantity of Carbon 14 in the atmosphere. Immediately after death this balance is interrupted, and the Carbon 14 retained in the organism gradually disintegrates at a fixed rate. By comparing the amount of radioactive carbon in remains such as bone, wood, and vegetable fiber, the span of time from the date of death until these materials are unearthed can be calculated with reasonable accuracy.

Applying this technology, scientists at the University of Pennsylvania examined a series of wood samples taken from door lintels found in the ruins of Tikal in Guatemala, all of which bore carved date inscriptions. Even with the margin of error normally occurring in Carbon 14 analysis, the tests convincingly supported the Gregorian dates assigned to these inscriptions using the Goodman-Martínez-Thompson system. As a result, the GMT correlation (as it is often referred to in technical literature) has since gained almost universal acceptance among Mayanists, and it is therefore used as the basis of the dates in this book.

Important though the correlation problem has been in reconstructing the development of Maya civilization, it is by no means the only such guide available to archaeologists. Valuable insight was obtained through the careful study of ceramics, stylistic changes in art and architecture, and various social, religious, and economic factors. By utilizing such information along with radiocarbon dating, stratigraphy (the study of the sequence in which archaeological remains are deposited in the earth), calendrical inscriptions, and ethnohistoric documents, it has been possible to define the successive stages of Maya history and the approximate dates at which they occurred. Allowing for some degree of regional differentiation, since cultures rarely evolve uniformly over large geographical areas, this basic chronology and the generally accepted terminology applied to its periods can be outlined as follows.

Paleo-Indian		15,000?–8000 B.C.
Archaic		8000–1500
Formative (Also called Preclassic)	Early	1500–1000
	Middle	1000–300
	Late	300–A.D. 300
Classic	Early	300–600
	Late	600–900
Postclassic	Early	900–1200
	Late	1200–The Spanish Conquest

Regardless of everything scientists have learned about the Maya so far, we constantly encounter unanswered questions of fundamental importance. No one has satisfactorily explained where Maya civilization originated or how it evolved in an environment so hostile to human habitation. We have almost no reliable information on the origin of their calendar, hieroglyphic writing, and mathematics; nor do we understand countless details pertaining to social organization, religion, government, and everyday life. Even the shattering catastrophy leading to the sudden abandonment of their greatest cities during the ninth century A.D.—one of the most baffling archaeological mysteries ever uncovered—is still deeply shrouded in conjecture.

In view of unresolved problems of such magnitude, any synthesis of Maya history must necessarily draw to some extent upon tentative conclusions. Obviously the existing literature, scientific and popular alike, contains errors and omissions which are unavoidable given the current state of research. Hopefully these gaps in our knowledge will ultimately be closed by future discoveries, for this, after all, is the *raison d'être* of archaeology.

4

THE SEARCH
FOR ORIGINS

 Archaeologists now agree that man first entered America from Asia via the Bering Strait during the geological epoch known as the Pleistocene or Ice Age. Exactly when the earliest such migrations occurred is uncertain; we have conclusive proof that humans were roaming the New World at least by 10,000 B.C., but some authorities believe their arrival may date back twenty-five to fifty thousand years, or possibly even longer. Equipped with flint-tipped spears, crude stone implements, animal skin clothing, and a knowledge of fire making, these ancient hunters—the direct ancestors of the American Indians—slowly spread throughout most of this hemisphere, living in caves or rock shelters and subsisting on the meat of now extinct animals. Numerous sites where they had slaughtered camels, mastadons, bison, mammoths, and sloths have been unearthed in western Canada, the United States, South America, and at several localities in Mexico, especially in the vicinity of Mexico City near the villages of Tequixquiac, Santa Isabel Iztapán, and Tepexpán.

Yet virtually nothing is known about this stage of human

occupation in the Maya area. Only one meager clue to the presence of early hunters has turned up thus far inside its boundaries: an obsidian projectile point from San Rafael in south-central Guatemala. It is strikingly similar to a widely distributed type designated as Clovis fluted points (first discovered in 1936 outside Clovis, New Mexico), dating from ten to twelve thousand years ago, but because it was found on the surface its precise archaeological context is unknown.

By about 8000 B.C. drastic environmental changes combined with overhunting had caused the disappearance of many species of animals on which these nomads depended for survival. Gradually the emphasis of their economy shifted to the gathering of wild seeds, roots, and nuts supplemented by killing small game, and their existence became more sedentary, since they usually moved only seasonally and within a restricted geographical area. Eventually these fundamental changes ushered in a new era known archaeologically as the Archaic period (8000 to 1500 B.C.), a major manifestation of which was the rise of the Desert Culture tradition—so named because it evolved in arid sections of the western United States and Mexico.

Like their predecessors, the Desert Culture peoples lived in caves or beneath overhanging cliffs, but examination of their remains shows a steady progression from the rude lifestyle of the Ice Age hunters to the rise of incipient agrarian societies. Along with more technically advanced artifacts such as milling stones, ornaments, weaving tools, ritualistic objects, and basketry, agriculture also appeared in these obscure horizons. In fact, the oldest examples of plant domestication found anywhere in America occur in Desert Culture sites in Mexico. Excavations in the states of Tamaulipas and Puebla conducted by the Canadian archaeologist Richard S. MacNeish have established that the principal staples of ancient Mexico—maize, squash, beans, chili peppers, and pumpkins—were under cultivation there by about 2000 B.C., with some of these plants dating back two or three thousand years earlier.

But even Archaic sites are extremely scarce in the Maya region, and those which have been found yielded very little information. A rock shelter known as Santa Marta, situated northwest of Tuxtla Gutiérrez in Chiapas (technically just outside the Maya area), contained artifacts similar to items unearthed in Tamaulipas and

Puebla, and radiocarbon dates placed their age in the same general time scale—7000 to 3000 B.C. Other sites probably belonging to the Archaic period include a cave near Comitán in Chiapas and several shell middens on the Pacific coast of Guatemala and Chiapas. What sparse data has been gleaned from these locations suggest the existence of peoples whose mode of life was basically the same as the Desert Culture groups to the north, except that agriculture does not seem to have been introduced into the area until sometime after 2500 B.C.

Actually, then, we have no idea who the earliest ancestors of the Maya really were or where they originated. Nor is it certain when they arrived in the region, although a possible answer to this question has resulted from the recent application of lexicostatistics and glottochronology, two newly developed techniques used to determine the age of languages.* One of the pioneers in this field of linguistics, Norman A. McQuown, has utilized these approaches to propose a sequence of specific dates for the appearance of various Maya dialects. If McQuown's findings are correct (and they have been seriously challenged by some scholars), he estimates that the first Maya-speaking groups settled in what is now the Department of Huehuetenango in northwestern Guatemala around 2600 B.C.

Not until the dawn of the Formative or Preclassic period (1500 B.C. to A.D. 300) do we encounter archaeological remains of peoples who were definitely ancestral to the Maya. Such evidence is presently limited to a few scattered sites, and the material uncovered in these horizons is extremely fragmentary. Indeed, scientists have so far been able to piece together only enough facts to reconstruct the barest outlines of life during this remote epoch.

We know that Formative villages already exhibited traits which remained largely unchanged throughout Maya history. Essentially they consisted of loosely knit clusters of single-roomed habitations intended to accommodate small family groups. Usually these dwellings were

---

* Lexicostatistics is a method of analyzing selected linguistic factors such as cognates, grammatical structure, and vocabulary, thus enabling specialists to determine which languages belong to the same basic stock and to measure the degree of variance between them. Glottochronology is used to estimate the time span involved in these changes. It operates on the principle that certain linguistic elements evolve at a predictable rate, and the more divergence that exists between related languages, the longer the time required for these differences to have occurred.

built of a framework of poles lashed together by vines and plastered
with mud (though stone, reeds, or other materials may sometimes have
been used); their roofs were high pitched and made of thatched palm
leaves or grass, and many units stood on low mounds to insure adequate
drainage. Set apart from the domestic houses were special structures
designed for ceremonial purposes. The earliest buildings of this type
were simple earthen platforms and terraced, flat-topped pyramids,
which often supported temples or shrines similar in appearance and
construction to the peasants' huts. Gradually this religious architecture
became increasingly elaborate, incorporating masonry, sculptural embellishments, and stairways; and important temples were arranged
around open courtyards to form ceremonial precincts within the core
of each settlement.

Artifacts unearthed in the oldest Formative sites reflect a level of
technology comparable to certain Neolithic cultures in Europe and
Asia. Among these objects are an assortment of stone implements,
including scrapers, knives, spear points, hammers, axes, drills, and
milling stones called *metates* and *manos* used to grind maize. Ornaments such as beads, earplugs, and pendants fashioned out of stone,
pottery, or shell are commonly found, together with tiny clay figurines
representing animals, birds, and humans, especially female forms which
presumably had some connection with fertility cults. Few examples of
more fragile articles have survived, but Formative peoples undoubtedly
utilized antler, bone, and wood to make awls, needles, weaving tools,
looms, simple furniture, and other specialized items. Henequen fiber
(also called sisal or hemp) and cotton supplied raw materials for
baskets, matting, bags, nets, and fabric, and animal hide was used in
making sandals.

While it is not known when or by what means pottery first
appeared among the Maya, large quantities are recovered in Formative
sites. One of the most ancient ceramic sequences came from the
earliest levels of occupancy at La Victoria on the Pacific coast of
Guatemala—the so-called Ocós phase which began about 1500 B.C. By
at least 900 B.C. pottery was in use at Seibal and Altar de Sacrificios in
the Petén, and elsewhere in this region the earliest ceramics unearthed
to date—a type known as Mamon—are widely distributed in sites that
were in existence by 600 B.C.

Formative pottery generally consisted of rounded jars called *tecomates*, cylindrical vases, bowls, and shallow, flat-bottomed plates with slightly flaring sides, though in the Guatemalan highlands effigy vessels, tripod jars, and incense burners were quite common. One particularly notable expression of early ceramic art—the famous Las Charcas ware produced at Kaminaljuyú near Guatemala City during the Middle Formative—was characterized by exquisite bowls embellished with monkeys, grotesque masks, and abstract elements superbly painted in red on a white background. Otherwise most Formative pottery was rather prosaic, and except for certain varieties decorated with incised geometric designs, appliqué, or simple painted motifs, it usually had plain surfaces ranging from white, cream, and gray to red, orange, buff, brown, and black.

Agriculture provided the principal economic basis of Formative cultures. Near every village fields were periodically cleared of vegetation to allow the cultivation of crops such as maize, squash, beans, pumpkins, and chili peppers. Abundant supplies of wild fruit, nuts, and seeds were available in most areas, and meat was obtained by hunting deer, peccaries, tapirs, monkeys, turkeys, iguanas, and other game animals. Groups living near the ocean supplemented their diet with crustaceans, sea turtles, and a variety of fish, probably caught in nets woven of henequen fiber and weighted with pottery disks or stones.

Life depended almost entirely upon the rhythm of seasonal change, upon sun and rain, and the uninterrupted sowing and harvesting of crops in amounts ample to support increasingly complex societies. Nature alone was recognized as the sole key to survival. Early in their history the Maya began to deify its manifestations through an elaborate pantheon; appeasing the gods inspired an endless round of ceremonial observances and eventually brought about the rise of a powerful priesthood. With these developments, the structure of Formative society—at least during the last half of the period—became steadily more stratified, and there are clear indications even at this early date of ruling classes whose wealth and authority set them considerably apart from the ordinary peasants.

More than any other factor, religion provided the prime stimulus for the upsurge of Maya culture. Overwhelming testimony to this fact

Design from a ceramic vase portraying a dignitary being carried in a palanquin, Ratinlinxul, Guatemala.

is seen in Late Formative horizons throughout the region. Nowhere is it better exemplified than by what is called the Miraflores phase at Kaminaljuyú, the period from about 300 b.c. to a.d. 200 that witnessed the transformation of this site from a relatively small village into an imposing ceremonial center whose influence dominated the highlands for centuries.

Today most of Kaminaljuyú's ruins lie buried under the outskirts of Guatemala City, but excavations conducted intermittently since 1935 by the Carnegie Institution have revealed over 100 pyramids and platforms erected during the Miraflores phase. Originally intended to support temples on their summits, these mounds ranged up to sixty-five feet in height and consisted of several superimposed structures built in successive stages over long periods of time. Some of them contained elaborate tombs—rectangular shafts cut into the tops of pyramids and roofed with heavy wooden beams, fiber matting, and reeds—in which important personages believed to have been rulers or priests were buried.

From the richness of the objects unearthed in these graves there can be no question that by Late Formative times the elite classes already enjoyed a highly exalted social position. The bodies were carefully wrapped in cotton shrouds, covered with red cinnabar, and placed fully extended on wooden litters before being lowered into the tombs. Sometimes adults and children (possibly servants or relatives of the deceased), who appear to have been sacrificial victims, were interred with the corpse, and the chambers were filled with funerary offerings of astonishing beauty. Two spectacular tombs concealed in a structure at Kaminaljuyú known simply as Mound E-III-3 yielded ornaments of jade, shell, and stone, translucent bowls carved of marble and chlorite schist, obsidian flakes, iron pyrite plaques, a mosaic mask made from albite, tiny soapstone bottles, effigies, a stone sculpture representing a mushroom rising from the back of a crouched jaguar, and approximately 455 pottery vessels (some were shattered beyond repair), including a jar in the form of a seated human decorated with polychrome stucco applied to its surface.

Levels of cultural development approximating the Miraflores phase at Kaminaljuyú have been found in Late Formative horizons in the Petén. Here our initial information on this period came to light in 1926 when archaeologists from the Carnegie Institution began excavating the important site of Uaxactún. Among the buildings selected for exploration was a cluster of twelve mounds in the city's eastern sector designated as Group E, and the seventh structure in this complex unexpectedly provided a discovery of major significance.

Outwardly this pyramid was typical of other Classic period ruins at Uaxactún. Its exterior was severely damaged by decay, but since it was the custom of Maya builders to frequently modify or enlarge their religious edifices, a considerably older pyramid in a nearly perfect state of preservation was disclosed underneath the outer shell. This exceptional structure—known as E-VII-sub—stood twenty-seven feet in height and was made of earth and rubble covered with a veneer of gleaming white stucco. Its terraced sides were ascended by stairways and adorned with ponderous, highly stylized masks representing jaguars and serpents; altogether eighteen of these curious masks decorated the pyramid, all skillfully modeled in stucco and measuring about six feet high by eight feet wide.

E-VII-sub is one of the finest examples of early religious architecture ever uncovered in the lowlands. It was probably constructed either in the first or second century A.D. and was associated with a type of pottery called Chicanel, which is characteristic of Late

Formative culture throughout the Petén. Equally important, the
discovery of E-VII-sub and Chicanel ceramics *underlying* Classic
buildings demonstrated not only the existence of well-established
ceremonial centers in the lowlands during the Formative period, but
also that these settlements had eventually expanded into the great cities
which flourished there between A.D. 300 and 900.

Further confirmation of this has since emerged at the huge site of
Tikal, twelve miles south of Uaxactún. Recent excavations by the
University of Pennsylvania have shown that Tikal was already
occupied by 600 B.C., with an accelerated emphasis in Late Formative
times on ceremonialism, elite social classes, architecture, and art.
Digging below the city's North Acropolis (one of the most incredible
achievements of Maya engineering), scientists unearthed the remains
of numerous temples and platforms dating from this period, along with
large quantities of Chicanel ceramics. Some of these structures were
surprisingly refined, and one outstanding example—a terraced pyramid-temple erected about 50 B.C.—was constructed of masonry and
ornamented with heavy apron moldings, two massive stucco masks,
and a complex sculptured frieze adorning its facade, which was
originally painted red, pink, black, and cream.

Splendid tombs were found in conjunction with these buildings at
Tikal. Usually situated beneath the floors or foundations of temple
platforms, they consisted of rectangular crypts built of cut stone and
often roofed with crude corbeled vaulted ceilings, a feature which later
became a hallmark of Classic architecture. As was the case at
Kaminaljuyú, such graves were intended for persons of high rank, and
they contained lavish mortuary offerings: jade and shell ornaments,
figurines, masks, ceramics, stingray spines (highly prized for ceremonial bloodletting), obsidian blades, and gourds covered with decorative
stucco, to mention a few typical objects. Several tombs also revealed
the badly decayed outlines of once magnificent polychrome frescoes
depicting humans wearing ornate headdresses and costumes.

Indications of Late Formative activity have turned up elsewhere in
the lowlands. Almost every site studied thus far in the Petén has
contained large amounts of Chicanel pottery, suggesting a sizable
population throughout this region during these centuries. Similar

evidence was found at various places in northern Yucatán, particularly at the important center of Dzibilchaltún near Mérida, where an expedition from Tulane University and the National Geographic Society excavated scores of Late Formative structures ranging from simple house mounds to multileveled aggregations of platforms, pyramids, and courtyards.

Obviously many details surrounding the rise of Maya culture out of the Formative period are still obscure. Yet archaeologists now have a reasonably accurate picture of the gradual transition from incipient agricultural villages to burgeoning ceremonial centers. Nor can there be any doubt that the basic traits which characterized Maya civilization at its height during the Classic period were deeply rooted in Formative traditions. Foremost among these were massive religious architecture, a complex pantheon coupled with formalized rituals, elite ruling classes, hieroglyphic writing, calendrics, a high degree of sophistication in art, and the so-called "stela cult" or "stela-altar complex"—the widespread practice of erecting dated monuments to commemorate important ritualistic events or mark the passing of specific time intervals, usually five, ten, or twenty year periods.

Scholars are not certain how or when the Maya acquired the calendar and hieroglyphic writing, though in recent years some fascinating clues bearing on this question have arisen. At first these inventions were believed to have been devised independently by the Maya, probably in the lowlands where their earliest inscriptions came to light. But lately many archaeologists have concluded that they originated among a shadowy people called the Olmec, who inhabited Tabasco and southern Veracruz at an extremely remote date.

Olmec culture is known mainly from three important ruins: La Venta, Tres Zapotes, and San Lorenzo. By roughly 1000 B.C. at least two of these sites—San Lorenzo and La Venta—were already flourishing settlements complete with pyramids, temple platforms, and highly evolved stone sculpture, thus making them the oldest ceremonial centers ever discovered in Mesoamerica. Another intriguing fact about the Olmec is that although their origin remains a mystery, their influence was extremely widespread. Unmistakable Olmec traits are found in numerous archaeological sites extending from the Valley of

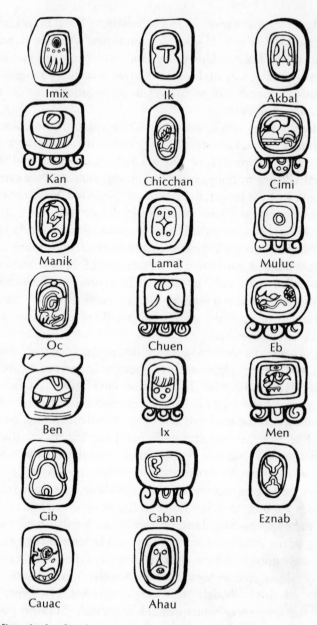

Imix | Ik | Akbal
Kan | Chicchan | Cimi
Manik | Lamat | Muluc
Oc | Chuen | Eb
Ben | Ix | Men
Cib | Caban | Eznab
Cauac | Ahau

Hieroglyphs for the twenty days of the Maya calendar with their Yucatec names.

Mexico to El Salvador, and some authorities view the Olmec as a kind of "mother culture" which played a vital role in stimulating the rise of civilization throughout the area.

Olmec craftsmen were exceptionally adept at cutting and polishing materials such as jade, serpentine, quartz, and steatite, and had mastered the art of carving basalt from which they made altars, stelae, and colossal human heads, some of which weigh up to eighteen tons. Olmec sculpture, noted for its vigor, originality, and emphasis on realism, is unique in Mexico and Central America, and students consider it the first major art style to have evolved anywhere in the region. It centered on full-figure and bas-relief depictions of fat, "baby-faced" humans, often displaying pronounced Negroid or Oriental features, and anthropomorphized monsters or werejaguars, with flat noses, flamelike brows, fangs, and snarling, down-turned mouths.

Apparently the Olmec also possessed the earliest calendar and hieroglyphic writing in Mesoamerica. In 1939 Matthew W. Sterling, excavating at Tres Zapotes under the sponsorship of the Smithsonian Institution and the National Geographic Society, dug up a broken monument known as Stela C. One side was carved with a relief mask representing a typical Olmec werejaguar, but to the astonishment of Sterling and his colleagues its backside contained a date inscription employing the same bar-and-dot numerals and Long Count calendrical system used by the Maya. It recorded a year equal to 31 B.C.—the oldest surely dated object ever found in Mexico or Central America!

Now another curious fact suddenly assumed new significance. In 1902 a small jade effigy of a duck-billed figure—the Tuxtla Statuette— was unearthed near San Andrés Tuxtla in Veracruz, only fifteen miles east of Tres Zapotes. Generally conceded to be of Olmec workmanship, this piece had puzzled archaeologists because it was carved with a Long Count date equivalent to A.D. 162. Since the inscriptions on both the Tuxtla Statuette and Stela C from Tres Zapotes were considerably older than any dates of positive Maya origin, speculation arose that it was perhaps the Olmec who actually invented hieroglyphic writing and the calendar. Added support was given to this idea by the discovery of numerous Olmec artifacts—mostly figurines, pendants, celts, and plaques—inscribed with glyphic symbols that suggest early forms of Maya hieroglyphs. Furthermore, the existence of extremely ancient calendrical texts, bar-and-dot numerals, and glyphs has been established at Chiapa de Corzo in central Chiapas and the famous Zapotec ruins of Monte Albán in Oaxaca, and in both cases these innovations are seemingly related to Olmec influences.

Recently an expedition from the University of Pennsylvania led by Robert J. Sharer uncovered a badly effaced monument at the Formative site of El Portón in the Salama Valley of central Guatemala. Nothing remained of its original carvings except eleven figures believed to represent glyphic elements, but several of these are strikingly similar to certain Olmec motifs. Other early dates and inscriptions associated with Olmec traits have been found elsewhere in Guatemala. Included among these are fragmentary calendrical glyphs on a sculptured stone at Abaj Takalik, a small ceremonial center on the Pacific slopes south of Quezaltenango. Another monument designated as the Herrera Stela from El Baúl, approximately fifty miles southeast of Abaj Takalik, exhibited a partially eroded Long Count inscription tentatively dated at A.D. 36. Excavators working at Kaminaljuyú stumbled upon a portion of a magnificent Late Formative relief carving—Stela 10—depicting an anthropomorphized jaguar and two lavishly costumed humans interspersed with bar-and-dot numbers and hieroglyphs, which appear to represent an antecedent of Maya script.

In each instance the monuments at Abaj Takalik, El Baúl, and Kaminaljuyú (the stela from El Portón is too damaged for comparison) reflect a sculptural style derived from an important center called Izapa, situated in southeastern Chiapas near the Guatemalan border. Izapan art is distinguished by its superbly executed, if somewhat florid, bas-relief sculpture, usually portraying mythological creatures, richly attired chieftains, and gods. Inherent in these works are a number of Olmec-inspired characteristics, and many archaeologists envision Izapa as a major entrepôt through which Olmec influences were infused into Maya culture during Late Formative centuries. Such arguments are strengthened by the early appearance at Izapa of several unique features subsequently adopted by the Maya: the stela-altar complex, images of a "Long Lipped God" who probably became the rain deity Chac, and various stylistic conventions incorporated into Early Classic sculpture.

Regardless of the inferences to be drawn from this evidence, not all scholars are willing to concede that the calendar and hieroglyphs used by the Maya were outgrowths of Olmec inventiveness. Opponents of the "Olmec theory" contend that inscriptions comparable in age or even earlier than those on Stela C at Tres Zapotes, the Tuxtla Statuette, and the Herrera Stela at El Baúl may still lie undiscovered in the dense lowland rain forest. Others have suggested that prior to the appearance of stone sculpture the Maya recorded inscriptions on perishable materials such as wooden tablets, leather scrolls, or bark paper which have long since vanished, or that the common practice of demolishing older monuments in the course of expanding architectural complexes might have caused the deliberate destruction of many if not all of the earliest texts.

Whatever the facts surrounding their origin, calendrics and hieroglyphic writing reached their highest development in the lowlands during the Classic period, especially in the thriving cities of the Petén and adjacent regions. The oldest Maya inscription found so far comes from Stela 29 at Tikal, which bears a Long Count date corresponding to July 6, A.D. 292. Along with hieroglyphics and the calendar, all of the other key determinants which marked the Classic florescence— monumental architecture, the corbeled vault, stone sculpture, polychrome pottery, and the stela cult—had appeared fully developed in the lowlands by the time Stela 29 was erected at Tikal, leaving no question that the Maya had attained a remarkably civilized state by the end of the third century A.D.

In spite of the obvious environmental advantages offered by the highlands of the Southern Area—its temperate climate, fertile soil, and abundant natural resources—this region remained curiously outside the mainstream of Classic Maya civilization. As J. Eric Thompson has pointed out, sculpture, architecture, and ceramics never approached the levels of excellence in the highlands that they did elsewhere, and the corbeled vault, one of the most fundamental concepts of Maya engineering, was restricted to several sites near the periphery of lowland influence. Even the auspicious beginnings in hieroglyphic writing and calendrics evidenced by the monuments at Abaj Takalik, El Baúl, and Kaminaljuyú mysteriously disappeared from the area sometime after A.D. 150, and no inscriptions positively belonging to the Classic period have occurred in any highland sites. Equally strange was

Pop   Uo   Zip   Zotz   Tzec   Xul

Yaxkin   Mol   Chen   Yax   Zac   Ceh   Mac

Kankin   Muan   Pax   Kayab   Cumhu   Uayeb

Hieroglyphs for the eighteen months of the Maya calendar and the five-day Uayeb.

the sudden abandonment of Long Count dates and the stela cult in the Southern Area by the end of the Late Formative era, both having previously played an important role in the development of its early cultures.

Archaeologists believe these puzzling circumstances are largely attributable to an influx of invaders from Teotihuacán, the huge ceremonial center near Mexico City so famous for its lavish palaces, long avenues of temples, and the Pyramids of the Sun and Moon. Large numbers of immigrants from Teotihuacán began infiltrating the highlands around A.D. 400, heralded perhaps by a full-scale military invasion. Strong Mexican influences were also felt about this time in various lowland cities, particularly at Tikal where Early Classic monuments and ceramics often reflect the unmistakable imprint of Teotihuacán's artistic conventions. But the impact of Mexican intervention was most pronounced in the Guatemalan highlands. In the two centuries immediately after A.D. 400, Kaminaljuyú was practically rebuilt in the image of Teotihuacán's architectural style. Much of the pottery from Classic tombs at Kaminaljuyú was either imported directly from Teotihuacán or copied after its characteristic wares, even to vessels decorated with images of Teotihuacán's gods or figures wearing typical costumes of its elite classes. Unquestionably, Kaminaljuyú, together with vast sections of the outlying territory, fell under the domination of Mexican rulers, sociopolitical institutions, and religious beliefs, and though certain Maya traditions continued to survive and extensive trade was carried on with lowland cities, life in this region was radically altered by these foreign contacts.

It was, therefore, in the lowlands of the Central and Northern Areas that Maya civilization reached the peak of its development. One can hardly imagine a more unfavorable setting for this extraordinary upsurge. Nearly all of the lowlands are plagued by poor soil, excessive heat and humidity, high rainfall (averaging 90 to 120 inches annually in some regions), limited natural resources, swarms of insects, and rampant disease. Except for a few enclaves of swamp, grass-covered savannas, and semiarid coastal plains, immense expanses are blanketed by thick rain forest consisting primarily of mahogany, ceiba, sapote, wild fig, logwood, rubber trees, breadnut, aguacate, palms, and a profusion of herbaceous plants, vines, and ferns. Yet in these inhospitable surroundings, especially in the densely overgrown Central Area, Maya civilization soared to superlative heights of intellectual, artistic, and technical achievements.

Here architects used the full potential of masonry, principles of stress, and the corbeled vault to design cities on a truly heroic scale. Such pursuits as mathematics, hieroglyphic writing, astronomy, and calendrics opened limitless new scientific and philosophical vistas. Stone sculpture gave permanent expression to aesthetic concepts previously impossible to execute, and skilled artisans began to produce ceramics, murals, ornaments, and textiles of exceptional refinement. Increasing populations encouraged the rapid spread of established traditions, restless building, and the founding of new settlements until the countryside was dotted with villages and ceremonial centers.

Almost everything the Maya accomplished during the Classic period continued to spring as it had in Formative centuries from deeply rooted sources of religious inspiration. Even their cities were gigantic shrines encompassing all they envisioned as darkly mysterious in the universe. Despite regional variations in certain aspects of Maya culture—particularly art and architecture—the fundamental precepts of cosmology, ritualism, iconography, hieroglyphics, and calendrics remained essentially alike throughout the lowlands, a fact suggesting a high degree of orthodoxy and single-minded devotion to spiritual ideals. Everywhere the nature of Maya society displayed a similar uniformity: a rigid class structure dominated by powerful priests and nobles in whom all authority resided. Leading the way before masses of illiterate peasants, these elite groups established the tenets around which the daily existence of the people revolved. Under their direction life for the common man was an endless round dedicated to cultivating the soil, public service necessary to construct, maintain, and enlarge the ceremonial centers, and adoration of the gods through strict observance of rituals, offerings, and sacrifices.

In the beginning the peasants were content to subject themselves to this powerful elite. Willingly they upheld the mandates of priest-kings who they believed were divinely chosen to guide their destinies. Ample reward was to be found in the Golden Age their ingenuity had ushered into reality and that now burst upon them with intoxicating brilliance.

5
THE CLASSIC PERIOD: SIX CENTURIES OF ACHIEVEMENT

Above everything else the Maya accomplished during the Classic period, their ingenuity was most pronounced in the fields of astronomy and calendrics. As such pursuits were closely connected to religion, they expended unlimited effort to achieve mastery in these realms of knowledge. No other people in history were so obsessed with the passing of time, and they labored tirelessly to understand its mysteries and control its awesome influences. Ultimately these endeavors led them to evolve a calendrical lore extending back millions of years into the past and encompassing a profoundly complex philosophy.

To the Maya time was never a purely abstract means of arranging events into an orderly sequence. It was envisioned as a supernatural phenomenon involving omnipotent forces of creation and destruction, with all of its aspects directly influenced by gods who were believed to be either benevolent or evil. Such deities were associated with specific numbers and took forms by which they could be portrayed in hieroglyphic inscriptions. Each division of the Maya calendar—whether days, months, years, or larger segments—was conceived as a "burden" carried on the backs of these divine guardians of time; at the conclusion of their allotted cycles the burdens were assumed by whatever god represented the next appropriate number as determined by the calendar.* If a malevolent deity happened to acquire the burden of a particular cycle, grievous consequences could be expected until it was relinquished to a more favorable bearer. Whether or not a certain month or year held promise of good or bad fortune was a matter predetermined by the temperament of the god on whose back it was transported.

It was a curious belief, and one which explains in part the far-reaching power of the priesthood over the populace, who must surely have considered survival impossible without learned mediators to interpret the gods' irrascible tendencies. Only the astronomer-priests stood between the normal continuation of life and catastrophes brought about by misjudging divine inclinations. Having recognized the attributes of the gods and plotted their restless paths across the highways of time and space, they alone could determine when beneficial and harmful deities ruled a specific period or, as was frequently the case, when the number of benevolent gods outweighed the less sympathetic ones. Thus this obsession with time was tantamount to a grand-scale quest for lucky and unlucky periods in the hope that, once forewarned of future prospects, events could be guided along a propitious course.

Altogether the Maya observed three distinct year measurements: the 260-day sacred year or *tzolkin*, the *tun* or 360-day year, and the *haab* or vague year, which was composed of 365 days divided into eighteen months of twenty days each, with the addition of an extra five-day month known as the *uayeb*. Ordinarily the vague year (often referred to as the "civil year") was used in secular affairs; the *tzolkin*

---

* To illustrate this principle, imagine that at midnight on October 31 the god of the number thirty-one unloads his burden—the month of October. Immediately the god of the number one picks up the month of November, carries it on his back for twenty-four hours, then releases it to the god of the number two, who the next day gives it to the god of the number three, and so forth. The same procedure would also apply to the years, decades, centuries, and millennia, all of them moving through eternity on the backs of various gods responsible for their proper numerical sequence.

determined certain matters pertaining to ceremonials and prophecy, and the *tun* was employed in computing Long Count dates.

Great ritualistic importance was placed on the so-called Calendar Round, or the meshing of the vague year with the *tzolkin*. To accomplish this it was necessary to synchronize the days and months of the 365-day vague year with repeating sequences of twenty days and the numbers from one to thirteen, which comprised the 260-day *tzolkin*. A total of 18,980 possible combinations of days, months, and numbers were involved in these permutations, and the Calendar Round—the interval required for a particular date to return to its original position—occurred only once every fifty-two years. Actually, the Calendar Round was not an exclusively Maya innovation. It was widely used throughout Mesoamerica both for recording time and as a divinatory almanac, and though its origin is unknown, there is evidence of its appearance among the Zapotecs at Monte Albán in the fifth century B.C.

Unquestionably, the outstanding achievement of Maya calendrics was the Long Count—also called the Initial Series. Generally considered to be the most accurate calendar ever devised in the ancient world, it was surprisingly complex in structure and consisted of recurring cycles of nine interrelated periods which made it possible to keep track of enormous time spans in somewhat the same way as we compute decades, centuries, and millennia. The basic unit of the Long Count was the day or *kin*. Since there is no evidence that it was divided into anything comparable to hours, minutes, or seconds, we must assume a day was the smallest segment of time recorded by the Maya. Beginning with the *kin* the sequence of Long Count intervals was as follows:

20 *kins*	= 1 *uinal*	(20 days)
18 *uinals*	= 1 *tun*	(360 days)
20 *tuns*	= 1 *katun*	(7,200 days)
20 *katuns*	= 1 *baktun*	(144,000 days)
20 *baktuns*	= 1 *pictun*	(2,880,000 days)
20 *pictuns*	= 1 *calabtun*	(57,600,000 days)
20 *calabtuns*	= 1 *kinchiltun*	(1,152,000,000 days)
20 *kinchiltuns*	= 1 *alautun*	(23,040,000,000 days)

Each of these cycles revolved independently, expanding from *tuns* to *alautuns* by multiples of twenty. Virtually every Long Count inscription included only the first five divisions, or *kins* through *baktuns*, plus the position of the Calendar Round on which the date terminated. Hieroglyphs representing these periods were inscribed in double rows of vertical columns descending in order from *baktuns* at the top to *kins* at the bottom. Numeral coefficients accompanying the glyphs indicated the number of times each cycle had occurred since the beginning of Maya chronology. Hence a typical date as written by archaeologists would read 8.14.10.13.15 7 *Ahau* 3 *Xul*, or 8 elapsed *baktuns*, 14 *katuns*, 10 *tuns*, 13 *uinals*, and 15 *kins*, together with a Calendar Round position equal to the day 7 *Ahau* of the *tzolkin* and the third day of the month *Xul* in the vague year—in this case a date corresponding to April 9, A.D. 328. In addition, Long Count inscriptions were usually augmented by what is known as a "Supplementary Series," which included glyphs denoting such information as the length of the lunar month, the phase of the moon, and the patron deities associated with the specific date involved.

One of the major problems faced by epigraphers was to determine the starting point of the Maya calendar. This question was successfully resolved by the discovery that every Long Count inscription was calculated from a base of 13.0.0.0.0 4 *Ahau* 8 *Cumku*, now interpreted as 3113 B.C. It is referred to as the "zero date" of all Long Count computations, and its function is analogous to the birth of Christ in the Gregorian calendar. Because this date occurs over three millennia before the earliest known Maya inscription on Stela 29 at Tikal, it undoubtedly represents a hypothetical rather than an actual historical event. Sylvanus Morley suggested that the Maya might have considered 13.0.0.0.0 4 *Ahau* 8 *Cumku* the day of the world's creation or the birthdate of their gods, but if we allow that the Olmec actually invented the Long Count, its origin may be rooted in Olmec mythology.

While unraveling the complexities of the calendar, scholars quickly became aware of the astonishing skills possessed by Maya astronomers. Using fixed lines of sight or buildings aligned so as to provide observation points, they had meticulously plotted the movements of the sun, the moon, and Venus; there is some evidence they might also have probed Mars, Jupiter, and Mercury, and they undertook intensive studies of solar eclipses, enabling them to accurately predict these phenomena. They were acutely aware that seemingly minute discrepancies in certain computations would eventually lead to irreconcilable flaws, and as a result of cautious observations their margin of error was remarkably slight. For example, their measurement of the length of the tropical year was 365.2420 days as compared with our present estimate of 365.2422; and they calculated the average synodical revolution of Venus at 584 days, whereas its actual span is 583.92. Adjustments may have been made to allow for fractional increases in the duration of the solar year (which we eliminate by the addition of leap years), and their error in synchronizing the Venus cycle with the 260-day *tzolkin* and the 365-day vague year amounted to only one day in approximately 6,000 years. Moreover, the Maya appear to have envisioned time in infinite terms: examples of calendrical inscriptions have been uncovered reaching back 90,000,000 to 400,000,000 years into eternity.

Achievements of this magnitude would obviously have been impossible without a system of mathematics. As was the case with many other hieroglyphs, the Maya employed two means of representing numbers—head variant symbols and the more commonly used bar-and-dot notations. With the latter method numbers from one to nineteen were written as follows:

Numbers above nineteen were noted according to their placement in vertical columns, with each ascending position increasing by multiples of twenty, or a sequence of 1, 20, 400, 8,000, 160,000, 3,200,000, and 64,000,000. Numerals placed in any one of these positions automatically increased in value as determined by the corresponding multiple, and the column was then added to formulate the total. To write a number such as 827, two dots were placed in the third position denoting two units of 400, one dot in the second position to indicate twenty, and a bar and two dots (the number seven) in the first position. A vigesimal system of this type made it relatively simple to add and subtract, and recent studies have demonstrated that it could also be adapted to multiplication, division, and square root extractions, although to what extent the Maya understood these more complicated procedures is unknown.

Another notable feature of Maya mathematics was the principle of the zero. In fact, this abstract concept, essential to all but the most rudimentary calculations, was invented by only two other peoples in history—the Babylonians and Hindus. Even the Greeks and Romans had no knowledge of the zero, and it was not introduced into Europe until the Middle Ages. Whether the zero's invention in Mesoamerica can be attributed to Olmec or Maya ingenuity is closely tied to the controversy surrounding the origin of the calendar and hieroglyphic writing. Yet the Maya made extensive use of its potential, and it was represented in their inscriptions by a stylized shell, an open hand, or several variant glyphs.

As was true of so many facets of Maya civilization, archaeologists have amply demonstrated that religion was a major factor behind the development of the calendar, mathematics, and hieroglyphic writing. Art and architecture added still other dimensions to this quest for the supernatural—a means of glorifying the gods and enshrining sacred beliefs, iconography, and traditions. Such considerations were equally inherent in the basic concept of Maya "cities," which throughout their history were primarily—though not exclusively—ceremonial rather than urban in function.

Although the cities were not laid out according to formalized plans, they included certain characteristic types of structures—primarily open courtyards, terraced pyramids, temples, palaces, and shrines.

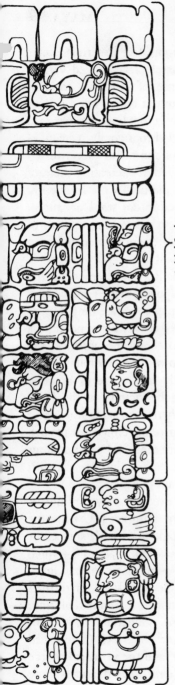

Initial Series Introducing Glyph

Grotesque head in center is the only variable element of this sign. This is the name glyph of the deity who is patron of the month (here Cumhu) in which the Initial Series terminal date falls

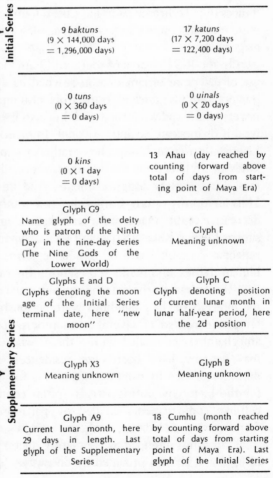

Initial Series

9 *baktuns* (9 × 144,000 days = 1,296,000 days)	17 *katuns* (17 × 7,200 days = 122,400 days)
0 *tuns* (0 × 360 days = 0 days)	0 *uinals* (0 × 20 days = 0 days)
0 *kins* (0 × 1 day = 0 days)	13 Ahau (day reached by counting forward above total of days from starting point of Maya Era)

Supplementary Series

Glyph G9 Name glyph of the deity who is patron of the Ninth Day in the nine-day series (The Nine Gods of the Lower World)	Glyph F Meaning unknown
Glyphs E and D Glyphs denoting the moon age of the Initial Series terminal date, here "new moon"	Glyph C Glyph denoting position of current lunar month in lunar half-year period, here the 2d position
Glyph X3 Meaning unknown	Glyph B Meaning unknown
Glyph A9 Current lunar month, here 29 days in length. Last glyph of the Supplementary Series	18 Cumhu (month reached by counting forward above total of days from starting point of Maya Era). Last glyph of the Initial Series

Often these buildings were extraordinarily impressive in terms of size, design, and external decoration, and Maya architects utilized various techniques to impart an overwhelming sense of grandeur to their creations. Nearly always they enhanced important temples and palaces by elevating them on pyramids, platforms, or acropolises. Widespread use was made of tall, crestlike appendages called roof combs, usually of open-work design, which adorned the rooftops and further accentuated the illusion of height. Great effort was expended in decorating the roof combs and upper facades of many buildings, and both were frequently ornamented with sculpture or friezes executed in cut stone or stucco. Traces of polychrome paint have been found on the remains of some of these embellishments, indicating that they were originally coated with bright colors.

In the Río Bec area of southern Quintana Roo and Campeche, the use of elaborate ornamentation reached its apogee, with emphasis on pseudopyramids attached to the front of temples to create the effect of towers, and facades adorned with huge stylized masks surrounded by a wealth of intricate sculptural detail. Immediately to the north, in the Chenes district of Campeche, another group of ruins exhibits similar kinds of architectural flamboyance, especially in the use of gigantic masks and restless design elements. And in the vicinity of the Puuc Hills in northwestern Campeche and southern Yucatán, this florid decorative tradition attained a remarkable degree of refinement in such sites as Uxmal, Kabáh, Sayil, and Labná, where the facades of buildings reflect a veritable maze of geometric forms, false columns, serpents, human figures, and masks representing the rain god Chac.

In contrast to the external splendor achieved by Maya architects, the interiors of their buildings were curiously uninspired. Usually the temples consisted of several small rooms, sometimes with shrines or antechambers concealed within them, whereas the "palaces"—which may actually have been elite residences, administrative buildings, dormitories used by candidates studying for the priesthood, or retreats for the hierarchy during rituals—often contained a number of tiny, cell-like compartments divided by partitions. Generally the rooms were narrow and damp, without windows or chimneys (a few had small openings intended as ventilating ducts), and the principal source of light and air was provided by doorways. Sometimes the walls were decorated with murals, hieroglyphic inscriptions, or graffiiti, but for the most part interior rooms were plastered with white stucco and left unadorned.

In virtually every city there was a ball court in which a popular game known as *pok-to-pok* was played, and many of the larger centers had several such courts. As a rule they were shaped like a capital I, with a flat playing surface about 100 to 150 feet long and 25 to 50 feet wide flanked on two sides either by sloping or vertical walls. Elaborate rituals accompanied the playing of *pok-to-pok*, and the courts were often associated with temples where appropriate ceremonies were enacted in conjunction with the games. Quite possibly these temples also served as viewing stands for the elite classes, while ordinary spectators watched the matches from atop the enclosing walls.

Numerous cities contained structures identified as sweat baths—rooms fitted with stone benches, drainage troughs, and hearths for boiling water to make steam. Another interesting feature of some sites are groups of buildings arranged to serve as astronomical observatories; each of these consisted of a pyramid oriented due east opposite which stood three temples positioned to give observers on the pyramid's stairway stationary points for viewing the sunrise in order to determine equinoxes and solstices. Among other types of structures found in Maya cities are artificial reservoirs designed to store rainwater, and underground, bottle-shaped pits called *chultuns* probably used as cisterns, storage places, and burial vaults. Elaborate drainage systems for carrying off excess water from buildings and courtyards were quite common, and several sites have yielded the remains of aqueducts and bridges.

Maya engineers excelled in the building of roads and causeways. Known by the Yucatec word *sacbeob* ("white roads"), these were constructed of large stones overlaid by rubble and surfaced with a smooth layer of stucco or cement. Usually they were raised about two to four feet above ground level (sometimes up to eight feet where the roadways crossed swamps) and varied in width from approximately twelve to thirty-two feet. *Sacbeob* frequently connected important buildings or complexes, forming avenues through the heart of the city's ceremonial precincts. Many centers were linked to outlying districts by a network of roads extending for miles into the countryside, and the longest *sacbe* yet discovered stretches from Cobá in Quintana Roo westward to Yaxuná in Yucatán, a distance of slightly over sixty-two miles.

Unquestionably the expenditure of labor required to erect the ceremonial centers was enormous. Trees and underbrush were first cleared from prospective sites, and if necessary the land was leveled to permit the construction of foundations. Tons of stone had to be quarried and transported either by hand or on log rollers before it was cut, shaped, and set into place by masons. Limestone supplied the predominate building material throughout the lowlands, but elsewhere dolomite, tuff, sandstone, slate, adobe, and kiln-fired bricks were substituted. Wood from sapote and mahogany trees was utilized for making lintels over doorways, crossbeams to reinforce vaults, and joists under masonry roofs; stucco, mortar, and concrete could easily be obtained by burning limestone until it was reduced to powder and mixing it with water, gravel, or a sandlike substance called *sascab*.

In erecting substructures such as pyramids, acropolises, and platforms, the customary method was to build up the central core using rubble and earth, then secure it with masonry retaining walls. By contrast, the temples and palaces, with their interior space and vaulted ceilings, presented complex problems involving balance and stress, and the use of corbeled arches in place of the true arch (which the Maya never perfected) required a tremendous amount of downward thrust to support. Initially, these difficulties were resolved by means of large stones which extended through the entire width of the building's walls and sustained the weight of the superstructure. But by about A.D. 600 walls composed of smaller stones set in concrete and faced with a thin veneer of cut masonry were introduced, an innovation that increased structural stability and afforded greater flexibility of design—though because the older technique continued to be employed, it is not uncommon to find a single building incorporating both types of walls. Nor did the Maya ever completely abandon the use of wooden poles, wattle and daub, and thatch for certain religious structures; even in Classic and Postclassic sites there are platforms and pyramids with postholes on their summits, indicating that perishable buildings of this kind, doubtlessly patterned after Formative prototypes, were occasionally constructed.

Diego de Landa: Third Bishop of Yucatán, relentless destroyer of Maya culture, author of the *Relación de las Cosas de Yucatán.*

(From a portrait in the Catholic church at Izamal; reproduced by permission of the Peabody Museum of Archaeology and Ethnology, Harvard University.)

John Lloyd Stephens: the "father of Maya archaeology."

(From Harper's Monthly Magazine, January, 1859; reproduced by permission of Harper & Row, Publishers.)

Above, Copán as it appeared at its height during the Late Classic period.

(Restoration drawing by Tatiana Proskouriakoff.)

Left, Stela H, Copán.

Left, backside of Stela A, Copán, showing hieroglyphic inscriptions.

(Drawing by Frederick Catherwood; reproduced by permission of Harper & Row, Publishers.)

Below, the Hieroglyphic Stairway, Copán.

Left, Stela F, Quiriguá.
(From a photograph by Alfred P. Maudslay.)

Below, Altar P, Quiriguá. A zoomorph representing a two-headed monster.
(From a photograph by Alfred P. Maudslay.)

Limestone disk found at Chinkultic, Chiapas, depicting a ball player enclosed by a band of hieroglyphs.
(Courtesy of the Museo Nacional de Antropología, Mexico.)

The Great Palace, Palenque.

Right, stucco relief showing an elite figure attended by two retainers, the Great Palace, Palenque.

Below, sculptured figures in the East Court of the Great Palace, Palenque.

Temple of the Cross, Palenque. Note the use of a roofcomb to accentuate the building's height.

Limestone plaque found in the Great Palace, Palenque.
(Courtesy of the Museo Nacional de Antropología, Mexico.)

Temple of the Inscriptions, Palenque.

View of the Great Plaza at Tikal showing Temple I (rear) and Temple II. *(Courtesy of the University Museum, University of Pennsylvania.)*

Temple III, Tikal.

Alfred P. Maudslay in his camp at Chichén Itzá in 1889.
(From a photograph by H. N. Sweet.)

The Acropolis at Piedras Negras, Guatemala, about the beginning of the
ninth century A.D.

(*Restoration drawing by Tatiana Proskouriakoff.*)

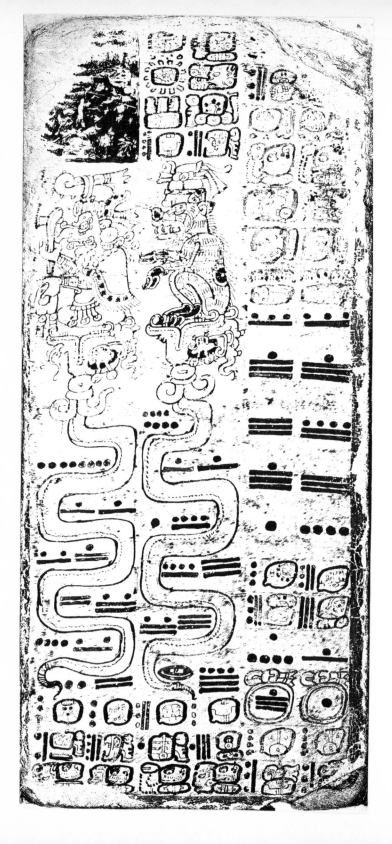

Left, a page from the Dresden Codex.
(Courtesy of the University Museum, University of Pennsylvania.)

Below, lintel 26 from Yaxchilán carved with elite figures in characteristic poses.
(Courtesy of the Museo Nacional de Antropología, Mexico.)

Ceramic figurines found in tombs on the island of Jaina, Campeche. Objects of this type—which date from the Late Classic period—were frequently decorated with red, yellow, blue, white, or black paint.

(Courtesy of the Robert Woods Bliss Collection of Pre-Columbian Art, Dumbarton Oaks, Washington, D.C.)

Ⅎ

Left, late Classic polychrome bowl embellished with the figure of a bird, probably from Campeche.

(Courtesy of the Robert Woods Bliss Collection of Pre-Columbian Art, Dumbarton Oaks, Washington, D.C.)

Below, limestone relief found at Jonuta, Tabasco. Note the artificially deformed forehead, pronounced nose, and almond-shaped eyes typical of Maya profiles.

(Courtesy of the Museo Nacional de Antropología, Mexico.)

Wooden figure of a kneeling priest or dignitary, Tabasco. An exceptional example of Maya woodcarving, this piece probably dates from the Early Classic period.
(Courtesy of the Museum of Primitive Art, New York.)

≣

Above, jade plaque, Late Classic, Nebaj, Guatemala.
(Courtesy, Middle American Research Institute, Tulane University.)

Below, marble vase carved with scrolls and animal effigy handles, Postclassic, Ulúa Valley, Honduras.
(Courtesy, Middle American Research Institute, Tulane University.)

Late Classic polychrome vases, Tepeu style.

(Courtesy of the Museum of Primitive Art, New York.)

Left, eccentric flint in the form of a human wearing an elaborate headdress, Guatemala. Probably used as a scepter.

(Courtesy of the Museum of Primitive Art, New York.)

Below, polychrome bowl, Late Classic, Yucatán.

(Courtesy of the Robert Woods Bliss Collection of Pre-Columbian Art, Dumbarton Oaks, Washington, D.C.)

Interior of the burial vault in the Temple of the Inscriptions at Palenque showing the carved slab in place over the sarcophagus.

(Courtesy of the Instituto Nacional de Antropología y Historia, Mexico.)

The sarcophagus containing the skeleton of a high priest or noble surrounded by jade ornaments.

(Courtesy of the Instituto Nacional de Antropología y Historia, Mexico.)

We do not know whether architects worked from predetermined plans or sketches, or what units of measure might have been used in their designs; but the size and complexity of many buildings make it difficult to believe they were erected without detailed drawings as a guide. Other mechanical aids available to Maya builders were extremely limited by modern standards, particularly since they had no wheeled vehicles to haul materials, no draft animals, and no metal tools.* Instead, they relied solely on manpower, stone implements (including axes, celts, hammerstones, chisels, and drills), henequen fiber rope to help in lifting heavy objects, and perhaps plumb bobs for aligning walls. Yet regardless of these limitations, the magnificence of Maya architecture almost defies the imagination. One needs only to view the spectacular structures at Tikal, Copán, Palenque, Uxmal, Chichén Itzá, or dozens of lesser-known ceremonial centers to appreciate their phenomenal impact, or to comprehend the dedication of the artists, craftsmen, and peasants who labored so diligently to execute such grandiose conceptions.

Similar technical restrictions surrounded the development of Maya art. Sculptors fashioned their materials—whether it was the much favored limestone or other media such as trachyte, sandstone, wood, stucco, or clay—with nothing but stone tools and wooden mallets. The carving and polishing of jade, bone, and shell, or the production of featherwork, mosaics, and inlays were accomplished with equally primitive instruments, and weaving was done on simple backstrap looms, using needles and battens of wood or bone. Even the potter's wheel, introduced in the Old World over 4,000 years ago, was never invented in Mesoamerica, although a crude device called a *kabal*—a wooden turntable rotated between the potter's feet—was used for shaping ceramics in colonial Yucatán and may have been known in this region prior to the Conquest. Nevertheless, the Maya created a unique artistic tradition displaying originality, prodigious vigor, and

---

* The use of the wheel in Mesoamerica constitutes an interesting paradox. Absolute proof exists that the principle of the wheel and axle was known in the region: ceramic figurines in the form of toy animals mounted on wheels have been excavated in several parts of Mexico. But there is no evidence that the wheel ever had practical applications in Mesoamerica or anywhere else in the New World prior to the arrival of Europeans.

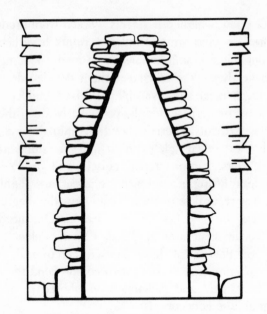

A corbeled arch used in Maya buildings.

incredible aesthetic refinement, an art whose genius was unexcelled in pre-Columbian America.

From earliest times Maya artists were primarily concerned with religious ideas. Yet within this prescribed framework highly innovative approaches gradually evolved, and many cities developed easily recognizable styles and specializations. Amid the rich and often abstract symbolism inherent in a religiously oriented art, the Maya did not hesitate to experiment in conveying perspective and a sense of movement, or to depict such activities as rituals, human sacrifice, warfare, and scenes from daily life with a startling degree of realism. Even in the most formalized works, with their hieratic mysticism, strangely aloof figures, and aura of impersonality, there is a tremendous sense of restrained vitality.

The conventionalized aspects of Maya art were most pronounced in sculpture. Undoubtedly this is attributable to its use in embellishing temples and religious monuments, particularly stelae and altars commemorating events of ritualistic or historical significance. Inspired by the sacrosanct nature of their creations, sculptors produced powerful images of deities, mythological creatures, animals in supernatural contexts, and, most important, elegant human figures representing ruling lords or priests. Invariably these regal personages are portrayed in a manner contrived to accentuate their lofty status: attired in elaborate costumes and jewelry, holding emblems of authority, attended by retainers, receiving tributes, presiding over captives or slaves, seated on thronelike daises, or being carried in litters. Generally they are shown in profile or with their bodies slightly angled toward the viewer; sometimes they face straight forward with only the head in profile and the feet turned out. Great attention was lavished on details of clothing, headdresses, and ornaments, which are often so ornate as to virtually obscure the figure itself, and because the remaining space within the composition was frequently covered with hieroglyphs or decorative elements, the total effect resulted in a visual opulence reminiscent of Oriental art.

Large-scale monuments were usually carried out in bas-relief, but the Maya were equally capable of working in the round. Among the best examples of full-figure modeling are numerous ceramic effigies noted for their elegant style and execution. Made either by hand or in molds (occasionally both techniques were combined) and fired in kilns, these took the form of animals, supernatural creatures, or humans in the guise of elite men and women, warriors, ball players, musicians, or dancers. Some of the most sophisticated types come from the island of Jaina off the west coast of Campeche, where they were placed in richly appointed tombs as funerary offerings. Jaina figurines often portray unusual subjects, including dwarfs, hunchbacks, aged persons with wrinkled faces and toothless jaws, and erotic scenes of old men caressing young girls; but the finest pieces represent elite dignitaries whose aristocratic features, magnificent costumes, and imperious *hauteur* suggest the same lofty positions they assume in stone sculpture.

Another supreme triumph of Maya art is reflected in the so-called Tzakol and Tepeu ceramics made in the Petén and neighboring regions during the Early and Late Classic periods respectively. Each of these styles is characterized by a variety of shapes—primarily jars, bowls, plates, and vases—and exhibits absolute mastery over such decorative techniques as incising, appliqué, modeling, and polychrome painting, all applied with astonishing sensitivity and draftsmanship. Aesthetically, Tzakol and Tepeu vessels rank among the most beautiful pottery made anywhere in the ancient world, especially Tepeu wares, which are often adorned with highly refined figurative paintings. Executed principally in orange, red, yellow, white, brown, and black on a buff-colored background, these remarkably animated designs focus upon deities, grotesque monsters, animals, nobles and priests, ceremonies, human sacrifice, and imaginative tableaux believed by some students to illustrate legends.

The narrative quality so evident in the scenes on Tepeu ceramics frequently carried over into murals that sometimes covered the interior walls of temples and palaces. Regrettably, few of these are known to have endured the ravages of decay; the most extensive are the celebrated frescoes at Bonampak in Chiapas (discussed in Chapter 9), but interesting paintings were also found at Uaxactún, Palenque, Chichén Itzá, Santa Rosa, and Tulúm. Judging from surviving examples, Classic period murals—in contrast to the more rigidly stylized or symbolic frescoes dating from later centuries—were surprisingly dynamic, treating a wide range of subjects in vividly realistic terms. Often they exhibit innovative experiments in perspective and the use of foreshortening to create an illusion of depth, and some of them have provided archaeologists with a wealth of otherwise obscure details pertaining to rituals, costumes, musical instruments, sacrifices, warfare, and occasional vignettes into everyday life.

Among the minor arts at which the Maya excelled was the working of jade, a mineral greatly prized for its intrinsic beauty and ritualistic connotations. Offertory caches and tombs of important persons yield large quantities of jade in the form of jewelry, effigies, plaques, and mosaics. It was frequently used as inlays in stone and shell or as decorations set into human teeth (a mark of social prestige), and many jade artifacts are engraved with low-relief designs comparable on a small scale to the most accomplished stone sculpture. Maya craftsmen were also adept at carving bone, shell, and wood from which they fashioned a variety of ornaments and ceremonial items, and some cities manufactured exquisite vessels of alabaster and marble embellished with incising or reliefs. Skillfully made knives, spearpoints, and other implements were chipped out of flint and obsidian, though the most intriguing objects of this type are known as "eccentric flints"—oddly shaped blades resembling crescents, exotic plants, scorpionlike insects, or profiles of humans and animals, which were apparently used in rituals.

We have almost no information about perishable arts such as weaving and featherwork, since nothing of this nature has survived except a few fragments of cloth. But considering the resplendent costumes and headdresses worn by elite figures depicted in sculpture and paintings, there is no doubt that these crafts were exceptionally advanced. Vivid pictorial details confirm that the Maya produced excellent cotton textiles decorated with dyed and embroidered designs, as well as gorgeous feather capes, mantles, panaches, shields, banners, and fans. Unfortunately, countless specimens of other fragile crafts, including basketry, leather goods, wood carvings, and lacquered gourds, were destroyed as a consequence of burial under moist conditions, leaving few traces of what must have once been a remarkable artistic legacy.

Only during the Postclassic period after A.D. 900 did metals assume any importance to the Maya. For the most part these were restricted to copper and gold imported from Panama, Costa Rica, Colombia, and Mexico (a few specimens of silver, zinc, and tin have come from the Guatemalan highlands), and metalworking techniques consisted primarily of filigree, lost wax or *cire perdue* casting, and *repoussé*. Objects of copper recovered from various sites include tiny bells, axes, celts, tweezers, figurines, tubes, disks, rings, earplugs, a small mask, and a single example each of an arrowhead and a fish hook. Gold was limited to ornaments and ritualistic items, and the largest number of gold artifacts discovered to date—primarily rings, beads, effigies, bowls, cups, and embossed disks—were brought up from the famous Sacred Cenote at Chichén Itzá (see Chapter 12) into which they had been thrown as sacrificial offerings. Recently a tomb uncovered in the ruins of Iximché, the former capital of the Cakchiquel tribe located fifty miles west of Guatemala City, yielded another spectacular cache of gold: forty beads, ten masks representing jaguars, and a headdress ornament resembling a crown.

Even a cursory view of Maya art reaffirms what we have observed in almost everything else about their culture: a staggering outpouring

*Design from a ceramic vessel, Tepeu style, Northern Petén. (After
M.D. Coe.)*

of time, energy, and resources inspired by religion and directed by a
powerful ruling hierarchy. Conspicuously absent are images of the
common man—the peasant farmers, the laborers who worked tirelessly
to erect the ceremonial centers, or the anonymous artists whose talents
so eloquently perpetuated the ideals of Maya civilization. Quite rightly,
the late artist-scholar, Miguel Covarrubias, called it an "official" art
intended primarily for the glory of the gods and the aggrandizement of
the elite classes. Only rarely does it abandon its obsession with deities,
rituals, mythology, or exalted rulers and priests to offer glimpses into
the lives of ordinary people.

Somehow the aloof figures staring out from stone sculpture are as
impersonal to us today as they must have seemed to an illiterate peasant
centuries ago. We marvel at the sophisticated scenes painted on
ceramics, the immense friezes adorning temples and palaces, or the
innumerable treasures unearthed in tombs of long-forgotten chieftains.
Yet for all that science can tell us about these superlative works of art,
the overall impression they create is one of absolute mystery. We are
unfailingly awed by their technical brilliance, aesthetic ingenuity, and

the unique vision of human existence they represent, but we cannot escape their overwhelming sense of utter remoteness.

Despite the large quantity of Maya art in museums throughout Europe and America, archaeologists are constantly haunted by the spectre of creations long since lost to the effects of time: undiscovered murals already hopelessly effaced, sculptured monuments eroded or smashed beyond recognition, or hieroglyphic codices rotting into oblivion in the earth-filled vaults of collapsed buildings or tombs. Moreover, countless objects of art are presently endangered by looters willing to commit acts of vandalism and theft in order to reap lucrative financial rewards offered by dealers seeking to exploit the inflated market in antiquities. Suddenly pre-Columbian art has become *de rigueur* among collectors; everything from ceramics and figurines to major monuments are being purchased on a no-questions-asked basis, often by persons to whom their "status" or investment potential far outweighs aesthetic or historical considerations. Ironically, this situation, rather than environmental factors, now poses the most immediate threat to the preservation of Maya archaeological sites, and the problem is so serious that it has prompted legal action by various international law enforcement, scientific, and cultural agencies in an attempt to end the ruthless decimation of this incomparable artistic heritage.

6
PALENQUE YIELDS
A "ROYAL" TOMB

 In 1952 a sensational discovery at Palenque
dramatically illustrated the artistic and archi-
tectural heights achieved by the Maya during the Classic period. Along
with Yaxchilán and Piedras Negras on the Usumacinta River, Palenque
represents the climax of the Classic florescence in the western sector of
the Maya area. Its sedate buildings and monuments reflect the ultimate
aesthetic ideals toward which the city's inhabitants had progressed for
centuries, and many archaeologists consider it the most beautiful of all
Maya ruins.

Today Palenque appears quite different than it did when Stephens
and Catherwood explored the site in 1840. Its perimeter is still
obscured by rain forest and numerous structures lie buried under
mounds of rubble, but the core of the ceremonial center has been
excavated and partially restored. Instead of the hazardous journey by
muleback formerly required to visit Palenque, it can now be reached

via railroad from various points in Veracruz, Tabasco, and Yucatán, or by automobile over a paved highway from Villahermosa, seventy miles to the northeast. A landing field has also been opened in the nearby village of Santo Domingo del Palenque, and from there taxis are available for the five-mile drive to the ruins along a narrow road that was once an Indian footpath.

What is presently known about Palenque's history has resulted from the efforts of numerous investigators pursuing varied phases of research. Among the early explorers who conducted surveys at the site were Alfred P. Maudslay, William H. Holmes, and Teobert Maler; and in 1923 the Mexican government assigned the American archaeologist Frans Blom to excavate the Great Palace, which he attempted to restore as near to its original splendor as possible. Other noted Mayanists, including Alfred Tozzer, Herbert Spinden, Sylvanus Morley, and J. Eric Thompson, have subjected Palenque to intensive studies, and large-scale excavations were eventually carried out by the Instituto Nacional de Antropología y Historia under the supervision of Miguel Fernández. Four years after Fernández's untimely death in 1945, the continuation of the project fell into the capable hands of Alberto Ruz Lhuillier, a Cuban-born scholar now affiliated with the Center for Maya Studies at the Universidad Nacional Autónoma de México. It was extremely fortunate that Ruz should have applied his talents to Palenque; his tireless enthusiasm and intense determination were perfectly suited to the challenge awaiting him.

Ruz was particularly intrigued by the Temple of the Inscriptions, the imposing structure standing atop a high terraced pyramid in which Stephens and Catherwood had discovered five superbly carved hieroglyphic tablets. Ruz's curiosity was first alerted by the flagstone floor of the temple's interior chamber. Near the center of the room was an unusually large stone with two rows of circular holes drilled around its edges, all of them filled with plugs to conceal their presence. Archaeologists had long debated the possible significance of these holes, but no one could offer a satisfactory explanation for their use.

Ruz's examination of the chamber soon revealed a curious circumstance overlooked by earlier explorers: its walls appeared to continue on beneath the floor, as though another room lay below the upper level. Ruz decided to raise the drilled stone from the floor on a hunch that it might provide a key to some undisclosed architectural feature within the pyramid itself.

No sooner had his workmen lifted the heavy slab than the outlines of a narrow opening completely filled with rubble were visible underneath. At first it was impossible to tell whether it was actually a passageway connected to a lower room or simply a small subsurface crypt. But as the debris was removed a series of stone steps plastered with stucco began to appear, leading down through a vaulted tunnel into the core of the pyramid. Ruz immediately resolved to follow the elaborate subterranean stairway to its end, despite the exhaustive labor involved in such an undertaking.

The task of clearing the stairs proceeded with maddening slowness. Heavy rocks blocking the passage had to be loosened and hauled up with ropes and pulleys. The heat and humidity in the vault were stifling, and fumes given off by the excavators' gasoline lamp mixed with choking dust made it impossible to dig for long periods at a time. By the conclusion of the first season's work in the summer of 1949, only twenty-three steps had been exposed, but the outlines of the descending passageway were essentially clear.

As yet there was no way of knowing toward what the staircase was leading, though something had come to light that rekindled Ruz's expectations. Along one wall of the tunnel was a curious feature—a square hollow shaft or duct made of small stones set into lime mortar. What purpose it might have served was not known, but there doubtlessly had to be some motive for its construction concealed still lower in the pyramid's depths.

As the passage was deepened the obstructing rocks became heavier and tightly cemented by encrustations of lime. Undoubtedly the tortuous difficulty in reaching the bottom of the stairway resulted from a deliberate intent on the part of its builders. When the passageway ceased to be used it had been carefully sealed against intrusion by piling masses of rubble along its entire length. The flagstone was then set in place over the entrance in the temple floor, and the drilled holes by which it was lowered into position were filled with stone plugs. After Palenque was abandoned, the knowledge of the

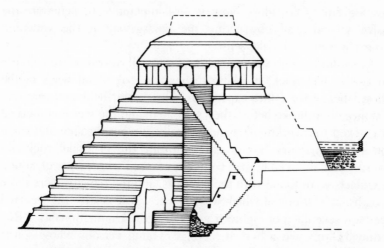

Cross section of the Temple of the Inscriptions showing the passage-
way and location of the burial chamber. (After Ruz.)

subterranean vault disappeared with its inhabitants. That much of the
enigma now seemed certain.

By the end of the third season the stairway was opened to a depth
of seventy-three feet. Still there was not the slightest clue as to its
original function. No inscriptions were found along the walls, and not a
single fragment of sculpture had turned up in the tons of debris cleared
from the vault. So far the only thing unearthed was a small masonry
box containing two jade earplugs lying on a red painted stone, a
discovery which if anything further complicated the questions in Ruz's
mind.

During the summer of 1952 the excavators broke through into a
corridor blocked at one end by a thick wall of tightly packed rubble.
Beyond this they encountered another wall of cemented stones, and on
the floor in front of it lay an offertory cache consisting of seven beads
and two earplugs made of jade, three ceramic dishes, two shells filled
with cinnabar, and an exquisite tear-shaped pearl a half inch in
diameter. Obviously these objects were intended as a ceremonial
offering, but toward what mysterious end had they been placed in the

otherwise empty corridor? Now it was imperative to penetrate the massive second wall obstructing the passageway if the widening dilemma was ever to make sense.

According to Ruz's own account, "the wall turned out to be more than twelve feet thick; breaking through it took a full week of the hardest labor of the entire expedition. The mortar held so firmly that the stones often broke before they separated, and the wet lime burned and cracked the workmen's hands. Finally we got through and came upon a rude masonry box or chest." Inside this cryptlike enclosure were six badly decayed human skeletons covered with a layer of stones. No artifacts were found with these burials, and the remains were those of youths, at least one of which was female, whose deaths had occurred at perhaps seventeen or eighteen years of age. "Unquestionably," Ruz continued, "this was a human sacrifice, young persons whose spirits were forever to guard and attend him for whom all this entire massive pyramid had been made—and whom we now soon hoped to find."

From this point on the excitement mounted in intensity. The corridor to which the steps led appeared at first to have no further outlet. But a closer investigation revealed the presence in the north wall of a low triangular doorway sealed by an enormous stone. With considerable effort it was loosened enough to be moved to one side, enabling Ruz to see beyond it into a vaulted room completely enveloped in blackness.

Now a drama occurred that was curiously reminiscent of Howard Carter's startling entrance into the treasure-laden burial chamber of Tutankhamen in 1922. Huddled together in the dimly lighted passage, Ruz and his workmen grew tense with an expectation only this kind of archaeological high adventure can evoke—the sudden discovery of splendors left by past civilizations, unseen for hundreds or thousands of years. Holding a floodlight, Ruz entered the darkened vault, and an instant later he knew his four seasons of patient labor had been lavishly rewarded.

It was some time before Ruz could aptly describe the sight confronting him: "Out of the dim shadows emerged a vision from a fairytale, a fantastic, ethereal sight from another world. It seemed a huge magic grotto carved out of ice, the walls sparkling and glistening like snow crystals. Delicate festoons of stalactites hung like tassels of a curtain, and the stalagmites on the floor looked like drippings from a great candle. The impression, in fact, was that of an abandoned chapel. Across the walls marched stucco figures in low relief. Then my eyes sought the floor. This was almost entirely filled with a great carved stone slab, in perfect condition.

"As I gazed in awe and astonishment, I described the marvelous sight to my colleagues . . . but they wouldn't believe me until they had pushed me aside and had seen with their own eyes the fascinating spectacle. Ours were the first eyes that had gazed on it in more than a thousand years!"

The sculptured stone on the floor of the chamber measured slightly more than twelve feet long by seven feet wide, and its entire surface was carved with a complex bas-relief design. In its center was the sensitive figure of a young man heavily laden with jewelry and wearing an elaborate headdress, reclining on the grotesque head of an earth monster. Above him arose a large ornate cross, its horizontal arms representing a two-headed serpent; at the top of the cross sat an exotic quetzal bird, and enclosing this tableau was a series of hieroglyphs containing the date A.D. 633.

Its cruciform design is quite similar to relief carvings found elsewhere at Palenque in the Temple of the Cross and Temple of the Foliated Cross. As Ruz pointed out, these crosslike devices were probably symbolic of growing maize. Referring to the example in the Temple of the Inscriptions, he wrote: "We may presume that the scene synthesizes fundamental concepts of the Maya religion: the veneration of maize, a plant that needs human aid for its life, and, in turn, assures man's life; the mortal destiny of man, from whose sacrifices springs life in the aspect of the cruciform motif . . . [and] the cosmic frame that surrounds human existence, in which the stars govern the unalterable course of time." Ruz believed this theme might also symbolize "the yearning of man for an afterlife. One can't be sure whether the figure depicts mortal man in general or a specific individual for whom the monument was built. He is doomed by fate to be swallowed by the earth, on which he reclines. But in the hope of eternal life he gazes fervently at the cross, the symbol of corn and therefore of life itself."

The chamber in which this gigantic carving rested was roughly

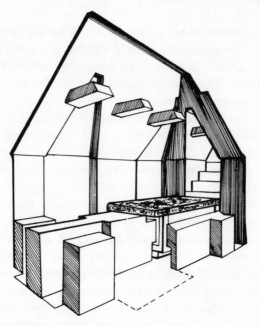

Interior of the burial chamber with sculptured slab in position over the sarcophagus. (After Ruz.)

twenty-nine feet long by thirteen feet wide. Its steeply vaulted ceiling reached a height of twenty-three feet and was reinforced by five ponderous stones placed as buttresses against the crushing weight of the roof. Adorning the walls were nine human figures modeled in stucco relief, probably representing the gods of the underworld. For almost thirteen centuries these images had peered out from beneath a curtain of white stalactites formed by lime deposits to preside over the silent chamber. Had they been placed there to witness rituals enacted by solemn priests, rites too sacred to perform before the multitudes? Or were they guardians of some undisclosed secret within the vault?

Examination revealed that the sculptured slab, which at first appeared to lie on the floor of the room, actually rested on an immense block supported by six rectangular pieces of stone. A suspicion awakened in Ruz's mind that the gigantic monolith under the slab held the solution to the original purpose of the hidden chamber. To test his inclination it was first necessary to ascertain whether or not the block was solid. By drilling a hole into one corner Ruz quickly determined that it not only had a hollow core, but its interior contained traces of red paint. Obviously the carved slab would have to be raised.

Utilizing the only suitable equipment at his disposal, Ruz had jacks placed under each corner of the five-ton stone, reinforced by logs to provide added leverage. "As the slab was lifted, inch by inch," he recalled, "we were surprised to find that a smaller inside cover lay below it. Also of stone and smoothly finished, this inner cover was about seven feet long and thirty inches wide. It was of a peculiar curved outline, with one end flared like a fishtail. And at either end was a pair of round holes, fitted with stone plugs exactly like those we had found in the temple floor far above us. By now we knew that these were lifting holes.

"We worked on, breathless with excitement. Every time we jacked the great carved top up an inch we slipped a section of board under it so that, if a jack slipped, the massive sculpture would not fall. When we had raised it about fifteen inches, my curiosity got the best of me. . . ."

Ruz squeezed his way under the slab and removed the plugs from the inner cover. Through the tiny openings he could barely distinguish what lay inside. "My first impression," he wrote, "was that of a mosaic of green, red, and white. Then it resolved itself into details—green jade ornaments, red painted teeth and bones, and fragments of a mask. I was gazing at the death face of him for whom all this stupendous work—the crypt, the sculpture, the stairway, the great pyramid with its crowning temple—had been built. . . . This, then, was a sarcophagus, the first ever found in a Mayan pyramid."

Undoubtedly the remains were those of an esteemed noble or priest. Although the bones were badly decayed, Ruz estimated his age at forty to fifty years and his height at approximately 5 feet 8 inches, unusually tall considering that Maya men averaged around 5 feet 2 inches. His teeth had been painted red, but they were not filed or inlaid with jade, obsidian, or pyrite in accordance with the widespread practice among elite classes, and Ruz could not determine if his skull was artificially deformed as was customary.

By far the most spectacular aspect of the burial was the rich treasure of jade ornaments placed on the dead man at the time of interment. Among these was a diadem fashioned of tiny disks, headdress decorations, and earplugs shaped like flowers with dangling appendages made from two pieces of mother-of-pearl fitted together and polished to give the illusion of enormous pearls. Around the neck was a collar of beads in the form of spheres, flowers, pumpkins, and a snake's head, and below this a breastplate or pectoral consisting of 189 finely polished jade tubes. Every finger of both hands was adorned by jade rings still in place over the bones; on the wrists there were cufflike bracelets, each composed of 200 small round beads, and near the feet lay two large beads perhaps once attached to sandals. Originally the corpse had held a spherical jade ball about three inches in diameter in its left hand and a cube of jade in the right (possibly symbols of rank), and scattered among the remains were two beautifully carved human effigies and a plaque representing a bat. In keeping with Maya burial rites, a single jade bead had been placed in the mouth to insure that the man's spirit could purchase food in the afterlife.

Before interment the body was wrapped in a cotton shroud and sprinkled with red cinnabar, traces of which adhered to the skeleton, the ornaments, and the interior of the sarcophagus. The face had then been covered by a magnificent mask made entirely of jade mosaic except for shell and obsidian inlays used to simulate the eyes. Now considered one of the most superb creations of Maya art, this mask has a strikingly lifelike aura about it, and Ruz suggested that it may be an actual portrait of the deceased prepared beforehand in anticipation of his death. When the sarcophagus was sealed and the great sculptured stone lowered into position, a polished slate necklace and a small jade mask were left on the floor of the crypt. Finally, pottery bowls, probably containing food and water, were placed in the chamber, along with two exquisite human heads molded in stucco and apparently broken from their original bodies.

Having at last clarified the reason for constructing the stairs and subterranean room, Ruz suddenly understood the baffling circumstances encountered during his excavations. In a manner befitting the pharaohs of Egypt, the preparation of the tomb must have assumed the proportions of a massive communal effort, requiring years to complete. As it would have been impossible to transport the sarcophagus and the

Figure from a ceramic vase, Nebaj, Guatemala.

immense sculptured slab down the finished stairway, the grave had obviously been prepared prior to the burial, after which the pyramid and the Temple of the Inscriptions were erected over it.

One question in particular puzzled Ruz in his attempts to reconstruct the preceding events. Had the priest or chieftain for whom this prodigious outpouring of labor was intended actually supervised the construction of the tomb during his lifetime? Or was it an act of homage conceived after his death? A probable answer lies in the existence of the passageway leading to the crypt, for had he died before the pyramid-temple was built, it is doubtful if such an elaborate means of access to the tomb would have been necessary. Almost certainly the stairway indicated the burial chamber was part of a preconceived plan, intended to remain in readiness until the revered man's death.

Eventually that long-planned-for day came to pass. The death of an individual so highly regarded must have presaged an occasion of tremendous importance, but unfortunately there are no records of the event. We are left to speculate on its solemnity, to imagine the crowds of peasants gathered in the plaza at the foot of the temple to mourn, while inside the burial rites were enacted.

On the prescribed day, the body, festooned with jade and encased in its shroud, was borne down the stairway to the crypt by a procession of priests bedecked in splendid ceremonial attire. Nobles followed closely behind the funerary cortege, accompanying the six youths whose spirits were to guard the dead man. Eerie shadows danced across the torchlit walls; a droning chant sounded above the shuffling of sandaled feet, and there were prayers spoken in barely audible murmurs. The descent into the afterlife was long and terror-filled, and their incantations asked: "May the gods protect and guide the honored one who now embarks."

When the procession entered the tomb, the body was lowered into the sarcophagus, the interior of which had been painted red—the color of death; at this time the corpse may also have received its coating of powdered cinnabar as a final gesture. Moments later the inner cover was carefully fitted over the coffin, and the massive carved slab was slowly moved into position. The two human heads modeled in stucco were placed near the sarcophagus along with the slate necklace, jade mask, and pottery vessels. Rubble was then piled around the edge of the sculptured slab, and the chamber was sealed by sliding the triangular stone door into place in the narrow entrance. In the corridor just outside the crypt, the six youths were killed in whatever manner was considered propitious for such an occasion, and their bodies interred in the masonry box under a layer of cemented stones.

But the memory of the deceased was not allowed to fade with the passing of time. For the survivors it was desirable to maintain a link with his still-hovering spirit, so the curious stone duct Ruz had encountered along the wall of the stairway was constructed to serve this purpose. Beginning at the side of the sarcophagus in the form of a stucco serpent's head, it extended into the adjacent corridor and continued up the entire length of the passage to the floor of the temple.

It is assumed that through this hollow tube passed the incantations of priests to the dead man below, and perhaps they received in turn some darkly mysterious confirmation of their acceptance. Ruz termed the remarkable device a "psychic duct"—a direct line between the living and the unknown realm of death.

We cannot be sure exactly when the stairway leading to the crypt was filled with debris and permanently sealed. At first it was thought to have been a preordained act to insure the tomb against any immediate threat of desecration. However, later excavations showed that Palenque was subjected to a strong wave of outside influence from Mexico's eastern coast during the century just prior to its final abandonment. Hence there is reason to suspect that the tomb—certainly the city's most important religious shrine—might have been closed only as a precaution against the threat of foreign intruders.

Even though numerous details such as this may never be fully clarified, Ruz's discovery provided an enormous amount of information about various aspects of Maya civilization. The structural complexity of the Temple of the Inscriptions, with its elaborate stairway, hidden tomb, and "psychic duct," offers perhaps the most convincing proof yet of Maya architectural skills. Furthermore, its very existence forces allowances in the long-accepted belief that the function of pyramids in Mesoamerica was solely for the purpose of elevating temples; in this case a pyramid was clearly built for funerary use as well, and similar tombs may lie concealed in other sites. New dimensions were added to our knowledge of Maya art, for the great carved slab covering the sarcophagus, together with the two stucco heads placed near it as offerings, are among the finest examples of Classic sculpture ever uncovered, not to mention the magnificent array of jade ornaments taken from the grave. Also inherent in Ruz's findings were further indications of the position enjoyed by the hierarchy, a circumstance dramatically illustrated by the Herculean concentration of effort inspired by the veneration of a single priest-king—engineers, artists, stonemasons, and laborers working devotedly over a period of years to construct his final resting place.

So much concerning Palenque's history remains, as it does in countless other Maya cities, in a state of suspension, awaiting excavation and significant breakthroughs in research. Nonetheless, a discovery such as the one made by Ruz sometimes provides archaeologists with far-reaching insights in a relatively short time. Often it is largely a matter of luck, and in undertaking his exploration of the Temple of the Inscriptions, Alberto Ruz had indeed been fortunate.*

---

* Using techniques of hieroglyphic decipherment originally worked out by Tatiana Proskouriakoff of the Peabody Museum (see Chapter 7), the archaeologist David H. Kelley and the linguist Floyd Lounsbury announced in 1975 that the nobleman who was entombed in the Temple of the Inscriptions has been positively identified. According to their findings, his name was Pacal (which means "Shield"), and he ruled Palenque from A.D. 615 to 683. Moreover, there is little question that the figure carved on the gigantic slab in the burial crypt represents an actual portrait of Pacal, and he is even depicted with what seems to be a deformed right foot, which apparently resulted from a birth defect. Inscriptions found elsewhere in the city indicate that Pacal may have married his sister, Ahpo Hel, and that his throne was inherited in the year 684 by a son named Chan-Bahlum. In addition, scholars believe they have thus far identified fifteen other members of Palenque's ruling elite, including two queens by the name of Kan Ik and Zac Kuk—the first evidence ever disclosed showing that Maya women sometimes ascended to positions of high authority.

7
GODS, PRIESTS, AND RULERS

 Who were the gods whose veneration inspired the Maya to such marvelous accomplishments? Unfortunately, what information on this subject has been extracted from ethnohistoric documents, hieroglyphic codices, and excavations is both complex and ambiguous, largely because the Maya worshipped a bewildering array of deities. Even their order of importance is not clear. Inconclusive evidence suggests that a god named Hunab Ku may have stood at the pinnacle of the Maya pantheon, yet everything about Hunab Ku's role is strangely amorphous. Various authors refer to him abstractly as a supreme being, the creator of the universe, and a deity so sacred he was incorporeal and played no part in everyday human affairs. Some students believe Hunab Ku was actually a post-Conquest phenomenon, invented by the Maya under the influence of the Christian concept of a single, all-powerful creator.

Other sources tell us the supreme god was called Itzamná. Quite possibly Itzamná and Hunab Ku were manifestations of the same diety, and Itzamná has sometimes been identified as Hunab Ku's son. Whatever their relationship, if any, Itzamná was looked upon as the creator of mankind, the inventor of books and writing, and the patron of science and learning. In the codices he appears as an aged man with a pronounced Roman nose, toothless jaws, and hollow cheeks. Elsewhere he assumes unmistakable reptilian traits; in fact, the name Itzamná literally means "iguana house," and he is commonly depicted in sculpture as an anthropomorphized lizard, snake, crocodile, or a dragonlike monster. Itzamná frequently consorted with a wife usually said to be Ix Chel, the patroness of the moon, childbearing, weaving, medicine, and floods; but in his recent book, *Maya History and Religion*, J. Eric Thompson identifies her as Ix Chebal Yax, a goddess associated with the arts of brocading and painting.

Immediately below Itzamná in prominence were Ah Kinchil or Kinich Ahau, the powerful sun god; Ah Puch—the Lord of Death—whose fleshless nose and lower jaw, exposed spine, and spotted body symbolized the fearful spectre of death; Ek Chuah, the guardian of merchants and travelers; Xaman Ek, ruler of the North Star; and Yam Kax or Ah Mun, the youthful corn god who is always portrayed wearing a headdress representing the life-giving maize plant. Rainmaking and the control of thunder, lightning, and storms were under the auspices of Chac, a long-nosed creature with volutes or fangs in the corners of his mouth, whom we see in the codices producing rain by urinating on the earth or pouring water on it with gourds or pottery vessels. Important gods called *Bacabs* functioned as impersonators and patrons of bee keeping, and exercised influence over lucky and unlucky years; often they were shown as old men with upraised arms, since it was believed they also held up the sky. Special deities presided over hunting, fishing, war, poetry, music, and suicide, in addition to which there were various gods associated with the earth, the sky, human sacrifice, calendrics, numbers, agriculture, and commerce.

Because these supernatural beings exhibit a curious mixture of human physical features with those of animals, reptiles, and birds, they appear in Maya iconography like fantastic monsters conjured out of the depths of some unearthly realm. Inherent in their nature were dualistic traits which expressed themselves in conflicting attitudes toward mankind, resulting in acts of kindness or wrathful vengeance according to unpredictable whims. Some gods readily altered their physical characteristics and roles or assumed manifestations during the day that changed radically at night. To further complicate matters, most gods were envisioned both individually and in groups of four. For example, Itzamná was thought of either as a discrete entity or as four separate deities, each with its own name and specific functions. Native sources speak of the rain god Chac singularly or as having four distinct aspects, and this idea is again illustrated by the four *Bacabs*, one of whom is stationed at each corner of the sky.

In Maya cosmology the world was conceived as a flat, square surface suspended between thirteen successive heavens and nine underworlds, all of them presided over by gods. At the geographical center of the earth grew a huge ceiba tree, with smaller trees located at its four outlying corners. Each direction corresponded to a particular color: white to the north, yellow to the south, red to the east, and black to the west. Specific deities were associated with these directions and colors, and a bird of the appropriate color supposedly nested in the trees at the corners of the earth. Apparently the Maya believed that the world rested on the back of a gigantic crocodile floating in a lily pond (a view shared with the Aztecs), and that the earth had been created several times in the past only to be destroyed again by calamities.

Naturally, ordinary men could scarcely hope to correctly interpret the will of the gods or devise the proper means of placating them. Instead this was the function of a sacrosanct priesthood whose training, specialized powers, and understanding of magic, ritual, science, and prophecy enabled them to intercede with the divinities on man's behalf. Entrance into the clergy was usually a matter of heredity, and since priests did not practice celibacy, their offices were inherited by their eldest sons or other close male relatives. It was also possible for the second sons of nobles to become priests if they showed an inclination for this profession.

According to Landa's *Relación*, the highest ranking priests in Yucatán were called *Ahau Can Mai* or *Ah Kin Mai*. Some post-Conquest documents refer to them simply as *Ah Kin* ("He of the Sun"), and they unquestionably enjoyed an extremely powerful position in Maya society. Landa's description of the high priests' functions includes divination, prophecy, medicine, and the execution of

Maya gods as represented in the codices: (a) Itzamná; (b) Yam Kax, the maize god; (c) Chac, the rain god; (d) Ah Puch, the god of death. (After Morley.)

ceremonies; other important aspects of their responsibilities involved instructing candidates for the priesthood in astronomy, mathematics, hieroglyphic writing, calendrics, and rituals, as well as assigning new priests to fill vacant offices.

Aiding the high priests with these tasks were *chilans* or prophets (sometimes spelled *chilams*), whose duty was to study divinatory almanacs, interpret mystical omens, and predict future events. Another class of priests—the *nacoms*—was charged with the grisly job of cutting out the hearts of sacrificial victims, and they were assisted in this by elderly subordinates known as *chacs* (named after the rain god), who held the victims' arms and legs at the moment of sacrifice. Shamans called *h-men* or *ahmen* specialized in prayer making and curing illness, and several early sources mention that various duties within the temples such as sweeping floors and tending sacred fires were performed by the equivalent of "vestal virgins"—young, unmarried girls of noble birth.

It is doubtful if the populace in general had much comprehension of the deeper philosophic aspects of their religion or the intellectual pursuits of the priesthood; almost surely they did not have access to important temples and shrines, except perhaps during special rituals. Mass participation was probably limited to rites focused primarily upon crops, hunting, fertility, and childbirth as determined by a strictly observed ceremonial calendar of events. Each of the eighteen months and the five-day *uayeb* comprising the vague year or *haab* had its specified rituals, as did certain periods of the *tzolkin*, the endings of *katuns*, the new year, seasons for planting and harvesting, and numerous other occasions. At such times the ceremonial centers were crowded with peasants whose homage expressed itself through prayers, dances, chanting, offerings to idols, and the burning of copal incense. Nearly every ritual was preceded by fasting (meat, chili peppers, and salt were particularly taboo), sexual abstinence, and purification rites. Once underway, however, many ceremonies involved feasting, drinking an intoxicating beverage called *balché*, bloodletting (usually done by piercing the ears, nose, lips, tongue, or sexual organs with stingray spines, thorns, or obsidian blades), and possibly the use of hallucinogenic mushrooms or peyote.

Sacrifices played a vital part in Maya ritualism. Animals such as iguanas, crocodiles, turtles, dogs, peccaries, jaguars, and turkeys were sacrificed in great numbers, and Landa observed that these offerings involved either whole animals—alive, freshly killed, or cooked—or in some cases only their hearts. But the supreme sacrifice was human life itself, and all too frequently humans were consigned to be slaughtered in the course of elaborate rituals. Such scenes are clearly depicted on sculpture, ceramics, and in murals, and this gruesome practice grew out of the conviction (adhered to throughout Mesoamerica, especially among the Aztecs) that human blood was essential to sustain the gods. Victims for these rites were provided by slaves, captured enemy soldiers, bastards, criminals, or orphans, and included adults and children of both sexes. Actually, children were often preferred because of what Landa termed their lack of "carnal sin"; if necessary they were sometimes abducted or even purchased from neighboring cities, the usual price ranging from five to ten *cuentas* (red beans) per child.

Landa gives a vivid description of a common method of human sacrifice wherein the victim, his body painted blue (the sacrificial color), was led to the summit of a pyramid and stretched over a stone altar, with his arms and legs firmly held by four *chacs*. Next the *nacom*, using a flint or obsidian knife, cut open his chest, tore out the heart, and handed it to a high priest whose task it was to anoint the faces of idols with its blood. Finally the corpse was thrown down the temple steps to a waiting priest who flayed it and danced in the skin, after which the onlookers ate the rest of the body, reserving the hands and feet for the officiating priests.

During another ritual known as the "arrow sacrifice," the victim—stripped and painted blue—was tied to a stake amid a group of dancers armed with bows and arrows. Upon a signal from a priest, each dancer passed in front of him, shooting at his heart until, according to Landa, "they made his whole chest . . . like a hedgehog full of arrows." Other sacrificial techniques included hanging, drowning, beating, mutilation, and decapitation, and one particularly grisly scene painted on a Tepeu vase shows a victim being disemboweled.

Maya society appears to have never been closely integrated, at least not with regard to seemingly inflexible barriers of heredity, education, and wealth separating the ruling hierarchy from the majority of the populace. Each of these groups lived at opposite poles from the other, and it is unlikely that commoners ever gained access to

*A priest cutting out the heart of a sacrificial victim, the Temple of the
Jaguars, Chichén Itzá.*

the upper echelons of political and ecclesiastical power. Archaeological
and documentary evidence alike indicate the existence of social strata
largely divided between an hereditary elite (nobles and priests) and
lower classes consisting of peasants and slaves, with another category
made up of artists, tradesmen, and minor civil administrators probably
occupying a somewhat middle position in the social scale.

Information on the structure of Maya society during the Classic
period is extremely limited, but various post-Conquest sources give us a
rough idea of its organization as it existed early in the sixteenth
century. In Yucatán the most influential member of the ruling elite was
the *halach uinic* or "true man." Anyone holding this position did so for
life, and upon his passing the office was inherited by his eldest son or
brother; in the event he had no suitable heir, a successor was elected by
a council of lords from candidates chosen among noble families. Each
major city was governed by a *halach uinic* in whom supreme political
authority rested, including ultimate responsibility for civil affairs,
dealings with neighboring cities, and the administration of justice. So
esteemed was his position that a cloth was always held up before his

face to prevent anyone from speaking to him directly. As there were ceremonial aspects to many of his duties, the *halach uinic* was also a priest (or at least well versed in ritual procedures), and he may have been considered a god-king endowed with semidivine powers.

To assist in governing outlying villages the *halach uinic* selected magistrates known as *batabs* (axe bearers). Essentially they functioned as provincial mayors, keeping a close rein on local government, judicial matters, and overseeing the collection of tributes paid by the peasants to the hierarchy. Occasionally the *batabs* commanded detachments of soldiers, which served as a kind of palace guard, but ordinarily in time of war the military forces were led by specially elected officers.

Immediately under the *batabs'* jurisdiction were administrative assistants called *ah kulelob*. Each town also had several *ah cuch cabob* or councilors who acted as representatives of local precincts. Other officials included the *tupiles* or constables charged with law enforcement, and the *ah holpopob*, whose position involved mediation at public meetings, leading dance rehearsals, chanting during festivals, and taking care of musical instruments.

All of these posts were held by members of the nobility (known collectively as the *almehenob*) and were attained either through inheritance or by selection on the basis of family and social status. Aside from their political and religious authority, some nobles were undoubtedly merchants, military leaders, slaveholders, and private landowners; others may have been renowned artists or architects under whose supervision important public works were executed. Abundant confirmation of their privileged status is seen in the aloof manner in which they are portrayed in sculpture and paintings, and the extreme disparity between the splendid costumes, jewelry, lavish tombs, and other symbols of personal wealth displayed by the ruling hierarchy as compared with the meager possessions of the peasants. Furthermore, all knowledge of astronomy, mathematics, hieroglyphic writing, and the more esoteric aspects of ritualism apparently remained entirely in the hands of the upper classes, leaving the vast majority of peasants totally illiterate.

Interesting insight into the archaeological background of this hereditary aristocracy grew out of an important breakthrough in glyphic decipherment announced in 1960 by Tatiana Proskouriakoff, one of the foremost students of Maya art and architecture. While studying a collection of sculptured stelae from Piedras Negras on the western border of the Petén, she noticed that on the basis of similarities in subject matter they could be divided into groups, each of which had been erected at consecutive intervals in conjunction with specific temples or palaces. Unfailingly, the earliest stela in a given series depicted a young man seated in a niche enclosed by astronomical signs and the body of a two-headed, dragonlike monster. These figures were originally believed to represent deities, but upon careful examination they actually proved to be "portraits" of rulers identified by name glyphs. The longest periods of time covered by the dates on any single group of stelae fall within the average human's life span, and accompanying the calendrical inscriptions are glyphs dealing with events such as the ruler's birthday, the date of his accession to power, and in some cases the names of his wife and children. In effect, then, these stelae recorded a succession of dynasties which governed Piedras Negras during the seventh, eighth, and ninth centuries A.D.—a discovery of far-reaching implications, since it offered definite proof that certain inscriptions pertain to historical occurrences rather than information limited solely to ritualism, astronomy, and calendrics, as was previously assumed.

Subsequently Proskouriakoff was able to demonstrate the existence of similar material on lintels and stelae from the neighboring city of Yaxchilán. Inscribed on these monuments were narrative scenes and hieroglyphs involving the birth and ascension of a powerful "Jaguar" dynasty, especially a prominent individual named Bird Jaguar whose military exploits over an adversary known as Jewelled Skull were clearly portrayed. Several years later, David H. Kelley, applying the principles worked out by Proskouriakoff, reported inscriptions on monuments at Quiriguá tracing a sequence of at least three, and possibly five, separate dynasties; Kelley's findings also hinted at a relationship between some of Quiriguá's elite and the rulers of nearby Copán. Most recently, evidence of dynastic accession has appeared in carvings from Palenque and Tikal, and future studies may show that such representations are widespread in Maya art.

Although little is known about systems of government during the Classic period, archaeologists have long held the view that each ceremonial center, together with its outlying peasant settlements, constituted a politically autonomous city-state. Nothing has really altered this basic concept, but later research has shown the situation to have been considerably more complex than was generally suspected. An extensive survey of sites in the northeastern Petén conducted by William R. Bullard, Jr., demonstrated that peasant dwellings outlying the cities, once thought to be located at random, actually form distinct territorial subdivisions. The smallest of these—designated as *clusters*—usually included from five to twelve households and covered an area of perhaps 250 to 350 square yards. Next in size were *zones* comprising a number of contiguous *clusters* plus a minor ceremonial center containing small pyramid temples, platforms, and courtyards. Several adjoining *zones* were then grouped together to form a *district*, an expanse of approximately forty square miles dominated by a major city. A similar type of settlement pattern was observed in the valley of the Belize River (though the relationship of dwellings, minor ceremonial centers, and cities to definite subdivisions was less well defined here than in the Petén), and many scholars feel some method of formalized territorial organization, along with a high degree of sociopolitical, religious, and economic interaction between its units, was quite widespread in the lowlands.

Eventually some of the larger centers achieved a status approaching urban cities, with a sizable population of merchants, artisans, and technicians. Indications of this are particularly strong at Tikal, where hundreds of structures believed to be residences of persons other than peasant farmers were mapped within the city's central precincts. No doubt the existence of this diversified social organization also brought about complex administrative problems necessitating a host of civil servants (magistrates, tribute collectors, law enforcers, etc.) who—along with the artists, craftsmen, and merchants—almost surely constituted the equivalent of a "middle class." Occasionally peasants might have been employed in the lower levels of this bureaucracy or filled certain posts on a rotating basis. Such an arrangement functions today among the Tzotzil Indians of central Chiapas—the so-called "cargo system" whereby positions of authority are periodically rotated, allowing adult males to work their way up a hierarchical ladder by

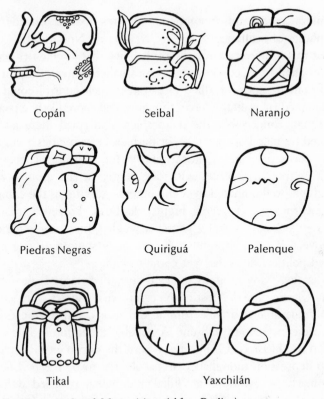

| Copán | Seibal | Naranjo |

| Piedras Negras | Quiriguá | Palenque |

| Tikal | Yaxchilán |

Emblem glyphs of Maya cities. (After Berlin.)

holding a series of increasingly prestigious offices. In fact, some students feel a system of this type even afforded peasants access to posts within the ranks of the ruling elite, a view the majority of their colleagues reject for lack of supporting archaeological evidence.

Finally, a few major ceremonial centers seem to have exercised a degree of political control over neighboring cities. In 1958 the eminent epigrapher Heinrich Berlin discovered the existence of what he termed "emblem glyphs"—hieroglyphic symbols presumably denoting either the names of individual cities or their ruling dynasties, which were used somewhat like an official seal or coat of arms. So far the emblem glyphs of Copán, Quiriguá, Palenque, Tikal, Yaxchilán, Piedras Negras, Naranjo, and Seibal have been identified, and the emblems of several of these centers appear on monuments in sites located outside their normal spheres of influence.

What this means is simply the probability that some cities became powerful enough to exact allegiance from smaller centers, thus forming a kind of confederation of allied city-states. Such control could have been maintained by military force, though it was more likely a peaceful process. Quite conceivably the hierarchies who ruled these alliances were related by blood or marriage, or perhaps certain cities voluntarily united to form a viable political entity for reasons of economic advantage or mutual defense, with one center in the group—whose emblem glyph predominated over the others—serving as the capital or seat of government. It seems highly doubtful, however, that this far-flung network of city-states was ever welded into a single nation or empire governed by a supreme ruler, or at least nothing suggesting widespread political unity has yet come to light.

Nor is there anything to indicate sustained, large-scale warfare during the Classic period. Most of the ceremonial centers were situated in terrain vulnerable to attack from all directions, and fortifications of any type are conspicuously absent. A possible exception to this occurs at Becán in southeastern Campeche, where the entire city is encircled by a deep depression thought by archaeologists to be the outline of a moat. Similarly, excavations at Tikal and Seibal revealed defensive earthworks obstructing certain approaches to these cities. Otherwise, specialized military structures such as fortresses, protective walls, and outposts have not been found in the Classic sites explored to date.

But this does not imply the complete absence of war. Raids and skirmishes constantly took place, touched off perhaps by territorial disputes, feuds between rulers of neighboring cities, or the need for sacrificial victims and slaves. Such a conflict is vividly portrayed in murals at Bonampak, and scenes on pottery and sculptured monuments frequently depict military exploits and figures of prisoners or slaves kneeling before their captors.

Whatever its motivation, war was considered a ritualistic activity. It was invariably accompanied by ceremonies intended to enlist the support of appropriate gods (whose images were carried into battle by priests), and it occurred in an atmosphere of elaborate pageantry.

Warriors shown in the Bonampak frescoes are clad in gorgeous headdresses, jade ornaments, and jaguar-skin capes, and are attended by individuals blowing wooden trumpets and holding feathered banners or parasols above their heads. Sixteenth-century Spanish chronicles tell of encounters with Maya soldiers—their bodies painted red and black— arrayed in plumed helmets, lavish costumes, carrying brightly colored standards, and attacking amid the eerie din of drums, conch-shell horns, whistles, and yells.

In addition to mercenaries known as *holcans*, warriors were conscripted from among the peasants, a task assigned to the *ah holpopob*, who acted as recruiters. Special scouts called *zabin* (road weasels) were relied on to secure information regarding enemy defenses, and prior to every campaign women prepared large quantities of food which the troops carried on their backs. Judging from representations in sculpture and paintings, Classic-period weapons were limited to short spears tipped with flint or obsidian points, wooden clubs, flint knives, and shields; but in the Postclassic era when warfare assumed an increasingly important role, a number of innova- tions entered the Maya arsenal: *atlatls* or spearthrowers, slings, two-handed wooden swords edged with obsidian blades, cuirasses made of quilted cotton or tapir hide, and the bow and arrow, all of them introduced from Mexico. Military tactics centered on ambushes, frontal assaults, or maneuvers designed to outflank the enemy, but once a conflict was underway it involved mostly hand-to-hand combat. Wars were generally of short duration, and fighting never took place at night—a truce being declared each evening until the following day. Anyone killing or capturing an officer of the opposing side was greatly honored; if a commander was killed or severely wounded his troops usually retreated.

In the field, armies were supervised by officers known as *nacoms* or "war captains" (not to be confused with the priests responsible for carrying out human sacrifices). *Nacoms* were elected for a period of three years, and throughout their tenure in office they could not indulge in sexual relations, eat meat, or drink intoxicants. Enormous prestige was accorded a *nacom*, especially one renowned for his success in battle. Once a year a festival was held in his honor, during which,

Landa reported, "they bore him in great pomp, perfuming him as if he were an idol, to the temple where they seated him and burned incense to him. . . ."

Landa further relates how victorious warriors cut off the lower jaws of dead enemy soldiers, skinned them, and wore the bones on their arms as a token of military prowess. Yet the primary goal was to capture rather than kill as many of the enemy as possible, particularly high-ranking officers and nobles. Usually prisoners of elite status were reserved for sacrifice, while the commoners were sentenced to slavery. Aside from captives taken in battle, orphans, debtors, and individuals convicted of theft or murder were cast into bondage, and the children of slaves were automatically condemned to their parents' fate. Occasionally a person enslaved for indebtedness was allowed to purchase freedom by paying the debt, and slaves were sometimes ransomed by their families, but slavery generally meant a lifetime spent as laborers, household servants, or farmers in the service of the elite classes.

What warfare did occur in the Classic period was not of sufficient magnitude to severely disrupt normal activities. On the contrary, there is overwhelming evidence that throughout these centuries the lowlands witnessed expanding populations, uninterrupted building, the free exchange of ideas, and extremely vigorous trade. Ever since Formative times, commerce had played a key role in the development of Maya civilization and contributed enormously to its political stability. Landa observed that "the occupation to which they had the greatest inclination was trade," and sixteenth-century explorers marveled at the vast network of commercial routes linking the entire region.

Such commodities as flint, beeswax, honey, cotton textiles, rubber, copal incense, vegetable dyes, tobacco, vanilla, polychrome pottery, tortoise shells, feathers, and jaguar and ocelot skins were regularly exported from the lowlands to cities in the uplands of Chiapas, Guatemala, and El Salvador. In return, merchants from those areas brought jade, albite, obsidian, hematite, quetzal feathers, pottery, and cinnabar to sell in lowland centers. Groups living in coastal regions supplied salt, dried fish, shells, stingray spines, and pearls to inland districts. And some time after A.D. 900 objects of turquoise, copper, and gold began to be imported from Mexico, along with a variety of metal items manufactured in Panama, Costa Rica, and Colombia. Virtually all commerce seems to have been controlled by wealthy merchants, most of whom were presumably members of the nobility. Goods were transported on the backs of slaves along well-established land routes, or by sea and rivers in large canoes measuring up to fifty feet in length. Cacao beans constituted the principal currency and had a fixed market value; occasionally payment was made in stone or shell beads, red beans, feathers, or small hatchet-shaped copper celts, and transactions based on credit were apparently quite common.

Some Postclassic cities contained specially designed marketplaces —most notably the Mercado at Chichén Itzá, a spacious building supported by round columns where items for sale were displayed in individual stalls. No markets have been positively identified in any Classic sites (a group of structures in the East Plaza at Tikal appears to have been designed for this purpose), but they may frequently have consisted of nothing more than thatched-roof shelters or stalls set up in open courtyards, in which case their remains would have long since disappeared. We do know, however, that certain cities on the periphery of the Maya area—Xicalango, Soconusco, Cimatán, and several more—grew into important commercial centers. Xicalango, on the shores of Laguna de Términos in Campeche, was especially famous as a port of entry for goods passing back and forth from Mexico to Yucatán, Guatemala, and Honduras.

Ancient Maya markets must have differed little from those of the present day: crowded, noisy, filled with visual delights and exotic smells, their stalls overflowing with a dazzling array of products ranging from food, clothing, and household wares to luxury items. Undoubtedly they served a secondary purpose as meeting places and public forums for the exchange of ideas. In native markets today, whether in Mérida, Antigua, San Cristóbal de las Casas, or anywhere else in the area, one hears discussions covering every imaginable subject of interest to local Indians. So it surely was in past centuries, for along with the intellectual and religious endeavors of the hierarchy, commerce assumed a vitally important function in Maya culture by encouraging contact with outside peoples, stimulating craftsmanship and specialization, and providing a broader economic base for large populations.

8

FARMERS
AND BUILDERS:
GLIMPSES OF
EVERYDAY LIFE

 In sharp contrast to our knowledge of the upper classes of Maya society, archaeology has revealed few details concerning the ordinary people. Rarely do inscriptions, sculpture, and paintings focus on their activities, and excavations of former peasant dwellings have underlined the comparative simplicity of their lifestyle. Among the sparse remains found in these so-called "house mounds" are large quantities of utilitarian pottery used for cooking and storage, plus a variety of household implements—such things as axes, celts, knives, scrapers, spindle whorls, and grinding stones. Occasionally, decorated ceramics, figurines, and ornaments are also unearthed, but these meager artifacts hardly compare with the extravagant array of treasures typical of elite burials.

Overshadowed as they were by the spectacular architecture, works of art, and intellectual feats surrounding them, it was nevertheless the peasants, the *yalba uinicob* (lower men), as they were known in Yucatec, who actually formed the backbone of Maya civilization. Without the benefit of their labors, the priest-rulers could scarcely have afforded leisure time for excursions into astronomy, calendrics, mathematics, or literature. Yet so few are the traces of the peasants' existence that we must rely upon early ethnohistoric works—primarily Landa's *Relación*—for almost everything we know about their lives.

No event held greater significance for the average Maya than the birth of a child. Not only were children considered a measure of personal wealth and good fortune, they implied the direct sanction of the gods, especially Ix Chel, the patroness of childbirth, whose image was placed under expectant mothers' beds during labor. One's birthday was counted from the day of the *tzolkin* or sacred year on which he was born, a factor also determining what deities were most inclined to favor or malign an individual throughout life. Infants were given a childhood name by a priest, who then cast a horoscope to aid in their upbringing. Later they assumed a *coco kaba* or nickname used by family and close friends, and took a formal name derived from their parents' surnames. Masculine names always began with the prefix *Ah* and feminine names with *Ix*, but after a man married he adopted the prefix *Na*.

According to Maya concepts of beauty, it was highly desirable to be cross-eyed; thus a nodule of resin or a small bead was attached to a child's hair which hung between the eyes and conditioned the pupils to focus inward. Shortly after birth an infant's head was tightly bound to wooden boards in order to flatten the forehead, as this too was considered a mark of attractiveness. Older children had their earlobes, septum, lips, and one nostril pierced so they could wear a variety of ornaments.

When a boy reached the age of five a white bead was braided into his hair; a girl of the same age received a string with a red shell dangling from it to wear around her waist. As symbols of virginity, these could not be removed until an elaborate rite marking the beginning of adolescence, which was performed when the boys were fourteen years old and the girls twelve. Drawing upon Landa's description, Sylvanus Morley recounts the details of this ritual in his book, *The Ancient Maya*:

The day of the puberty ceremony was carefully selected; pains were taken to ascertain that it would not be an unlucky day. A principal man of the town was chosen as sponsor for the children participating; his duty was to help the priest during the ceremony and to furnish the feast. Four honorable old men were selected as *chacs*, to assist the priest. . . . On the appointed day, all assembled in the court of the sponsor's house, which had been newly swept and strewn with fresh leaves. An old man was assigned to act as godfather for the boys, and an old woman as godmother for the girls. When this was done the priest purified the dwelling and conducted a ceremony to expel the evil spirit.

When the spirit had been expelled, the court was swept out again, fresh leaves were strewn about, and mats were spread on the floor. The priest changed his vestments to a handsome jacket and a miter-like headdress of colored feathers, taking in his hand an aspergillum for sprinkling holy water. This latter consisted of a finely worked short stick with rattlesnake tails hanging from it. The *chacs* approached the children and placed on their heads pieces of white cloth, which their mothers had brought for this purpose. The older children were asked if they had committed any sin or obscene act. If they had, they were separated from the others. . . . This concluded, the priest ordered everyone to be seated and to preserve absolute silence, and after pronouncing a benediction on the children, he sat down. The sponsor of the ceremony, with a bone given him by the priest, tapped each child nine times on the forehead, moistening the forehead, the face, and the spaces between the fingers and toes with water.

After this anointing, the priest removed the white cloths from the children's heads. The children then gave the *chacs* some feathers and cacao beans which they had brought as gifts. The priest next cut the white beads from the boys' heads. The attendants carried pipes which they smoked from time to time, giving each child a puff of smoke. Gifts of food, brought by the mothers, were distributed to the children, and a wine [*balché*] offering was made to the gods; this wine had to be drunk at one draught by a specially appointed official.

The young girls were then dismissed, each mother removing from her daughter the red shell which had been worn as a symbol of purity. With this, the girl was considered to have reached a marriageable age. The boys were dismissed next. When the children had withdrawn from the court, their parents distributed among the spectators and officials pieces of cotton cloth which they had brought as gifts. The ceremony closed with feasting and heavy drinking. . . .

Detail of Stela A, Copán. (After Maudslay.)

Until they were married, girls continued to live with their parents, learning from their mothers how to cook, spin cotton yarn, weave, and perform other household duties. Unmarried men painted themselves black to denote their station in life and lived in communal houses where they were instructed in various crafts, studied the arts of warfare, played games, and openly consorted with prostitutes. Referring to these "bad public women," Landa reported that "the poor girls who happened to ply this trade . . . although they received pay for it, were besieged by such great numbers of young men, that they were harassed to death."

Marriage was permitted anytime after the puberty ceremony, but normally it did not take place until the men were about eighteen years of age and the girls reached fourteen or fifteen. Arrangements were made through the parents (sometimes years in advance), with the father of the prospective bridegroom initiating the search for his son's wife. To facilitate this, a professional matchmaker was employed to represent the husband in the matter of a worthwhile dowry and details of the ceremony. Great emphasis was placed on finding a girl properly trained in the domestic skills and manners befitting a suitable wife. When passing a man she was required to lower her eyes, turn her back, and step aside. A wife never ate or drank with her husband; she did not laugh at him or engage in long conversations, and only rarely during certain festivals did she dance with him. Girls were expected to be chaste before marriage, and those who violated this rule were whipped, rubbed with pepper, and held up to public ridicule.

Strict taboos prohibited unions between persons with identical paternal surnames, and a man could not marry his maternal aunt, his brother's widow, his stepmother, or, if he was a widower, his dead wife's sister. Very likely the restriction against marrying anyone with the same patronymic indicates the former existence of exogamous clans. Vestiges of such clans survive today among several Maya-speaking tribes in Guatemala and Chiapas, and a statement by Landa would seem to confirm their presence in Yucatán in the sixteenth century: ". . . the Indians say that those bearing the same name are all of one family, and they are treated as such, and on this account when one comes to a place which is not known to him and he is in need, he at once makes use of his name, and if there are any of the same name there, they receive him at once and treat him with the greatest kindness. And so no woman or man was ever married to another of the same name, for that was in their opinion a great infamy."

Once a marriage had been arranged, the wedding ceremony involved reciting the terms of the agreement as worked out by the participants' families, the blessings of a priest, and a banquet given by the bride's father. Afterward the husband was required to live with his wife's parents (or at least in a nearby house) for a period usually ranging from three to six years, assisting his father-in-law and thereby proving his abilities. Since marriage could be dissolved at any time merely by a declaration on the part of either the husband or wife, divorce was quite common. Only first marriages were celebrated by a formal ceremony; thereafter persons who had been divorced or widowed were free to simply take up residence with a new mate, an event customarily marked by a banquet given for their relatives and friends.

If a man was wealthy enough to afford multiple wives—almost always a member of the nobility—he sometimes did so, and slaves were frequently kept by the elite as concubines. Monogamy was the generally accepted custom among the peasant classes, and Maya women were reported to be exceedingly jealous. "Some carried it so far," wrote Landa, ". . . that they lay hands on the women of whom they are jealous. And so angry and irritated are they . . . that some tear their husband's hair no matter how few times [he] may have been unfaithful."

Adultery on the part of men was considered a serious offense, punishable under certain circumstances by death at the hands of the outraged husband, who had the right if he so desired to kill his wife's lover by dropping a rock on his head "from a great height." One Yucatecan chronicler, Gaspar Antonio Chi, related how adulterers were "killed with arrows" and "he who corrupted any maiden or violated any woman received the death penalty." Even so, adultery and sexual promiscuity were fairly widespread, and Landa complained bitterly about the Indians' susceptibility to "weakness of the flesh."

Throughout Maya history the design of the typical domestic house remained essentially unchanged. Basically it consisted of a single-roomed unit—oval, square, or rectangular in shape—with walls made of poles, plastered earth (wattle and daub), or occasionally undressed stones; the roof was sharply pitched and constructed of thatched palm leaves supported by a framework of beams and saplings tied with lianas. High partitions divided the interior into two sections, allowing the rear half to be used as sleeping quarters and leaving the front for everyday activities. Adjacent to the main house there may have been auxiliary buildings or shelters which served as kitchens or storage areas, and to insure proper drainage, all of these structures stood on low platforms built of earth and stones. Often several households were situated around a courtyard to form a compound, and such arrangements probably included extended families, members of the same clan, or some other kinship group.

What furniture the Maya used in their dwellings was apparently restricted to wooden stools, benches, and low beds made of tightly lashed poles covered with fiber matting. (It is not certain whether the ubiquitous hammocks so popular throughout the region today date from pre-Conquest times or if they were introduced later.) Food was cooked on stone hearths or in ceramic vessels, and meals were eaten while sitting on stools or mats spread on the floor. Every household also contained an array of utilitarian pottery, gourd receptacles, baskets, wooden chests, woven storage bags, assorted implements, and *metates* and *manos* for grinding maize.

Landa's description of the way Maya cities were laid out indicates that the location of one's house was determined by social prestige: "In the middle of the town were their temples with beautiful plazas, and all around the temples stood the houses of the lords and priests, and those of the most important people. [Next] came the houses of the richest and those who were held in the highest estimation nearest to these, and at the outskirts of the town were the homes of the lower class. And the wells, if there were but few of them, were near the houses of the lords. . . ."

Unlike the splendid attire of the nobles and priests, the peasants' clothing reflected their humble status. Ordinarily the men wore nothing but a cotton loincloth (called an *ex* in Yucatec) and rawhide sandals tied about the ankles with thongs or hemp cords, though for cool weather or special occasions they had sleeveless jackets and mantles of cotton fabric. Women's clothing consisted of short skirts, *mantas* or shawls, and square-cut dresses worn with a petticoat—a garment identical to the *huipiles* so popular in Yucatán today. Men kept their hair long or pulled back, with a bare spot burned on the top of the head; the women's hair was braided in a variety of ways and sometimes decorated with ornaments. Generally the only jewelry peasants could afford were necklaces, earplugs, pendants, and nose buttons made of jade, albite, shell, and amber. But the use of perfumes, body paint, tatoos, and decorative scars was widespread among both elite and peasant classes, as was the practice of filing the teeth to points, which, Landa said, "they considered elegant." Often the nobility carried this obsession with adornment a step further by inlaying their front teeth with iron pyrite, obsidian, jade, or shell.

Scholars have long questioned how Maya civilization could have been supported by an agricultural system that hardly progressed beyond the earliest stages of its inception. Irrigation and crop rotation were not practiced. Farming implements remained of the crudest imaginable variety, and techniques of plant cultivation were extremely limited. As their ancestors had done in Formative centuries, the Maya

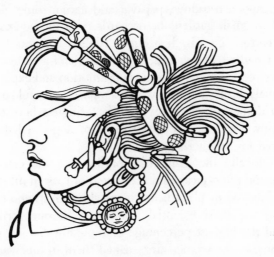

Head of an elite figure, Yaxchilán. (After Maudslay.)

periodically cleared the forest from small plots of land called *milpas* (an Aztec word meaning "cornfields"). Stone tools were used to cut down underbrush, saplings, and vines, but since it was virtually impossible to fell large trees with flint axes, they may have been ringed with fire several years in advance and left to die. When the bush was sufficiently dry it was burned off, and just before the onset of the summer rains, seeds were planted in shallow holes made with sharpened digging sticks. Using this method, a farmer could grow enough food in about three months to supply his family and pay tributes for the rest of the year. But after several seasons the land's productivity was depleted, making it necessary to prepare new fields; only by allowing worn-out plots to lie dormant for long periods and repeating the process of clearing and burning could they be recultivated. Known as *milpa* or slash-and-burn agriculture, this technique remained unchanged for thousands of years, and except for the appearance of steel axes, machetes, and iron-tipped digging sticks, the same system is widely practiced in the region today.

The most important crops raised by the Maya were maize, beans, squash, pumpkins, sweet potatoes, chili peppers, tomatoes, *chayote,* avocados, sapote, breadnut, papaya, and cacao, some of which were cultivated in small gardens or orchards near the houses. In addition, tobacco, cotton, gourds, henequen, rubber (natural latex extracted from the *Castilla* tree), vanilla, copal resin, and a variety of wild fruit were harvested for both domestic consumption and export. Aside from game animals, birds, and fish, which supplied plentiful sources of meat, the Maya domesticated turkeys, ducks, stingless bees (kept in hives inside hollow logs), and several species of dogs, including a barkless variety bred for sacrificial use.

Traditionally the main meal of the day was eaten in the late afternoon, and the typical menu consisted of roasted meat, spicy stews, tamales, chili, red or black beans, vegetables, fruit, and chocolate. Yet maize was the most essential staple and in one form or another constituted the highest percentage of the daily diet. In preparing the kernels for use, the women first soaked them in limewater to remove the hulls. Next they were ground with *metates* and *manos* into a thick dough called *zacan* which served as the base for various dishes, especially thin cakes or *tortillas* eaten in large quantities during the evening meal and for breakfast. *Zacan* mixed with water made a greatly relished drink known as *pozole*, and a thicker version of this—a corn gruel or *atole*—was served hot and sometimes sweetened with honey.

Every family paid its share of tributes in goods and services intended to maintain the "establishment." Landa recounts how the houses of the lords (which were considerably more elaborate than ordinary dwellings) were built by the peasants "at their own expense." Apart from this they planted, tilled, and harvested fields belonging to the nobility and shared with them the bounty from hunting and fishing. A portion of every season's crops—especially maize—was contributed to the hierarchy, along with regular tributes of commodities such as salt, cloth, honey, copal incense, fruit, and domestic animals. And since only a few months of the year were devoted to food production, the average man had a good deal of free time for construction projects, keeping the jungle cleared from the ceremonial centers, and undertaking repairs to buildings and roads.

Regardless of the burden of tributes, manual labor, and their inferior social status, it does not appear that the peasants were harshly mistreated. For one thing, all commoners may not have shared the same lifestyle or economic level. Quite possibly some achieved a higher degree of prosperity and social mobility through specialized skills or minor bureaucratic posts. In a recent article on this subject, Richard E. W. Adams listed a number of "middle class" occupational categories almost surely filled by peasants: scribes, accountants, musicians, entertainers, potters, sculptors, painters, costume makers, armorers, and stone masons. Others might conceivably have become petty merchants, and J. Eric Thompson believes there was nothing to prevent a peasant who was particularly successful in a specialty from exchanging his goods for luxury items, acquiring a measure of personal wealth in the process.

Nor was all of the peasant's time consumed with work. Each month brought its religious ceremonies, festivals, and banquets, some of which, if the descriptions given by Spanish informants are correct, involved excessive drunkenness and sexual debauchery. Many rituals included dances with large numbers of participants arrayed in lavish costumes and carrying brightly colored banners and streamers. In most cases men and women danced separately, but Landa noted at least one exception to this—a dance called the *naual,* which he denounced as "not very decent." Another historical document, the *Relación* of Campocolche, states that the Maya had more than a thousand different dances, and it was not uncommon for these festivities to attract over 15,000 spectators. Other popular entertainments featured satirical plays and comedies performed on stages or in courtyards by masked actors and clowns, and there were storytellers who recited fables and legends to the accompaniment of drums, orchestral music, and songs.

Everyone took a passionate interest in the ball game known as *pok-to-pok,* a sport played throughout Mesoamerica in courts similar to those described in Chapter 5. Basically, the object of the game was to knock a solid rubber ball about four to six inches in diameter through a stone ring placed midway along the wall of the court just above the players' heads. (Since stone markers were used in place of rings in Classic sites, the rules may have differed somewhat at that time.) Under no circumstances could the ball be thrown by hand; it had to bounce off the hips, shoulders, or forearms, which were heavily padded for protection. Two teams competed in these matches, and players demonstrating unusual skill were held in great esteem. Incredibly high stakes were wagered on the outcome of every game—including jade, gold, houses, and slaves—and the winning players were entitled to the jewelry and clothing of the spectators, who naturally fled the scene as quickly as possible once the match was decided.

All misfortune and illness was viewed by the Maya as resulting from evil spirits or disfavor of the gods. Even today witchcraft and dangerous omens are greatly feared, and many villages have medicine men whose duties include guarding against such forces. Among the Yucatec, gourds filled with food are regularly put out for the invisible dwarfs who are believed to cause sickness. Extreme caution is taken to avoid the *pishan* or souls of the dead, and the *x-tabai*—spirits in the form of beautiful young women with the power to lure men deep into

The god of human sacrifice as shown in the codices. (After Morley.)

the forest and steal their souls. Sylvanus Morley noted that if a Yucatecan dreams of red tomatoes it means the death of a baby. Dreams involving a broken water jar signify death in one's family, and dreaming of pain, having a tooth pulled, or floating on air means a close relative will die. If a hunter sells the head, liver, or stomach of a slain deer he will endanger his chances of killing other game; selling an animal he has killed to someone who throws its bones into a *cenote* will bring him ill fortune. Superstitions regarding lucky and unlucky days survive in the belief that anything undertaken on Tuesdays and Fridays is doomed to failure, or that the best time to plant *milpas,* gamble, or get married is a Monday or Saturday. Nine and thirteen are considered lucky numbers, a belief possibly stemming from their association with the nine underworlds and thirteen heavens of ancient Maya cosmology.

When illness occurred a sorcerer or priest was called upon to examine the victim. He might prescribe a variety of treatments involving fetishes, divination, rituals, or potions, often with extremely beneficial results. Extensive use was made of medicinal herbs, plants, and mineral substances, together with such unsavory ingredients as bat wings, red worms, animal excrement, urine, blood, crocodile testicles, and bird fat. In his book, *The Ethno-Botany of the Maya,* Ralph L. Roys gives a number of typical remedies translated from post-Conquest native sources, several examples of which are quoted as follows:

Toothache
   Crumble the soot that clings to cooking stones and wrap it with cotton wool; if it is a broken tooth, then let it be applied. The throbbing will cease. Or else grate with a fishskin the tooth of a crocodile and let it be wrapped with cotton-wool . . . and applied to the tooth that throbs. It will cease by this means. . . .

Pulling a Tooth
   There is an iguana that is yellow beneath the throat. Pierce its mouth, tie it up and burn it alive on a flat plate until it is reduced to ashes. These ashes of the iguana you are to anoint. You shall set your forceps and then you shall draw the tooth without pain. Try it first on a dog's tooth, before you draw the man's tooth with the ashes of the iguana which is yellow beneath its throat.

Excessive Sneezing
Anyone who sneezes excessively so that it will affect the joints and veins, will, one day or night, die of it. You take a handful of orange leaves, boil them, apply (the liquid) to the foot and then you rub the body with the liquid also.

Insanity
Take the testicles of a black cock, mash and dissolve them in cold water and give it to him to drink at dawn before he takes his breakfast. Every day at dawn he is to drink it.

If the appropriate treatment failed and death seemed imminent, a final confession was made to the attending priest, who then prophesied how long the patient could be expected to live and what his prospects were regarding the afterlife. Death was greatly feared by the Maya, despite their belief that worthy individuals—those obedient to religious mandates and therefore favored by the gods—would eventually reside in an eternal paradise located among the thirteen heavens. Suicide, especially by hanging oneself, was looked upon as the greatest measure of personal sacrifice, an act insuring the unqualified pleasures of immortality. Women who died in childbirth, priests, warriors killed in battle, and sacrificial victims could look forward to equally propitious rewards. Evildoers, however, were condemned to *Mitnal,* the Maya equivalent of hell—a demon-infested realm in the underworld where the damned suffered never-ending cold, hunger, and torment.

In stark contrast to the elite classes, peasants were usually placed in simple graves under the floors of their houses, which were frequently abandoned after the owner's death. Occasionally burials were made in stone-lined cists, *chultuns,* or caves, and children were sometimes interred in large pottery jars. In northern Yucatán cremation was widely practiced among the aristocracy, perhaps because the limestone surface made the preparation of elaborate underground tombs too difficult. As a rule the bodies were wrapped in cotton shrouds, sprinkled with cinnabar, and buried either fully extended or in a flexed position, with the knees drawn up against the chest; in some cases the head was oriented toward the north, south, or east. Ornaments, pottery vessels (probably containing offerings of food),

Mosaic mask made of turquoise, jade, and bone, Yucatán. Late Postclassic.
(Courtesy of the Robert Woods Bliss Collection of Pre-Columbian Art, Dumbarton Oaks, Washington, D.C.)

Temple of Kukulcán, or El Castillo, Chichén Itzá.

Temple of the Warriors, Chichén Itzá.

The Observatory, Chichén Itzá. The dome-shaped tower contains a circular stairway leading to observation points from which certain astronomical phenomena could be studied along fixed lines of sight.

La Iglesia, Chichén Itzá. An excellent example of Puuc architecture predating the Toltec-Itzá invasions of Yucatán.

Detail of a mural portraying a battle between the Maya and Toltec-Itzá invaders, Temple of the Jaguars, Chichén Itzá.

(*Courtesy of the Museo Nacional de Antropología, Mexico.*)

Left, Edward Herbert Thompson. *(Reproduced from City of the Sacred Well, by T. A. Willard.)*

Below, the Sacred Cenote, or Well of Sacrifice, Chichén Itzá.

Below, reconstruction of Structure 1 at Xpuhil, Campeche. This building is typical of the Río Bec style in its use of massive ornamental masks and false towers.
(Restoration drawing by Tatiana Proskouriakoff.)

Right, a pyramid-temple showing a "flying façade" used to enhance the structure's height, Labná.

The Archway, Labná.

The Great Palace, Labná. The ruins of an ancient road or *sacbe* leading to the palace are visible to the left.

Right, incense burner found at Mayapán. Generally of poor workmanship and painted with garish colors, these objects exemplify the decadence of Maya art during the Late Postclassic period.

(Courtesy of the Museo Nacional de Antropología, Mexico.)

Below, the Palace, Sayil.

The Temple of the Frescoes, Tulúm, in which a series of Mexican-influenced murals was discovered.

(Drawing by Frederick Catherwood; reproduced by permission of Harper & Row, Publishers.)

The Temple of the Seven Dolls, Dzibilchaltún. This structure acquired its name from the fact that it contained an altar on which there were seven small ceramic figurines representing deformed humans.

An incense burner representing the Toltec rain god Tlaloc, Cave of Balankanché.

(Photograph by Richard H. Stewart. Copyright: National Geographic Society.)

Yucatec Indians worshipping in the cave of Balankanché.
(*Photograph by Richard H. Stewart. Copyright: National Geographic Society.*)

Stucco head discovered inside the burial vault in the Temple of the Inscriptions, Palenque.
(Courtesy of the Museo Nacional de Antropología, Mexico.)

A section of a hiero-
glyphic tablet from the
Great Palace, Palenque.

Detail of a mural depicting musicians playing trumpets, Bonampak.
*(From reproductions by Augustín Villagra Caleti in the Museo Nacional de Antro-
pología, Mexico.)*

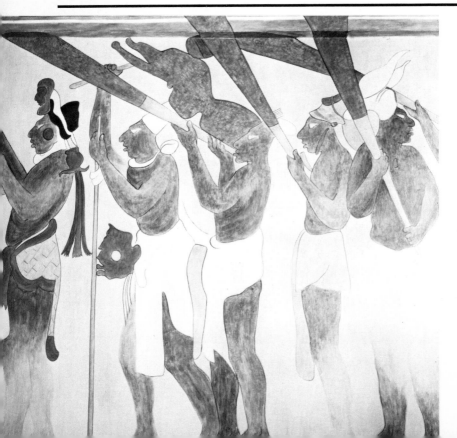

Jade mosaic mask found inside the sarcophagus in the Temple of the Inscriptions, Palenque. *(Courtesy of the Museo Nacional de Antropología, Mexico.)*

Details of murals, Bonampak. *Below*, priests or nobles in ceremonial costumes. *Right*, a procession of musicians playing rattles, a drum, and turtle carapaces. *(From reproductions by Augustín Villagra Caleti in the Museo Nacional de Antropología, Mexico.)*

Detail of the Palace of the Governors showing the intr
cate façade decorations typical of the Puuc style
architecture.

The Palace of the Governors, Uxmal.

Uxmal: the Nunnery Quadrangle (left); the Temple of the Magician (right),
as they appeared about A.D. 900.
(Restoration drawing by Tatiana Proskouriakoff.)

and objects formerly used by the deceased were put in the grave with the corpse, and cornmeal and a jade bead were placed in the mouth, a gesture intended to provide sustenance and money for the journey to the afterlife. "It was indeed a thing to see the sorrow and the cries which they made for their dead," wrote Landa, "and the great grief it caused them. During the day they wept for them in silence; and at night with loud and very sad cries, so that it was pitiful to hear them. And they passed many days in deep sorrow. . . ."

Overwhelming mysteries surrounded and awed the Maya peasant: the movements of the planets, the seasons, storms, birth, life and death itself, all the manifest powers of the gods thrown up around him like an infinite mirror in which was reflected the frailty of his existence. Life was spent placating the ancient fear of the unknown which had followed mankind since the dawn of history. Entrapped in uncertainty and superstition, the Maya constantly raised his eyes beyond his *milpas* and the terror-filled jungle to the gleaming temples of the ceremonial centers, where he sought the guidance of learned priests whose knowledge gave them greater insight into unknown realms. To achieve this assurance no sacrifice was too costly.

9

BONAMPAK:
THE MIRROR OF
A GOLDEN AGE

 Archaeologists have long been frustrated by
the scarcity of information pertaining to vari-
ous aspects of Classic Maya culture. Almost nothing in the way of
clothing, headdresses, furniture, or other perishable items has survived,
and many facts concerning rituals, dances, warfare, and everyday
activities could only be inferred from fragmentary data—mainly
pictorial representations in sculpture and ceramic painting. Unexpectedly, however, the discovery of an ancient temple in the rain forest
of eastern Chiapas afforded a much more graphic insight into such
details than anything previously unearthed.

For years this building was used as a shrine by a little-known
Maya tribe—the Lacandón—who kept their whereabouts carefully
guarded from intruders. Immediately after the Conquest the Lacandón
had retreated into the wilderness in an effort to resist the Spaniards,
and when an attempt to Christianize them in 1790 ended in failure,
they were for all practical purposes forgotten by the outside world.

Secluded in the depths of the humid, disease-ridden jungle, their remoteness stood as a barrier against the encroachment of foreign influences which they refused to tolerate.

But by the mid-1900s vast portions of Chiapas began to be exploited by chicle gatherers, mahogany cutters, and oil prospectors. As a result of this sudden influx, a variety of illnesses beset the Lacandón with disastrous consequences, and severe epidemics—added to a gradual exodus of younger Indians who migrated to nearby towns in search of improved living conditions—have sharply reduced their population. Now confined to the region between the Jatate and Usumacinta rivers, only about 200 Lacandón still survive and there is little hope their number will increase significantly in the future.

Even so, those who remain cling steadfastly to the primitive existence adopted by their ancestors during centuries of isolation. Few aspects of their economy, crafts, social customs, or daily life have changed radically as a result of outside contact, and native religious practices continue to play a dominant role in most settlements, despite the efforts of Catholic and Protestant missionaries to introduce Christianity. Although conscious links with their past are only dimly perceived, the Lacandón sometimes carry out rituals and place offerings of maize, *balché,* and copal incense in long-deserted temples amid the ruins of Maya cities. On these occasions they pause momentarily to pay homage to their plundered heritage, to worship effaced gods and recapture the venerable legacy lost in the desperate pursuit of seclusion which forced them to accept a way of life scarcely removed from the Stone Age. And there they have remained—impoverished victims of the bizarre mutations inflicted by history.

In the spring of 1946 the author-explorer Giles G. Healey entered the desolate frontier of Chiapas to photograph the Lacandón for a documentary film entitled *The Maya Through the Ages,* which had been commissioned by the United Fruit Company. While working among a group in the vicinity of the Lacanhá River, Healey observed that the men made regular pilgrimages to a secret shrine in a nearby ruin. The prospect of filming rites conducted in an archaeological site still revered by descendants of its builders offered an exceptional opportunity, but the Lacandón were reluctant to allow Healey to accompany them. Eventually he succeeded in bargaining for the location of the hidden shrine by giving the Indians shotguns and ammunition. He was led deep into the rain forest along narrow trails hacked out of the bush with machetes. In places no direct sunlight penetrated the overhanging vegetation, and one could easily have passed within a few yards of an entire city without suspecting its existence. Finally they reached an area enclosed by barely discernible ruins—temples, palaces, platforms, and monuments, rising like chalk-white phantoms out of a sea of jungle green.

In a courtyard at the foot of a terraced acropolis lay a massive sculptured stela broken into several pieces. Its central figure, etched in bold relief, depicted a dignitary laden with jade ornaments, holding a ceremonial staff, and surrounded by columns of hieroglyphic inscriptions. Flanking the stairway ascending the acropolis were two more elaborately carved stelae, and fragments of other monuments could be seen scattered about the ruins. On a platform near the northeastern corner of the acropolis stood an unpretentious flat-roofed building which, despite a thick mantle of trees and vines, had remained in a remarkably good state of preservation. Its three doorways opened into small interior chambers, and above each entrance was a niche containing fragments of seated stucco figures. Visible on the upper facade between two of the doors were remnants of a weathered relief showing a standing human, and the outlines of an ornate mask still adhered to a section of the wall.

Entering one of the doorways, Healey found himself in a narrow vaulted room. When his eyes adjusted to the chamber's dim illumination, he suddenly became aware of faces peering at him from the walls; gradually they assumed sharper delineation and muted colors, and he could see figures of richly costumed priests, nobles, musicians, and strangely masked impersonators surrounding him on all sides. In the next room he came upon a tableau of opposing armies locked in a furious battle, while on an adjoining panel prisoners of war were being judged by haughty chieftains. Magnificent paintings of dancers in exotic costumes, an orchestra, and scenes of human sacrifice adorned the third room, along with a group of nobles attended by retainers. What Healey had stumbled upon was a dazzling array of murals completely covering the walls of the building's three chambers.

Unknown to Healey, the existence of this site had been reported only four months earlier by two travelers, John G. Bourne and Carl Frey. Actually, Bourne had prepared scale drawings of its structures, but the jungle was so thick he had completely overlooked the building containing the frescoes. Hence by sheer accident Healey became the first outsider to stumble upon the most extensive murals yet discovered anywhere in Mesoamerica—a veritable "gallery" of pre-Columbian paintings which instantly provoked excited interest on the part of archaeologists and art historians alike.

In the winter of 1947 an expedition jointly sponsored by the United Fruit Company, the Carnegie Institution, and the Instituto Nacional de Antropología y Historia began an intensive study of the frescoes. Included among its staff were Healey, an engineer named Gustav Strömsvik, the archaeologists Karl Ruppert and J. Eric Thompson, and two artists experienced in mural restoration, Antonio Tejeda and Augustín Villagra Caleti, who set about making accurate copies of the paintings—a task requiring another expedition the following year to complete. At Sylvanus Morley's suggestion, the site was given the name Bonampak, a Maya term meaning "painted walls."

Because of its relatively small size—encompassing eleven major buildings situated on an acropolis, a single courtyard, and various unidentified mounds—Bonampak had obviously been a ceremonial center of secondary importance. It was one of numerous settlements

Design from a ceramic bowl, Tepeu style, Chamá, Guatemala. (After M.D. Coe.)

which once flourished in the Usumacinta Valley, and it had received
cultural impetus from the nearby site of Yaxchilán, whose emblem
glyph appears in Bonampak's murals. Tatiana Proskouriakoff wrote
that Bonampak "could not have been more than a small center in a
region crowded with other towns. It was without doubt merely a
dependancy of the much larger city of Yaxchilán. The stamp of the
Yaxchilán style in its works of art is unmistakable, and the artists who
for generations gave Bonampak its singular distinction were probably
trained in the schools of the larger city."

Why Bonampak should have been graced with such outstanding
artistic achievements we shall perhaps never know. Without considering for a moment the incredible skill of its muralists, much of the
sculpture at Bonampak is of exceptional quality. Proskouriakoff
described the immense stela found in the city's main courtyard as "one
of the largest and finest monuments ever set up by the Maya." Several
of its other sculptured stelae and lintels are scarcely less sensitive in
design and workmanship, and when the murals were finally executed,
an already profound mastery of creative expression was brought to an
unparalleled climax.

What most distinguishes Bonampak's murals from frescoes elsewhere in Mesoamerica is their extraordinary realism. With a few
notable exceptions—especially some of the wall paintings at Chichén
Itzá—ancient murals in Mexico and Central America involve extremely abstruse iconography. Almost always they deal with gods,
ritualism, cosmology, and other esoteric motifs rather than scenes of
actual life. For this reason the Bonampak frescoes have added an
important scope to our knowledge of pre-Columbian art; they
represent a literal translation of scenes drawn from life and are possibly
based on factual historical events. Varied aspects of Maya culture are
vividly portrayed in a style unhampered by abstract symbolism or
florid decorative embellishments, and Bonampak's painters left archaeologists a wealth of information concerning such details as costumes,
musical instruments, warfare, human sacrifice, and rituals. In fact,
Sylvanus Morley declared that "some of the figures in the Bonampak
murals exhibit a degree of naturalism which western Europe did not
achieve until several centuries later."

In copying the frescoes, the artists Tejeda and Caleti ran into formidable difficulties. Some areas were completely obliterated by decay, and the entire surface of the paintings was obscured by a layer of calcium deposited by moisture seeping through the building's walls. Any attempt to clean the murals would obviously have damaged them, so it became necessary to find a way to render these deposits transparent and bring out the full brilliance of the underlying colors. After lengthy experimentation it was discovered that the liberal application of kerosene produced the desired effect.

While studying the paintings, an attempt was made to retrace the steps originally involved in their execution. Apparently the figures were first drawn with a light red line on the freshly plastered walls. Intervening areas had then been filled in with color, and the forms retraced and accentuated with heavier black outlines. Both Tejeda and Caleti believed the original cartoons were made on wet plaster, thereby achieving a true *al fresco* technique. Brushes made of animal hair or feathers were probably used to apply broad areas of color, and rabbit fur may have served for painting more exacting details. A fairly extensive palette of colors had been derived from natural substances: reds and pinks were compounded of iron oxide, yellow was extracted from limonite or ocher, black from carbon, and brown from bitumen or asphalt. Until recently the source of the vivid blue used extensively by the Maya was unknown, but scientists have now identified its composition as a mixture of indigo dye and a type of clay called attapulgite. Greens were presumably obtained by combining blue and yellow in varying amounts.

Of necessity the interpretation of the murals rests partly on conjecture, especially since the significance of certain details can only be guessed and some sections are permanently destroyed. Hieroglyphic inscriptions indicate that the frescoes were painted around A.D. 800, and it therefore seems reasonable to assume that they afford an accurate mirror of life near the end of the Classic period—at the very height of its splendor.

We see depicted on the walls of the east room a grand array of elite dignitaries dressed in full ceremonial attire, including what may be a *halach uinic* or supreme ruler surrounded by his wife and children. Nearby are dancers and their attendants in the act of putting on costumes adorned with exotic quetzal feather decorations in preparation for a ritual. On a lower panel appears a group of earth god impersonators wearing fantastic masks and flanked by musicians playing rattles, a drum, trumpets, and beating on tortoise shells with deer antlers.

The scenes on the south, east, and west walls of the central room portray a raid on an enemy town. Hordes of elaborately attired warriors have hurled themselves against their opponents with dazzling fury, seemingly for the purpose of taking captives. On the north wall the spoils of the preceding conflict are exhibited: the prisoners, stripped of all but their loincloths, sit before the victorious lords awaiting the pronouncement of their fate—whether slavery or sacrifice.

In the west room the supplication to which the scenes in the two previous chambers have led is finally enacted. The ecstasy of the participants has broken forth in the restless movements of dancers, the ebullient color of their costumes, and the sound of music. Amid them is a dead captive whose hands and feet are held by attendants; a priest flails his limp body with a wandlike object. Watching from an opposite wall a group of chiefs adorned in floor-length white capes are apparently discussing the event, and below them minor officials sit cross-legged, gesturing as if in conversation.

In appraising these frescoes, the French anthropologist Jacques Soustelle wrote: "Bonampak is a sort of pictorial encyclopaedia of a Maya city of the eighth century; the city comes to life there again, with its ceremonies and its processions, its stiff and solemn-looking dignitaries weighed down by their heavy plumed adornments, its warriors clothed in jaguar skins. Lively or violent scenes are there displayed side by side with gracious, familiar pictures of daily life. A complete cross-section of society—women, children, servants, musicians, warrior chiefs, dying prisoners, and masked dancers—that is what these painters . . . succeeded in depicting on those walls, lost today in the depths of one of the continent's most impenetrable jungles. . . . Only naïve illusion, born of egocentricity, could permit us to apply the word 'primitivism' to an art which, like any other, was, in its time and place, the supreme creation of a genuine culture."

A sense of urgency may have overcome Bonampak's artists as they labored to record the spectacle of their times. Proskouriakoff writes of a vague apprehension which pervaded their sensibilities: "As far as we know, this was the last brilliant chapter in the history of the region. We see at Bonampak its full pomp, its somewhat barbarous and elaborately designed ritual. . . . There is a bare hint, a mere suggestion in the dramatic scenes, and in the excitement of line foreign to the serenity of the Maya style, of an emotional tension which might have presaged a crisis; but there is, unfortunately, no sequel to the scenes. . . ."

Events throughout the Maya realm were rapidly assuming an ominous restlessness. Not long after A.D. 800 the crisis alluded to by Proskouriakoff erupted throughout the lowlands. Suddenly the Maya were on the brink of a shattering upheaval, and though their inhabitants could not foresee its consequences, most of the magnificent ceremonial centers in this region had but a few years longer to exist.

10

THE RIDDLE
OF THE
ABANDONED
CITIES

 Early in the ninth century, Maya civilization in the lowlands underwent a catastrophic decline. In one city after another artistic, intellectual, and religious activity gradually came to a halt. New construction ended so abruptly in some sites that buildings and monuments were left unfinished. Even the practice of erecting dated stelae was terminated at successive locations, a circumstance which has provided an accurate chronology of this dissolution throughout much of the region.

Within a span of about a hundred years—from roughly A.D. 800 to 900—all of the once populous cities in the Central Area were deserted. Incredibly, the buildings were left untouched, without destruction or alteration, almost as if their occupants had intended to return momentarily. Instead an immense stillness enveloped them from which they never awakened. Slowly underbrush overtook the court-yards; vines and the roots of trees engulfed the pyramids, temples, and palaces, forcing their stones to split apart and crumble. Ultimately the jungle reclaimed the ill-destined Maya cities, totally forsaken at the very height of their glory.

In the absence of any clear-cut explanation to account for a disaster of such magnitude, archaeologists have advanced a number of theories. Had conquering armies from Mexico invaded the lowlands? Did they succeed in overpowering the resplendent cities in their path of conquest, slaughtering many of their inhabitants and forcing the rest to flee? It was a distinct possibility in view of the Mexicans' inclination toward militarism, but one which was soon discarded for lack of evidence. Unexpected changes in climatic conditions, especially sharp increases in rainfall, were suggested as possible factors, and some students concluded that earthquakes had struck the lowlands with sufficient frequency to cause the abandonment of its cities. Epidemics of malaria, yellow fever, and hookworm were cited as another reason for the exodus, and several investigators believed an imbalance occurred in the sex ratio resulting from the birth of progressively fewer females, eventually triggering a severe population decline. But none of these hypotheses were borne out by later research; there are no indications of abnormal climatic changes, widespread earthquakes, or radical demographic alterations, and all of the previously mentioned diseases appear to have been introduced after the Conquest.

Since this perplexing mystery had not been satisfactorily explained by external calamities, Sylvanus Morley felt its solution lay within the framework of Maya civilization itself—social disintegration, civil strife, or economic failure. But what could have presaged an internal crisis of such far-reaching consequences? For Morley and some of his colleagues the answer was to be found in the theory of "agricultural exhaustion," the conviction that the *milpa* system, which Morley viewed as appallingly wasteful of land resources, simply could not produce enough food to sustain an expanding population. In *The Ancient Maya* he detailed this concept:

> The repeated clearing and burning of ever-increasing areas of forest to serve as corn lands gradually converted the original forest into man-made grasslands, artificial savannas. When this process was complete . . . when the primeval forest had been largely felled and replaced in time by these artificially produced grasslands, then agriculture as practiced by the ancient Maya came to an end, since they had no

implements whatsoever for turning the soil—no hoes, picks, harrows, spades, shovels, or plows.

The replacing of the original forest by man-made savannas . . . must have come about very gradually, reaching a really acute state at different cities and eventually causing their respective abandonments at different times, depending in each case upon variable factors such as the relative size of the population in question, respective periods of occupation, and general fertility of the surrounding areas.

Other adverse factors following in the wake of the decreasing food supply, such as accompanying social unrest, governmental disorganization, and even religious disbelief, doubtless all played their respective parts in the collapse . . . but it appears highly probable that economic failure—the law of diminishing returns, another way of saying the high cost of living—was chiefly responsible for the final disintegration. . . .

But did the Maya actually exhaust their reserves of arable land? It became increasingly difficult to accept this premise in view of later findings to the contrary. Studies by the distinguished archaeologist Alfred V. Kidder demonstrated a salient fact in this regard: the soil along the Motagua River in western Honduras is revitalized annually by flooding. Whereas it was usually necessary to allow depleted *milpas* to lie fallow for several years during which, according to Morley's theory, they reverted to grasslands, the Motagua Valley has been continually farmed for centuries. Yet this region's two most important cities—Copán and Quiriguá—were among the first to be deserted early in the ninth century.

Recent discoveries have also shown that some cities were not entirely sustained by *milpa* agriculture. Near certain lowland centers scientists found the remains of extensive hillside terraces, an innovation which substantially increased the amount of farmland in these regions. Elsewhere artificial earthern platforms or "raised fields" were erected in low-lying districts, thus allowing the cultivation of crops in seasonally flooded areas that remained permanently fertile.

J. Eric Thompson has observed that cultivated lands tend to revert to forest rather than grass, and the large savannas found in some parts of the lowlands (once thought to be former *milpas*) are almost never in close proximity to ruined cities, and therefore they cannot be positively attributed to ancient agriculture. Nor is it entirely reasonable to assume that a shortage of land would have caused the Maya to vacate their far-flung ceremonial centers in comparatively rapid succession, particularly if, as mounting evidence suggests, food sources not dependent on *milpas* were being widely exploited in Late Classic times—principally breadfruit, sweet potatoes, and possibly manioc, a root crop native to the tropical forests of South America. To judge from the abrupt termination of activity throughout the lowlands, the cities were abandoned much more hastily, as if presaged by events less predictable than the gradual exhaustion of the land.

Along the Usumacinta River the city of Piedras Negras in Guatemala lies almost completely hidden by jungle. Many of its

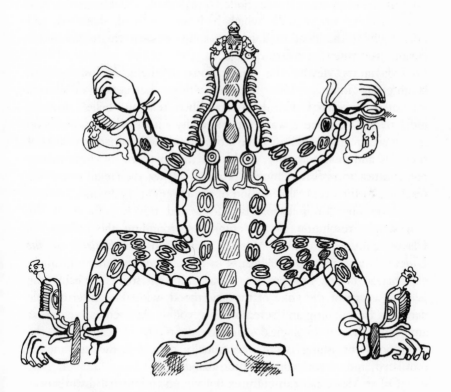

Figure of an anthropomorphized crocodile from Altar T, Copán. (After Maudslay.)

monuments are among the finest ever wrought by Maya sculptors, and one especially outstanding piece is a beautifully carved dais originally used as a "throne" by elite dignitaries. At some time in the past it had been intentionally smashed, but the exact date of its destruction could not be ascertained. Another work of marvelous craftsmanship was unearthed at Piedras Negras—a sculptured wall panel depicting a high priest or ruler presiding over a hierarchic conclave. Again, its severely damaged condition had not resulted from natural causes: the head of each individual figure—fifteen in all—was knocked off, leaving sharp breaks in the stone. Excavations at Tikal by the University of Pennsylvania have brought to light a number of stelae and altars showing deliberate mutilation similar to the monuments at Piedras Negras; a notable example was Stela 26 (called the "Red Stela" because it was painted bright red), which had been defaced, shattered, and buried under the floor of a temple amid its own fragments and a curious assortment of offertory objects.

Mayanists viewed the implications of these disclosures with heightening interest. Was not the willful destruction of objects intimately associated with long-established religious beliefs perhaps indicative of defiance toward the hierarchy under whose supervision they were created? And since the cities functioned primarily as seats of religious and civil authority, could not the smashing of these monuments attest to uprisings by the peasants against their elite overlords, resulting in the eventual desertion of the ceremonial centers?

A number of archaeologists advocated this hypothesis as the long-sought resolution to the enigma surrounding the collapse of Classic culture. J. Alden Mason, writing in the *Bulletin of the University of Pennsylvania Museum* in 1943, stated that the most likely explanation of the problem was "war and civil strife. Probably the people, weary of the yoke of the priesthood, with their interminable demands for building and ceremonies, revolted. At Piedras Negras, at any rate, the archaeological evidence definitely indicated that the ceremonial furnishings were intentionally damaged, the monuments mutilated, and its ceremonial center abandoned."

Other Mesoamerican cultures fell victim to internal disturbances at about the same time. Teotihuacán, once the most powerful city in Mexico, had been burned and deserted shortly after A.D. 650. In

Oaxaca the great Zapotec center of Monte Albán was overturned around A.D. 900, and within a century thereafter serious upheavals began to erupt in the Toltec capital of Tula in western Hidalgo, ultimately leading to its downfall. In each case the underlying causes appear to stem at least partly from weaknesses inherent in the nature of these societies, ostensibly brought on by the oppressive abuses of their ruling hierarchies.

In a revised edition of Morley's *The Ancient Maya* published in 1956, George Brainerd wrote: ". . . the causal element for the Maya decline may be restricted and defined if we assume that the contemporaneous decline of other Classic New World civilizations was influenced by historically related causes. . . . Just as peoples in widely spaced areas of aboriginal America developed similar formal governments ruled by priests, they may have tired simultaneously of this way of life. The lower classes must have revolted, and the word must have traveled. Such a drastic change may well have been caused by the formation of an organized set of new ideas as the purpose of existence—a new philosophy."

In his book, *The Rise and Fall of Maya Civilization*, J. Eric Thompson examined the question of why the power of the hierarchy might have been undermined. Among the ideas he suggested was the possibility that the mystique of their esoteric pursuits eventually wore thin in the eyes of the overburdened multitudes. What value to illiterate peasants were abstract realms of mathematics, calendrics, and astronomy, particularly when such knowledge was kept sequestered exclusively among the priest-rulers? Too long had the masses remained in a state of servitude; too exacting was the endless labor required to construct the ceremonial centers, tend the fields of wealthy nobles, pay tributes, and supply luxury goods. And too blatant were the tricks with which the priests wove their cabalistic patterns of psychological control, the system of religious punishments and rewards intended to awe the populace into strict obeyance.

For centuries the masses had willingly submitted to the ruling elite, until perhaps the shadow of despotism and degeneracy were glimpsed and the outcry for rebellion arose. Once this disenchantment set in, it is possible that something as simple as a crop failure in one or two localities, a natural catastrophe, or an astronomical phenomenon

Detail of Stela D, Copán. (After Maudslay.)

such as an eclipse which the priests failed to predict prompted a serious loss of faith in the hierarchy. Events of this kind could easily have touched off revolts, with the result that the authority of the elite (who seemingly had no effective means of controlling the peasants other than religious sanctions) was overturned, and the ceremonial centers—the supreme symbols of upper-class power—were sacked and abandoned.

Lately there has been a trend among Mayanists not to attribute the demise of Classic culture to any single cause, and a great deal of speculation has focused on a combination of underlying factors. Indeed, this was the prevailing viewpoint at a seminar held in October of 1970 at the School of American Research in Santa Fe, New Mexico, which brought together eleven leading scholars to discuss the subject in the light of current archaeological data.

Briefly, the papers read at this conference, as summarized by Gordon R. Willey and Demitri B. Shimkin,* emphasized a variety of social, political, and economic conditions thought to have rendered the Maya susceptible to a sudden upset and decline. For instance, recent excavations at numerous sites have underlined the extraordinary complexity of Late Classic society. By this time the aristocracy and

---

* Gordon R. Willey and Demitri B. Shimkin, "The Maya Collapse: A Summary View," in *The Classic Maya Collapse*, T. Patrick Culbert, ed. (Albuquerque: University of New Mexico Press, 1973). This important book contains eighteen papers delivered at the School of American Research seminar and represents the most exhaustive synthesis to date dealing with the decline of Classic civilization.

priests alike had become enormously powerful, wealthy, and self-serving, a fact amply confirmed by the lavish splendor of their tombs, representations of dynastic succession on monuments, and the proliferation of palace-type structures and luxury items. No doubt they directly controlled a vast segment of the economy, including foreign trade and possibly the local distribution of raw materials and food. Along with this sharp increase in elite power and prosperity, the number of retainers and minor administrators swelled tremendously, placing additional demands upon the peasants for food and commodities necessary to support the hierarchy. Very likely these conditions resulted in ever-widening gaps and antagonisms between the upper and lower classes, and much of the work required by the elite may have finally been carried out by enforced labor.

Everywhere there are indications in Late Classic horizons of greatly expanded population pressures, together with a marked acceleration in the size and number of ceremonial centers, some of which (especially Tikal, whose inhabitants are variously estimated to have numbered between 20,000 and 50,000 at this time) were almost certainly quite urbanized. Ritualism and intellectual pursuits had reached a peak of activity, and there was apparently a considerable amount of competition between the major cities and their respective hierarchies, a tendency to challenge each other in sheer magnificence of architecture, monuments, and luxury goods such as jade, feather-work, and ceramics. Eventually this rivalry may even have erupted into widespread inter-city warfare, leading to a further drain on manpower and food reserves.

All of these circumstances imposed a tremendous burden on land, natural resources, and available labor, particularly since Maya technology, which had remained basically unchanged for hundreds of years, lacked the capacity to accommodate these demands. In turn, this could easily have caused land use to be mismanaged, thereby bringing about acute shortages of food and a heightened susceptibility to disease. Significantly, skeletons from some Late Classic burials reveal evidence that peasants were smaller and less healthy than the aristocracy, suggesting that the latter had requisitioned more than its share of dwindling food supplies. And an analysis of skeletal remains from graves at Altar de Sacrificios by Frank P. Saul, an anatomist with the

Medical College of Ohio, showed abundant traces of scurvy, anemia, and periodontal disease, all attributable to malnutrition.

Each of these problems—overpopulation, exaggerated demands by the elite for goods and services, inter-city rivalry, widening gulfs between social classes, and decreasing food supply—contributed to what Willey and Shimkin termed "stress factors," which left Maya civilization precariously balanced on the edge of catastrophy. Given such circumstances, any of several situations might have provoked a chain reaction ending in a general collapse. Severe famine or outbreaks of disease could have resulted in a massive economic failure—a Maya version of the Great Depression—causing the cities to be deserted as repercussions from these events spread throughout various levels of society. If the peasants had finally revolted against authoritarianism, it is possible that they not only destroyed the elite class, but also disrupted the whole superstructure of trade, political administration, religion, and intellectualism controlled by the nobility, leaving the ceremonial centers without skilled leadership in any of these realms. Quite conceivably, all of the previously cited "stress factors" were involved simultaneously, interacting with each other to produce a situation of insurmountable chaos.

Further clues bearing on the problem have recently emerged from research by Harvard University at Seibal, located on the Río Pasión in the south-central Petén—findings which revived earlier speculations regarding outside invaders. Investigations revealed the sudden appearance of a complex of non-Classic traits at this city during the ninth century. Included among these are ceramic figurines of a strikingly alien type, and two varieties of pottery called Fine Orange and Fine Gray known to have originated along the Gulf Coast of Mexico, presumably somewhere in Tabasco. Even more intriguing, a series of stelae were erected at Seibal between about A.D. 850 and 900 portraying elite figures whose faces differ radically from those characteristically depicted in Classic sculpture, resembling instead carvings from eastern Mexico or Yucatán. Foreign architectural features are also associated with these monuments, particularly a curious round structure and the use of columns, which are both typical of certain archaeological sites in Mexico.

Inescapably, such facts point to some degree of intrusion into the

Central Area in the ninth century, either directly from Mexico or by way of Maya groups in Yucatán who had already been exposed to strong Mexican influences. Sizable quantities of Fine Orange and Fine Gray pottery have also turned up at Altar de Sacrificios, Yaxchilán, Piedras Negras, and Palenque, leading archaeologists to view these penetrations by outsiders as fairly extensive. Whether this influx of non-Classic elements took the form of a military invasion or a gradual infiltration of people and ideas is not clear. In any case, with the unstable conditions already existing in Maya society, such incursions could easily have spread havoc throughout the region and set in motion a conspiracy of malefic events: further overtaxation of food and other resources, disruption of normal trade relations, conscription of manpower for prolonged military service (effectively removing them from food production), displacing the hierarchy, and even forced resettlement of conquered populations, perhaps in northern Yucatán. If this was actually the situation, then the Maya may have ultimately succumbed to a combination of outside pressures and demoralizing internal tensions, a circumstance so often responsible for the downfall of civilizations elsewhere in the ancient world.

At present no one can say with certainty why Classic Maya culture collapsed so suddenly. Existing evidence is far too fragmentary for absolute conclusions to be drawn. Only one thing is certain: whatever the reasons behind the abandonment of the lowland cities, they were irreconcilable with the destiny of the Maya. Never again would their civilization regain its former brilliance; its once splendid Golden Age was forever lost.

11

CHICHÉN ITZÁ: THE HOME OF ALIEN GODS

 What, then, became of the survivors of these disastrous events? Had they continued to live in the midst of their decaying cities, eventually reduced by circumstances to a rudely primitive existence? Or had they deserted the region completely and moved elsewhere? For years most Mayanists envisioned the Central Area as having quickly reverted to an uninhabited wilderness in the aftermath of migrations which carried the remnants of its population into Yucatán. But a considerably different picture of the situation has emerged from subsequent research.

Excavators working at Uaxactún discovered that people had lived in or near that city long after it ceased to function as a ceremonial center, even using some of its buildings as dwellings and burial places. Similar findings were unearthed at several sites in Belize and the central Petén, especially at Tikal, where deposits of refuse in temples, intrusive graves beneath the floors of Classic structures, and the appearance of new types of ceramics all point to a partial occupation of the site after A.D. 900. Apparently many of Tikal's rich tombs had been looted at this time, and a number of its stelae and altars were reset in different locations, usually with total disregard for their original architectural context.

However, none of this information suggests anything like a revival of Classic culture in the Central Area. For reasons not entirely understood, this district seems to have undergone a steady decline in population from the end of the tenth century onward, leaving behind only small, semi-isolated groups. Despite half-hearted attempts to make use of deserted temples and resurrect religious monuments (presumably to maintain contact with ancient gods), its inhabitants never produced art or architecture remotely comparable to the creations of their illustrious predecessors. Every aspect of their existence reflects at best a weak imitation of former glories, an almost desperate effort to preserve rapidly fading links with their past without the benefit of an educated elite or strong political authority. At Tikal these survivors were so culturally impoverished that they had sometimes reset monuments upside down or backwards, as if their hieroglyphic texts could no longer be read. It was a sad postscript to the dazzling achievements of earlier centuries, all memory of which was slowly but inexorably engulfed by the ubiquitous rain forest.

Yet the presence of ruins of a different character throughout northern Yucatán affirms that Maya civilization endured there long after its demise in the Central Area. Originally this region was believed to have remained uninhabited during the Classic period, or at most had contained only widely scattered settlements which were nothing more than provincial outposts by comparison with the thriving ceremonial centers to the south. After the collapse of the Central Area's cities, large numbers of survivors were thought to have migrated into the upper half of the peninsula, imparting to this sector the intellectual, artistic, and technical genius of their lustrous heritage. Here between approximately A.D. 900 and 1200 these immigrants supposedly founded magnificent new centers: Uxmal, Chichén Itzá, Kabáh, Sayil, Labná, and dozens more whose ruins comprise one of the most spectacular arrays of archaeological monuments anywhere in America. With these hypothetical events there emerged what scholars called the "New Empire" (in contrast to the "Old Empire," a term formerly used to designate Classic culture in the Central Area)—a brilliant resurgence of Maya traditions infused with renewed vitality. Succeeding years of research have demonstrated the inaccuracy of this concept. When more was learned about the date inscriptions from Yucatán, some of those which could be securely fixed in Maya chronology fell between A.D. 475 and 889, a clear indication that long before the Central Area was deserted, Yucatán was inhabited by people versed in hieroglyphic writing and calendrics. As excavations in the region broadened in scope, a number of sites contained pottery closely related to the Tzakol and Tepeu wares found in Classic horizons to the south, including polychrome vessels imported directly from the Petén and adjacent areas; and several ruins in Yucatán have produced Formative period ceramics, notably at Dzibilchaltún where levels of occupation dating back to around 500 B.C. are unusually well defined.

Scholars had previously attached much importance to certain marked differences between Yucatán's ruins and those of the Central Area with regard to building techniques, decoration, and city planning, viewing these as proof that the northern cities were considerably later in date. Generally the arrangement of temples, palaces, and courtyards had been less formalized in Yucatán than was customary in the southern lowlands. Fewer terraced pyramids had been erected, and the elegant, comparatively simple embellishments used to decorate buildings in the south had been supplanted by highly ornate exteriors as exemplified by the Chenes, Río Bec, and Puuc styles. Great emphasis had been placed on the construction of concrete walls faced with a veneer of cut stones, the erection of multistoried "apartment" type structures was fairly widespread, and there was an increased use of columns, especially to support doorways. But as the evolution of Maya architecture became better understood, these peculiarities were viewed as less indicative of a radical departure from older traditions than had originally been supposed; it was shown that many of the architectural conventions seen in Yucatán sprang directly from Classic prototypes and represented regional variations that had developed at an early date.

All of these factors necessitated a broad revision of prior theories concerning the "New Empire." Contrary to the idea that Yucatán had remained either a desolate wilderness or a sparsely inhabited province during the Classic period, archaeologists now believe that all but a few of its cities flourished at the same time as those in the Central Area. No longer do they look upon such ruins as Uxmal, Chichén Itzá, Labná, and Sayil as crowning jewels in a "renaissance" wrought by survivors of the "Old Empire." Nearly every aspect of their art, architecture, inscriptions, and ceramics appears to have been firmly rooted in Classic traditions, and there is no doubt that the region had supported a heavy population even in Formative centuries.

Furthermore, many students feel that when the great ceremonial centers in the southern lowlands were finally surrendered to the rain forest, most of Yucatán's sites were also abandoned at about the same time and for equally mysterious reasons. Emigrants from the south probably did migrate northward after the collapse of their cities, but their fortunes may have been no more promising once they reached Yucatán. Very possibly the same disaster which overtook Yaxchilán, Palenque, Tikal, Uaxactún, Copán, and the rest of the Central Area's cities had spread into the northern end of the peninsula, leaving its centers empty and their inhabitants scattered in small agrarian communities.

Before his untimely death in 1971, E. Wyllys Andrews, who conducted an intensive study of Yucatán's prehistory under the auspices of the Middle American Research Institute, seriously disputed this hypothesis. He contended that a number of northern cities—specifically those in the Chenes, Río Bec, and Puuc districts—should be viewed in a different chronological context than was previously supposed. Based on artistic, ceramic, and architectural evidence, Andrews insisted that these sites had not risen to prominence until relatively late in the Classic period and were occupied for several centuries afterward. Actually, he saw them as representing an extension of Classic civilization which somehow survived its demise farther south, stimulated perhaps by an influx of refugees from the Petén and Usumacinta Valley who began migrating northward early in the ninth century. Given the ascendancy of the Chenes, Río Bec, and Puuc cities during what he termed the "Florescent" phase in Yucatán—dating from roughly A.D. 900 to 1100—Andrews argued that Maya culture never really "collapsed" in the north, undergoing instead a vigorous upsurge resulting in the rapid proliferation of new ceremonial centers for several hundred years after the downfall of the Central Area.

Andrews' provocative theory has touched off a far-reaching controversy between its supporters and those scholars who maintain that the Chenes, Río Bec, and Puuc cities were abandoned by about A.D. 900 along with neighboring centers to the south. Before it can ever be resolved, much of Andrews' research remains to be evaluated, complex problems involving chronological alignments must be worked out, and many sites which may shed additional light on the subject need to be adequately explored. But the question is one of fundamental importance, and it will have to be clarified if we are to understand fully the final centuries of Maya history.

Soon after this juncture was reached—that is, the abandonment of the Central Area and the confusing events that followed in the north—a curious new element appeared in Yucatán. Against the background of cultural change, social unrest, and shifting populations then plaguing the Maya, a radically different force seized their political and spiritual fortunes. It appears to have swept over them suddenly; in its very uniqueness Maya civilization found a temporary renewal of its former vigor redirected by alien ideals. It was a virile, cogent stimulus, but one whose origin was deeply cloaked in mystery.

Chichén Itzá, the sprawling ruined city seventy miles east of Mérida, had long been an archaeological puzzle. Its existence was known since the time of the Conquest, but other than the desultory efforts of a few early explorers, it was not systematically excavated until 1924 when the Carnegie Institution began a ten-year project there under Sylvanus Morley's supervision. Even before then, however, a curious paradox had been observed among its ruins: in contrast to numerous older buildings of predominantly Puuc style, much of the architecture at Chichén Itzá reflected strangely non-Maya elements.

These spurious structures included the impressive Temple of Kukulcán—also called El Castillo—the Temple of the Jaguars and its adjoining Ball Court, the Temple of the Warriors, the Mercado or marketplace, and a circular building known as El Caracol, an astronomical observatory not unlike its modern counterparts in outward appearance, with a spiral stairway leading to fixed observation points inside a domelike tower. Ironically, these famous buildings have

Detail of a carved lintel depicting a human head emerging from a serpent's mouth, Yaxchilán. (After Maudslay.)

come to epitomize Maya civilization in the minds of the general public, yet they incorporate foreign concepts wholly out of character with traditional Maya architecture: the use of colonnades, interior courts or peristyles, rooms divided by columns, and a type of exterior wall treatment known as *talud-tablero*—rectangular inset panels placed on an outward-sloping base.

Another unique innovation at Chichén Itzá was the construction of square platforms, two of which probably served as stages for ceremonies or theatrical performances. Nearby stands a third platform, T-shaped in outline and decorated with rows of human skulls carved in low relief. Nothing like it had ever been encountered in the Maya area (they have since been found at Uxmal and Dzibilchaltún), though similar platforms were excavated at several locations in central Mexico. In fact, Spanish chroniclers reported seeing a structure of this type in the Aztec capital of Tenochtitlán; it was known as a *tzompantli*, and it held racks on which the skulls of sacrificial victims were publicly displayed.

Aside from these architectural features, a number of new sculptural motifs were evident at Chichén Itzá. Adorning temple walls and columns were dozens of warriors whose dress and physical appearance differed sharply from the usual images portrayed by Maya artists—enigmatic figures wearing quilted cotton armor, with pectorals in the form of butterflies or birds, and carrying shields, *atlatls*, spears, and flint or obsidian-tipped clubs. Massive columns and balustrades sculptured to represent feathered serpents flanked the doors and stairways of temples. Rows of eagles and crouched jaguars clutching human hearts were carved in bold relief on walls, and several buildings contained effigies of seated men designed to hold standards or flags in their outstretched hands. Elsewhere were anthropomorphic statues with upraised arms known as "Atlantean" figures, used to support altars and door lintels, together with so-called *chacmools* or representations of reclining men with raised heads and knees, holding shallow basins on their abdomens.

Since all of these non-Maya architectural and sculptural traits were closely duplicated at sites in the Valley of Mexico and adjoining regions, only one plausible explanation seemed to account for their existence at Chichén Itzá: they were indelible imprints left by intruders from among Mexico's more warlike peoples who had invaded the city and implanted the seeds of a radically different culture. Indeed, a mural in the Temple of the Jaguars depicts lines of battle drawn between Maya defenders and invading warriors whose costumes and weapons match the ominous figures shown so profusely in Chichén Itzá's sculpture. For the first time in a graphic representation, the Maya are pictured falling in defeat before an enemy!

Now, too, a question that had long perplexed students began to clarify itself. Numerous post-Conquest documents, including the *Books of Chilam Balam* and Landa's *Relación*, mentioned the important role played in Yucatán by a tribe called the Itzá. Allegedly they had settled at Chichén Itzá in the tenth century and transformed it into a powerful capital whose influence dominated the surrounding territory. According to these accounts, the Itzá had originally lived in a mysterious city in central Mexico named Tollán—the legendary home of the Toltecs —from where they set out on a series of southward migrations, eventually settling in Yucatán.

Myths concerning Tollán were quite common in Mexican folklore. Among the first European chroniclers to mention this site was a Franciscan friar, Bernardino de Sahagún, who referred to it in his monumental work entitled *A General History of the Things of New Spain*, also known as the Florentine Codex. For years after the conquest of Mexico, Sahagún had labored at transcribing the language, history, and customs of the Aztecs into a bilingual record, using their own Náhuatl tongue and Spanish. With much the same determination as Landa had pursued his studies of the Yucatecans, Sahagún worked among the Aztecs, questioning them about every aspect of their culture. One point was consistently reaffirmed by his native informants: their art, architecture, calendar, and religion—in short, almost everything the Aztecs accomplished—had been strongly influenced by peoples who inhabited the Valley of Mexico long before they rose to power in the fourteenth century. Unfailingly, these precursors were identified as the Toltecs, whose capital of Tollán was reportedly one of the most magnificent cities in Mexico. So highly skilled were the Toltecs, wrote Sahagún, "nothing they did was difficult for them. . . . They cut green stone [jade], and they cast gold, and made other works of the craftsman and the feather-worker. . . . And these Toltecs enjoyed great wealth; they were rich; never were they poor. Nothing did they lack in their homes. . . ."

A sixteenth-century Aztec noble, Fernando de Alva Ixtlilxochitl, an interpreter for the Spanish viceroy in Mexico City, compiled a lengthy version of his people's history which corroborated the fact that the stimulus underlying the rise of Aztec culture was largely derived from the Toltecs. Ixtlilxochitl portrayed them as masters of art, architecture, calendrics, medicine, and engineering, with a fierce dedication to religion and a love of rich pageantry. Toltec laws were said to have been strict but justly enforced, and their most important priest-king was the famous Quetzalcóatl, the "living divinity who dwelled among the builders of Tollán."

In weighing the validity of these accounts, scholars were confronted with certain basic considerations. Native sources generally agreed that the Aztecs were profoundly influenced by Toltec culture as originally derived from Tollán. Moreover, scattered throughout the Valley of Mexico and its environs were archaeological remains far older than those of Aztec origin, the most spectacular being the ruins of Teotihuacán, thirty miles north of Mexico City. For lack of a more definitive term this ancient substratum was initially designated as "Toltec," and virtually every pre-Aztec site in central Mexico was directly attributed to Toltec inspiration.

But subsequent research has ruled out this once widely accepted concept. We now know that the Toltecs did not exclusively occupy the cultural stage in the Valley of Mexico prior to the coming of the Aztecs. Other peoples were equally responsible for its rich archaeological heritage, and the Toltecs themselves were relative latecomers. Like the Aztecs, they inherited much of their culture from earlier groups, especially the inhabitants of Teotihuacán, who had controlled central Mexico for centuries.

Until recently it could not be said with certainty who the Toltecs were; nor was it known where their capital of Tollán was located, or whether the long-missing city ever existed at all. Some archaeologists dismissed the whole problem as a myth and even denounced the hypothetical use of the word "Toltec," insisting that since no such culture had been positively defined, its application was unjustified. Others, however, were not so willing to disregard the value of legend in reconstructing historical events, and they proceeded to search for Tollán's ruins.

Roughly fifty-four miles northwest of Mexico City, in the state of Hidalgo, the small town of Tula nestles in a sun-parched valley. On a promontory overlooking the dusty village, dozens of rubble-covered mounds were all that remained of what was once a vast complex of terraced pyramids, temples, sunken plazas, and ball courts. Sahagún and Ixtlilxochitl had both identified this site as Tollán, and in 1880 the famous French traveler and antiquarian, Désiré Charnay, noted with more than passing interest how closely many of the monuments and

sculptural motifs he saw while visiting Tula were duplicated at
Chichén Itzá. But it was not until 1940 that excavations were
undertaken at Tula by the Mexican archaeologist J. R. Acosta, who
was to continue his research for almost fifteen years.

Hardly had Acosta started to dig before Charnay's astute
observations were resoundingly confirmed. Out of these explorations at
Tula gradually emerged the entire panorama of traits so clearly
identified with Chichén Itzá. Here were the same images of warriors
clad in quilted armor who had carried the bitter taste of conquest to
Yucatán. Identical reliefs of eagles and jaguars feeding upon human
hearts moved across the walls of Tula's pyramid-temples, and there
were buildings with colonnades, peristyles, *talud-tablero* facings, Atlantean figures, standard bearers, and *chacmools*. Although no *tzompantlis*
were unearthed at Tula, rows of carved skulls—grim reminders of the
Toltecs' obsession with human sacrifice—were prominently displayed
on monuments and walls, along with representations of feathered
serpents, the emblem of their adored god-king Quetzalcóatl. So
striking were the parallels between Tula and Chichén Itzá, it seemed as
though the same artists and architects had worked at both locations.

Acosta's findings left no doubt that Tula was the original site of
Tollán, and archaeologists were now able to clarify many aspects of
Toltec history. Apparently the city was founded by Nahua-speaking
tribesmen known as Tolteca-Chichimecas, who entered the Valley of
Mexico early in the tenth century A.D. Under the leadership of
sagacious priest-kings, Tula's influence spread throughout central
Mexico until virtually every tribe in the region proudly claimed Toltec
ancestry. Eventually Tula fell victim to ideological and political
rivalries, and sometime around 1168 it was permanently abandoned as
a result of internal conflicts and invading armies. If we can believe
native accounts, a large number of people had already departed from
Tula almost two centuries earlier, led by the celebrated Quetzalcóatl
after he was driven from his homeland by forces allied to the war god
Tezcatlipoca. This exodus presumably took place in the year 987, and
according to various sources, Quetzalcóatl and his subjects—probably
the group the Maya called Itzá—migrated to Yucatán and established
themselves at Chichén Itzá.

In essence, most of what the traditional Maya accounts said

Figure of a Toltec-Itzá warrior armed with spears, Temple of the Jaguars, Chichén Itzá. (After Maudslay.)

concerning the Toltec-Itzá seemed borne out by archaeology, though countless details of these epochal events are still obscure. We can only guess whether the Itzá were of pure Toltec extraction or a mixture of peoples united to them by political and economic ties. Nor do we know how long their migrations to Yucatán continued or by what routes they came. And towering above all these questions was the identity of their great culture hero Quetzalcóatl.

Numerous myths describe Quetzalcóatl's remarkable accomplishments. His name is a combination of the Náhuatl words *quetzal* (the magnificently plumed bird native to the Guatemalan highlands) and *cóatl* (snake); hence he is symbolically depicted as a serpent adorned with feathers. Native accounts refer to him variously as a deity of extreme importance and the first ruler of Tollán, and he was revered throughout Mexico and Central America for his wisdom, gentleness, and patronage of art, literature, agriculture, and science. Sahagún wrote that the Aztecs believed Quetzalcóatl "created the world; and they bestowed upon him the appellation Lord of the Wind, because they said that Tonacatecotli [a powerful creator-god] . . . breathed and begat Quetzalcóatl. They erected round temples to him. . . . They said that it was he who formed the first man. . . . He alone had a human body like that of men; the other gods were of an incorporeal nature."

When Quetzalcóatl was finally defeated by the jealous warrior god Tezcatlipoca and driven from Mexico, some legends say that he vanished into the sea near Veracruz. Others proclaim that he ascended into the heavens and became the planet Venus. Still another version states: "the man whom they called Quetzalcóatl . . . taught [his followers] by word and deed the way of virtue, saving them from vice and sin, giving them the laws and good doctrine; and to restrain them in their lusts and lewd ways, had instituted fasting amongst them. . . . But seeing how little fruit his doctrine brought forth, he had gone away by the same road he had come, which was to the East, vanishing on the coast of Coatzacoalcos, and as he departed . . . he had said to them that at a future time . . . he would return, and then his doctrine would be received, and his sons would be lords and owners of the land. . . ."

Quetzalcóatl's fame extended far beyond the limits of Toltec influence. He was worshipped at Teotihuacán long before Tula had supposedly been founded, as evidenced by images of feathered serpents on some of Teotihuacán's sculpture, murals, and ceramics. To the Maya of Yucatán he was known as Kukulcán, the Quiché called him Gucumatz, and his veneration became as profound in these regions as it was in Mexico.

Writing of Quetzalcóatl's appearance in Yucatán, Landa reported: "It is believed among the Indians that with the Itzás who occupied Chichén Itzá there reigned a great lord named Kukulcán, and that the principal building, which is called Kukulcán, shows this to be true [a reference to the Temple of Kukulcán or El Castillo]. They say that he arrived from the west; but they differ among themselves as to whether he arrived before or after the Itzás or with them. They say that he was favorably disposed, and had no wife or children, and that . . . he was regarded in Mexico as one of their gods and called Quetzalcóatl; and they also considered him a god in Yucatán on account of his being a just statesman; and this is seen in the order which he imposed on Yucatán after the death of the lords [the overthrow of Maya rulers by the Toltec-Itzá], in order to calm the dissensions which their deaths had caused in the country."

Had such a man as Quetzalcóatl actually existed? Native documents are quite specific in telling us how a leader by this name ruled Tollán shortly after its founding. Some historians feel that because of his renown as a statesman he may have been deified by succeeding generations, or his office may have carried with it the connotation of a god-king. What seems more likely is that long before the Toltecs' rise to power, Quetzalcóatl was already an important deity in Mexico (which would account for his veneration at Teotihuacán), and an early Toltec chieftain—possibly an entire dynasty—adopted his name, perhaps as a means of investing himself with Quetzalcóatl's powers.

Unquestionably the worship of Quetzalcóatl-Kukulcán in Yucatán was ushered in by the influx of Toltec-Itzá culture that swept over the area late in the tenth century. Archaeologists are not certain whether these influences emanated directly from Tula or filtered into the peninsula via less direct means. Early accounts pertaining to the Toltec-Itzá invasions are contradictory and lack a sound chronological basis. This is due in part to problems arising from the use during the Postclassic period of the abbreviated Short Count calendar or *u kahlay katunob* (explained in Chapter 3), which recorded only twenty-year *katun* cycles. Yet the *Books of Chilam Balam* place Kukulcán's arrival at Chichén Itzá in Katun 4 Ahau, one of the few Short Count dates that we definitely know corresponds to A.D. 967–987, and on the basis of information recorded in certain native manuscripts, many authorities believe 987 was the year Quetzalcóatl's banishment from Tula supposedly took place.

Some Mayanists are of the opinion that Quetzalcóatl-Kukulcán did not reach Yucatán until *after* the introduction of Mexican influences at Chichén Itzá, in which case the Toltecs and Itzá were almost surely separate groups. J. Eric Thompson, who has studied this problem in depth, identifies the Itzá as a tribe called the Putún or Chontal, a Maya-speaking people known to have inhabited the coastal regions of Tabasco and Campeche. Famed as traders and seamen whose ships ranged as far east as Guatemala and Honduras, the Putún had absorbed strong Mexican influences and probably spoke Náhuatl in addition to their own language. If Thompson's hypothesis is correct, the Putún expanded into Yucatán and settled at Chichén Itzá around A.D. 918, bringing with them many earmarks of Mexican culture. When Quetzalcóatl and his Toltec followers arrived at Chichén Itzá from Tula in 987, they were cordially received by the Putún-Itzá, whose own Mexican affinities encouraged them to enter into an alliance with the Toltecs.

In contrast to this viewpoint, other students see the Itzá as latecomers to Yucatán. In his book, *The Maya*, Michael D. Coe suggests that the Itzá (who he thinks were led by a later ruler also using the name Kukulcán) did not arrive from Mexico until A.D. 1224–44, long after the Toltecs infiltrated Chichén Itzá and were adopted into the mainstream of Yucatecan culture. Since Chichén Itzá was deserted by about this time, Coe believes the Itzá settled there only briefly before they moved eastward and founded the city of Mayapán, which figures prominently in the final phase of Maya history.

Whatever its source, there is little doubt that the Toltec-Itzá colonization of Yucatán first took the form of an all-out military conquest as shown by scenes at Chichén Itzá depicting battles and the sacrifice of Maya captives at the hands of Mexican invaders. Along with profound aberrations in art, architecture, religion, and sociopolitical structure incurred by this alien intrusion, some of Yucatán's cities may have been abandoned as a result of these external pressures. Yet many obviously continued to flourish under the new regime, and aside from Chichén Itzá, whose size and advantageous location encouraged the conquerors to seize it as their capital, such places as Izamal, Motul, Dzibilchaltún, Maní, and Cozumel Island became key centers of Toltec-Itzá authority.

Along with the sculptural and architectural features already mentioned, other significant innovations entered Yucatán as a consequence of foreign intrusion. Gold, copper, and turquoise were brought in from Mexico, and two distinctive varieties of ceramics came into

*Feathered serpent column representing Quetzalcóatl, Temple of the
Jaguars, Chichén Itzá. (After Holmes.)*

widespread use: highly polished vessels known as X-type Fine Orange
and a unique ware called Plumbate, the only glazed pottery ever
manufactured in Mesoamerica. Among the invading armies were
well-organized military orders using the eagle and jaguar as their
symbols. Newly introduced weapons included cotton armor, *atlatls*,
slings, and obsidian-edged swords, and there was an increased emphasis
on militarism in all phases of political and religious life. Human
sacrifice began to be practiced on a scale never approached in the
Classic period, with the ruthless Toltec-Itzá soldiers assuming a vital
ritualistic function as providers of captives for sacrificial purposes.

New gods and ceremonies appeared, involving not only the cult of Quetzalcóatl-Kukulcán but several other Mexican deities as well: Tonatiuh, the sun god; Chicomecóatl, the maize goddess; Tlaloc, the rainmaker; Xipe-Totec, god of sacrifice; and even Quetzalcóatl's arch rival, the powerful Tezcatlipoca or "Smoking Mirror." In his revision of Morley's *The Ancient Maya*, George Brainerd wrote: ". . . respect for the piety of Kukulcán and the luxuriance of religious construction at Chichén Itzá suggest that the Maya may have lent their talents and labors willingly to the furtherance of a new religion. Perhaps the Toltec conquest of Yucatán was accomplished as much by religious evangelization as by military force."

In time, Toltec-Itzá influences made their way into almost every aspect of Maya culture, and Chichén Itzá became the focal point from which they extended their control over a large section of the peninsula. Even so, native traditions did not disappear under this foreign domination; nor were they subjected to the kind of deliberate annihilation later inflicted by the Spaniards. Intermarriage and cultural exchange presaged a gradual fusion of Maya and Mexican traits, and the conquerors had enormous respect for Maya technology and craftsmanship. Everywhere at Chichén Itzá we see Toltec-styled buildings and monuments executed according to Maya techniques. Images of rigidly posed Mexican warriors and chieftains are shown opposite serene Maya lords, and there are buildings adorned with long-nosed Chac masks of typical Puuc design alongside the feathered serpent emblems of Kukulcán. Like the Roman conquests in Europe and the Near East, the Toltec-Itzá invasion of Yucatán resulted in a synthesis of artistic styles, religious beliefs, and customs in which the thread of Maya civilization continued to survive.

But the great Classic tradition remained forever dead, and it was not long before the Maya were beset by an increasing number of irresolvable problems. Even the infusion of new vigor by outsiders, innovative approaches to art and architecture, and the stimulation of Mexican gods could not forestall the disastrous events now awaiting them. Unknowingly, the pattern of cultural decay and political disunity that was to overtake them in the three centuries prior to the Spanish Conquest had already been set in motion.

12

THE WELL
OF SACRIFICE

Because of its prominence as the seat of Toltec-Itzá power, Chichén Itzá was the center of artistic, religious, and economic activity in Yucatán for over two hundred years. Several sixteenth-century Spanish authors claimed that it was equally renowned as a shrine, and in times of drought, pestilence, or similar misfortunes pilgrims from distant areas visited the city in order to carry out human sacrifices in which victims laden with jade, gold, and precious stones were hurled into the now celebrated Sacred Cenote, an ominous pool of water said to be the abode of gods, especially the rain deity Chac. For years, however, this intriguing tale had remained nothing but hearsay until a scholar-diplomat named Edward Herbert Thompson attempted to verify its grim details and in so doing made archaeological history.

When Thompson was appointed to the post of United States Consul in Yucatán in 1885, he was barely twenty-five years of age. A native of Worcester, Massachusetts, he had been educated in business and engineering, but as a young man he developed a consuming interest in archaeology, and when an opportunity arose for him to reside in Yucatán as a member of the consular service, he unhesitatingly accepted it. Like John Lloyd Stephens, Thompson regarded the responsibilities of a diplomatic career as secondary in importance to his enthusiasm for antiquities. Scarcely had he assumed his official duties in Mérida before he launched a series of explorations at various ruins under the sponsorship of the Peabody Museum and the American Antiquarian Society, but eventually the focal point of his research became the acres of overgrown structures and mounds marking the site of Chichén Itzá.

A few years after his arrival in Yucatán, Thompson negotiated for the purchase of the abandoned plantation on which Chichén Itzá was located. In his autobiography, *People of the Serpent*, he described his first impression of the ruined city that was to be his home for three decades:

> The gradual ascent and winding of the trail between the boulders and the big trees seemed so like familiar forest rambles at home that it came over me almost with a shock to realize that the boulders I passed by so carelessly had cut surfaces and were once carved columns and sculptured pillars. Then, just as I began to understand that the level, forest-covered surface beneath my feet was a terrace made by ancient man, I peered upward to a great stone mass that pierced the sky, and all else was forgotten. A pyramid with terraced sides, panelled walls of cut limestone, and broad stairways leading upward, was crowned by a temple. Other buildings, high mounds, and broken terraces, were buried in the forest and only the dark green knobs on the horizon told where they stood.
>
> Pen cannot describe or brush portray the strange feelings produced by the beating of the tropic sun against the ash-colored walls of those venerable structures. Old . . . furrowed by time, and haggard, imposing, and impassive, they rear their rugged masses above the surrounding level and are beyond description.
>
> The ruined group of Chichén Itzá covers a space of fully three square miles. Over all this territory are scattered carved and square stones in countless thousands and fallen columns by the hundreds; while the formless remains and outlined walls of huge structures fallen into decay are seen on every side. Seven massive structures of carved stone and

adamantine mortar still tower erect and almost habitable. Their facades, though gray and haggard with age and seamed by time, sustain the claim that Chichén Itzá is one of the world's greatest monuments of antiquity.

During his exploration of the city, Thompson's attention was drawn to the ruins of a pyramid similar in design to the nearby Temple of Kukulcán, except that it was much smaller in scale. Now called the Tomb of the High Priest, each of its four terraced sides was ascended by a stairway flanked with stone balustrades representing open-jawed serpents. In characteristic fashion, its summit formerly supported a small temple, although nothing remained of this ceremonial superstructure other than four elaborately carved columns. While clearing rubble from the base of these pillars, Thompson stumbled upon two highly polished capstones imbedded in what had once been the floor of the temple.

Beneath these stones he discovered a square shaft descending approximately twelve feet into the core of the pyramid. Faintly discernible on the floor of this vault were portions of a human skeleton surrounded by broken pottery bowls. The burial rested on a smooth flagstone similar to those which had sealed the crypt's entrance, and below this were four more graves superimposed upon one another. "In the third grave," wrote Thompson, "I found a handful of copper bells, small in size, and turned to verdigris. In the fourth grave I found a necklace of handsomely cut and finely polished rock-crystal beads. The floor of this last grave was on a level with the base of the pyramid, and I naturally concluded that, as the pyramid rested on the limestone ledge rock of the region, my work of excavation was automatically ended. Then I observed that the stone floor tiles still persisted, and, lifting them, I discovered to my surprise a series of steps hewn out of the living rock down into a chamber. . . . The stairs were covered and the chamber filled with wood ashes. The only way I could enter . . . was by lying flat on my back and pushing my feet ahead of me through the ashes and into the chamber. . . ."

Slowly Thompson worked his way into the narrow crypt. Intermingled with the refuse he cleared from the vault were a number of jade beads, some of which looked as though they had been burned. Otherwise the room turned out to be empty except for a square stone resting against one wall. When Thompson attempted to move the slab it unexpectedly gave way, revealing a black hole in the floor underneath it. A flood of cold air rushed out of the cavernous opening, blowing out the candles and leaving Thompson and his Maya assistants in "utter darkness in the bowels of the earth."

"Don Eduardo," cried his workmen, "this is surely the mouth of Hell!"

"Not so," he replied. "Since when has the mouth of Hell given forth a breath as cold as this wind?"

By a curious irony this logic appealed to the terrified Indians. Years of Christian teaching had instilled in them the concept of Hell as a blazing inferno where the condemned suffered fiery ordeals. Had they still adhered to the beliefs of their ancestors that *Mitnal* or the underworld was a place of unbearable cold, they would surely have fled in terror as the cold air issued from the ominous black pit.

The opening was roughly circular in outline and three feet in diameter. By lowering a lantern attached to a tape line, Thompson estimated its depth to be fifty feet. "I had two of the natives grasp each of my feet at the ankle," he recalled, "and then, head downward, my body swinging like a pendulum with my tape and light below me, I managed to get a good idea of the place. . . .

"After getting back my breath, I told my workers that we would quit for the day and go home, but would return very early on the morrow prepared to go down into that hole. I also warned them not to tell anybody what we were doing lest they laugh at us and call us crazy. As a matter of fact, I was certain that we had made a very important find, and I did not want any more witnesses than I could help."

By dawn Thompson's crew had assembled at the pyramid for the day's adventure. A block and tackle was mounted above the opening in order to haul up the debris from the pit. Equipped with a knife between his teeth, his pockets bulging with trowels, brushes, and candles, Thompson was lowered by a rope through the opening into the pit.

No sooner had he switched on his lantern than he encountered an unexpected treasure—an alabaster vase filled with polished jade beads and an exquisite pendant. Moments later his assistants scrambled down the rope to join him, and during the hours that followed they were lost in the feverish excitement of discovery. One after another magnificent relics were exhumed from the debris littering the floor of the crypt. Scattered about were shells inlaid with mother-of-pearl, pottery vessels, and a ceremonial flint blade which Thompson described as resembling "the votive stone sickles of the ancient Druids"; there were also numerous large oval pearls, many of which had lain undisturbed for so long that they fell to powder at the slightest touch. Later Thompson recorded an interesting postscript to these discoveries:

> We ate and drank as the spirit moved us and then continued with the work until I could feel that a weariness was creeping over us. I gave the signal to stop work and get ready to go up into the outer world. When we reached the temple platform with our trophies, we saw a strange sight.
>
> It was eleven o'clock in the evening. . . . A darkness as of midnight was all about us and on the plains beneath, the families of my workmen were crying and lamenting, with my wife and children trying in vain to calm them.
>
> "No use!" they wailed. "The master and all of our people are dead and gone. The Great Serpent has taken them and we shall never see them again!"
>
> Great was the rejoicing when we triumphantly appeared with our trophies and came down to them.
>
> This was one of the red-letter days in my life as an archaeologist. I had discovered and investigated what was probably the sepulchre of a high priest of the Mayas. . . .
>
> The five graves in the vertical shaft above . . . what of them? Whose bones, decayed and turning to dust, rested in the graves when I first uncovered them? Were they the acolytes or the servants of the high priest whose bodies were so placed as to guard in death as they served in life this high and sacred personage? Or were they priests of a lower order, whose friends sought for them by this last close contact a higher place in the future life? Who knows?

But a discovery of far greater magnitude awaited Thompson's restless curiosity. In the midst of his speculations he was seized by an obsession which was to endanger his life, subject him to ridicule, and

Figure of a Toltec-Itzá warrior, Temple of the Jaguars, Chichén Itzá.
(After Maudslay.)

ultimately result in disastrous legal difficulties. It was also to place him among the foremost contributors to Maya research.

Leading from the north side of the Temple of Kukulcán was the outline of an ancient road or *sacbe* known as the Sacred Way, which extends for 300 yards through the city's main plaza to a huge natural well. Formations of this kind, called *cenotes* (from the Yucatec term *dzonot*), provide the major source of surface water in northern Yucatán; they are fed by underground drainage systems and form wherever the porous limestone crust has collapsed to expose the subterranean water table. It was this particular *cenote* that gave Chichén Itzá its present name. Literally the Yucatec word *chi* is translated as "mouth" and *chen* signifies a "well," thus Chichén Itzá means "the mouth of the well of the Itzá." (Its original name may have been Uucyabnal or "seven great owners.") The oval-shaped *cenote* measured roughly 200 feet in diameter and was encased by vertical limestone walls rising to a height of sixty-five feet above the surface of its murky green water. Undoubtedly this was the well to which native folklore so often referred—the Sacred Cenote whose mysterious depths were rumored to contain a treasure.

Landa himself had stood at the brink of this evil-looking pool and recalled its awesome secrets as told by his Indian informants: "Into this well they . . . had the custom of throwing men alive as a sacrifice to the gods, in times of drought, and they believed that they did not die though they never saw them again. They also threw into it a great many other things, like precious stones and things which they prized. And so if this country had possessed gold, it would be this well that would have the largest part of it, so great was the devotion which the Indians showed for it."

Most antiquarians had dismissed Landa's statement as nothing more than a legend unworthy of serious consideration. But Thompson did not share their skepticism. ". . . The thought of that grim old water pit," he wrote, "and the wonderful objects that lay concealed within its depths became an obsession with me. . . ."

Then he came across another account written in 1579 by Diego Sarmiento de Figueroa, who had visted Chichén Itzá during his tenure as alcalde of the nearby town of Valladolid:

> The lords and principal personages of the land had the custom, after sixty days of abstinence and fasting, of arriving by daybreak at the mouth of the Cenote and throwing into it Indian women belonging to each of these lords and personages, at the same time telling these women to ask for their masters a year favorable to his particular needs and desires.
>
> The women, being thrown in unbound, fell into the water with great force and noise. At high noon those that could cried out loudly and ropes were let down to them. After the women came up, half dead, fires were built around them and copal incense was burned before them. When they recovered their senses, they said that below there were many people of their nation, men and women, and that they received them. When they tried to raise their heads to look at them, heavy blows were given

them on the head, and when their heads were inclined downward beneath the water they seemed to see many deeps and hollows, and they, the people, responded to their queries concerning the good or the bad year that was in store for their masters.

A daring plan was taking shape in Thompson's mind. If he was to test the validity of the myth that had so captivated his imagination, it would be necessary to probe beneath the *cenote's* waters for relics of the gruesome homage supposedly paid by the Maya to their gods. But before proceeding with his formidable undertaking, Thompson journeyed to Boston where he sought instruction in deep-sea diving and familiarized himself with various types of underwater equipment. Next he assembled a portable derrick and dredging apparatus suitable for his specialized needs, a device easily mounted at the well's edge and operated by a hand winch.

"Not until then," he wrote, "did I appear before the Honorable Stephen Salisbury of Worcester, Massachusetts, and Charles P. Bowditch of Boston, both officers of the American Antiquarian Society and of Harvard University of which the Peabody Museum is a part. To them I explained the project and asked the moral and financial aid of the two organizations they represented. . . . I found both of these gentlemen very reluctant to put the seal of their approval upon what they clearly believed to be a most audacious undertaking. They were willing to finance the scheme, but hesitated to take upon themselves the responsibility for my life.

"I finally argued them out of their fears, and all other obstacles having been overcome, the dredge and its equipment were duly installed on the platform to the right of the shrine and close to the edge of the great water pit, the Sacred Well."

With a group of Indians to manage the heavy machinery, the dredging operation was finally begun. Thompson had previously determined the area of the pool most likely to contain human remains by throwing in logs the approximate size and weight of a man attached to a rope and measuring the depth to which they sank. Slowly the rigid boom swung into position over the designated spot, and the dredge was lowered into the water.

For days the dredging continued with endless repetition; the heavy steel bucket disappeared into the *cenote's* somber depths only to reappear with nothing but mud, leaves, and decayed wood in its jaws. "At times," reported Thompson, "as if to tantalize me, the dredge recovered portions of earthen vessels undeniably ancient. I resolutely threw aside the thought that these might be the proofs I sought. Potsherds, I argued, were likely to be found anywhere on the site of this old city, washed from the surface deposits by rains."

Not long afterward something came to light that rekindled Thompson's fading expectations. ". . . I rose in the morning from a sleepless night," he wrote. "The day was gray as my thoughts and the thick mist dropped from the leaves of the trees as quiet tears drop from half-closed eyes. I plodded through the dampness down to where the staccato clicks of the dredge brake called me and, crouching under the palm-leaf lean-to, watched the monotonous motion of the brown-skinned natives as they worked at the winches. The bucket slowly emerged from the heaving water that boiled around it and . . . I saw two yellow-white, globular masses lying on the surface of the chocolate-colored muck that filled the basin. As the mass swung over the brink and up to the platform, I took from it the two objects and closely examined them."

Undoubtedly they had been fashioned by human hands, but Thompson was uncertain what their purpose might have been. He broke one in half and tasted it; then it occurred to him to hold the substance over a smoldering fire. Instantly a pungent fragrance filled the air, and Thompson suddenly remembered a detail from a native legend he had once read. "Like a ray of bright sunlight breaking through a dense fog came to me the words of the old *H'men*, the Wise Man of Ebtun: 'In ancient times our fathers burned the sacred resin—*pom*—and by the fragrant smoke their prayers were wafted to their god whose home was in the Sun.'

"These yellow balls of resin were masses of the sacred incense *pom* [copal], and had been thrown in as part of the rich offerings mentioned in the traditions."

Thereafter each dredge load of slimy mud contained new affirmation of his conviction. Out of the pit's murky water came a profuse array of objects bearing the unmistakable imprint of Maya craftsmanship: pottery vessels, incense burners, wooden spearthrowers,

fragments of stone sculpture, jade figurines, beads, and p
to Landa's prediction, there were dozens of artifacts ma
and gold, including tiny bells, rings, a golden bowl and c
sections of a mask, and skillfully embossed disks. "Object
pure gold," Thompson noted, "were encountered, both ca
and engraved in *repoussé*, but they were few in number and ..ativery
unimportant. Most of the so-called gold objects were of low-grade
alloy, with more copper than gold in them. That which gave them
their chief value were the symbolical and other figures cast or carved
upon them." Aside from this spectacular array of relics, the dredge
finally brought up the ultimate proof Thompson had hoped to recover:
human bones and skulls appeared amid the other treasures so long
immersed in the watery shrine—the remains of sacrificial victims cast
into the well in the manner Landa and Figueroa had reported.

After several months the dredging operations reached an impasse;
the basin began to emerge with nothing but silt and sticks caught in its
steel jaws, and Thompson knew it had eaten its way to the rocky floor
of the pool. Having anticipated such an eventuality, he now planned to
descend into the *cenote* and explore the hidden crevices which the
dredge was too large to reach. The necessary diving equipment was
already at his disposal, and he had previously engaged two Greek
sponge fishermen to assist with his precarious explorations. To the
horror of the Indians who crowded around the well's rim, the three
men embarked upon their subterranean quest. "As I stepped on the
first rung of the ladder," recalled Thompson, "each of the pumping
gang, my faithful native boys, left his place in turn and with a very
solemn face shook hands with me and then went back again to wait for
the signal. It was not hard to read their thoughts. They were bidding
me a last farewell, never expecting to see me again. Then, releasing my
hold on the ladder, I sank like a bag of lead, leaving behind me a silvery
chain of bubbles."

Gradually the water changed from amber to green and finally to
an impenetrable black. Thompson's submarine flashlight was unable to
pierce the veil of darkness in which he was shrouded. He groped
blindly along the floor until he located a ledge or crevice, then sifted its
contents by hand. Here and there were steep mud walls laden with
rocks and tree trunks; these proved to be a distracting hazard, for as

Thompson explained, "every little while one of the stone blocks, loosened from its place in the wall by the infiltration of the water, would come plunging down upon us in the worse than Stygian darkness. . . ."

For several weeks the divers continued their examination of the well. The Indians, who watched the proceedings with abject fascination, waited anxiously for the terrible disaster they were certain was imminent—outraged gods lurking in some unseen cavern beneath the surface would surely drag the intruders to a watery grave. But fortunately no serious mishaps occurred, and their dangerous venture resulted in more startling discoveries. Each time a diver reappeared from the depths his pouch brimmed with artifacts: pieces of carved jade, nodules of copal incense, pottery, objects of copper and gold, human bones, and fragments of cloth miraculously preserved in the mud. Among the most interesting treasures were three ceremonial knives of the type used to cut the heart from sacrificial victims; only one was unbroken and its beautifully chipped flint blade was mounted in a carved wooden handle overlaid with gold representing two entwined serpents. Of the identifiable skeletons retrieved from the *cenote*, twenty-one were children between the ages of eighteen months and twelve years, thirteen were adult men and eight were women.

Since almost all of the relics were broken, Thompson was of the opinion that the Maya had adhered to the common practice among ancient peoples of "killing" objects intended as votive offerings, smashing them so their "spirits" could accompany the deceased with whom they were entombed. But elsewhere in the Maya area the custom of breaking funerary items was not widespread, and much of the damage noted by Thompson might have been caused by the height from which they were thrown into the well.

Judging from the abundance of material recovered in the *cenote*, human sacrifices had taken place there with ominous frequency. And because of the obsessive emphasis on sacrificial rites in Mexican religion, scholars were at first inclined to view the use of the pool for this purpose as a Toltec-Itzá innovation, introduced after their occupation of Yucatán. But this may not have been the case. Some of the carved jades from the well are definitely of Classic period workmanship; one piece in the sculptural style of Piedras Negras was inscribed with a date of A.D. 706, and another, which is almost certainly from Palenque, bore an inscription equal to A.D. 690. Archaeologists are not sure whether these jades were brought to the Sacred Cenote from distant cities during the seventh and eighth centuries, or if they had been kept through the years as treasured heirlooms or looted from Classic tombs, then cast into the well at a later time.

Despite the immense scientific importance of Thompson's discoveries, his years of exploration at Chichén Itzá ended with a series of unfortunate occurrences. During a revolutionary uprising which swept Yucatán in 1921, the hacienda where Thompson lived was burned while he was away in Mérida. Lost beyond reclamation was his valuable library, as well as many priceless artifacts recovered from his excavations. A few years later the hacienda was rebuilt and leased to the Carnegie Institution as the headquarters for its extensive program of research at Chichén Itzá, and today its main building is part of the Mayaland Hotel situated adjacent to the ruins.

Legal difficulties then developed with the Mexican government over the rumored value of the articles reclaimed from the Sacred Cenote. Some estimates placed the worth of the much publicized gold objects in excess of $500,000, though Thompson steadfastly denied these reports, arguing that the actual value of the material could only be judged in terms of its contribution to science. But the Mexican authorities were unswayed by his protests, and because Thompson had shipped the collection to the Peabody Museum for safekeeping, he was promptly charged with stealing national treasures. Accordingly, his property in Yucatán was confiscated and held against payment of 1,300,000 pesos, an act which forced him to relinquish his ownership of the hacienda and forsake plans for future excavations at Chichén Itzá.

In his defense Thompson wrote: ". . . I should have been false to my duty as an archaeologist had I, believing that the scientific treasures were at the bottom of the Sacred Well, failed to improve the opportunity to bring them to light, thus making them available for scientific study instead of remaining in the mud and useless to the world. I should have been equally false to my duty as a scientist if, after bringing them to light, I had neglected to take all possible measures for their immediate security and permanent safety."

Although the litigation was unsettled at the time of Thompson's death in 1935, the Mexican supreme court later ruled that no existing laws had been violated by his actions. Even so, ethical questions surrounding the ownership of the material from the *cenote* remained a controversial issue, and in 1960 the Peabody Museum voluntarily returned ninety-four pieces from the collection to the Instituto Nacional de Antropología y Historia in Mexico City.

Ever since Thompson's operations at the Sacred Cenote ended in 1911, numerous proposals have been made to resume explorations there in the hope of finding more objects concealed beneath its waters. Finally, in 1960, an expedition jointly sponsored by the National Geographic Society and an organization of underwater sportsmen

Gold repoussé *disk from the Sacred Cenote showing a conflict between Mexican and Maya warriors, Chichén Itzá. (After Marquina.)*

known as CEDAM (Club de Exploraciones y Deportes Aquáticos de México) undertook such a venture. With them came professional archaeologists, scuba divers assigned to the project by the Mexican navy, and an array of up-to-date equipment—principally a motor-driven airlift with which the divers could vacuum the silt from the floor of the *cenote* and pass it through screens designed to catch even the smallest artifacts. But four months later the work was abruptly terminated because of a controversy over damage to valuable specimens caused by the powerful airlift, though by then some 4,000 additional relics had already been recovered, including more bones of sacrificial victims, ornaments of jade, amber, and crystal, gold-washed copper rings, and a ceremonial knife with a gold foil handle.

Another effort to explore the *cenote* was launched in 1967 by CEDAM and Norman Scott, an American underwater expert whose company, Expeditions Unlimited, had previously been involved in quests for sunken treasure in the Caribbean. With substantial financial backing supplied by a number of commercial firms and a wealthy Texan named F. Kirk Johnson, a twofold plan was devised. An attempt would first be made to drain the well using centrifugal pumps capable of handling 200,000 gallons of water an hour, thereby allowing archaeologists to excavate the thick deposits of silt covering the bottom. If this failed or proved too expensive, the alternate approach involved the use of complicated filtering devices to clear the water so divers could work unhampered by the pool's impenetrable darkness.

After repeated efforts the pumping operation was only partially successful; the porous limestone surface surrounding the *cenote* permitted the runoff to drain back through underground channels almost as quickly as it was removed. Nevertheless, the water level was lowered enough to expose what was called "Thompson's bank," a huge mound consisting of the silt and debris brought up by Thompson's dredge and later dumped back into the well. Under careful excavation and screening it was found to contain hundreds of artifacts overlooked by Thompson and his native workmen.

Fortunately, the plan to clear the *cenote*'s water by means of chemicals produced remarkably good results. Utilizing chlorine to kill the algae and other organisms normally infesting the well, its water was then circulated through filtering tanks filled with diatomaceous earth to remove impurities. Eventually the pool was rendered sufficiently clear to enable archaeologists with scuba gear to systematically probe the floor while underwater photographers recorded many of their finds *in situ.*

Among the objects retrieved by these procedures were two stone standard bearers in the form of crouched jaguars, gold effigies, disks, and rings, the soles from two sandals made of gold (presumably placed on the feet of sacrificial victims just before their death, since they showed no signs of wear), ceramic figurines, a carved antler representing a bird, and fragments of Tepeu polychrome pottery, their brightly painted scenes still clearly visible. Hundreds of human skeletal remains, a high percentage of them from children, were also found, along with the bones of deer, jaguars, turkeys, dogs, and other animals, indicating that these creatures were probably cast into the well as sacrificial offerings. Perhaps the most interesting items were the only known examples of ancient Maya furniture ever found—two low wooden stools, shaped somewhat like turtles and decorated with carvings of human faces emerging from serpents' mouths.

No doubt the Sacred Cenote has not revealed the last of its secrets, and future expeditions may challenge it again with even more sophisticated techniques. Quite possibly it was not the only well in Yucatán used for sacrificial purposes. In 1958 divers from the National Geographic Society explored another pool—the Xlacah Cenote—located amid the ruins of Dzibilchaltún. To everyone's amazement it yielded over 6,000 artifacts, including large quantities of pottery, several bone awls incised with hieroglyphs, a clay flute, jade ornaments, a small wooden mask, and the all-too-familiar human skeletons.

We can only guess whether or not other treasure-laden *cenotes* lie hidden elsewhere in Yucatán, but if the discoveries made by Thompson and his successors are any indication, the rapidly developing science of underwater archaeology may disclose countless surprises in the depths of these forbidding wells.

13

WARFARE, DISUNITY, AND DECLINE: THE MAYA "DARK AGE"

From about A.D. 1200 until the Spanish Conquest, the sequence of events in Yucatán is obscured in a mist of quasi-historical evidence gleaned from sources of questionable reliability. But one place reappears frequently in post-Conquest accounts relating to this era—the once populous city known as Mayapán, a sprawling maze of debris-littered mounds thirty miles southeast of Mérida. For years it had remained a mystery. It was often mentioned in the *Books of Chilam Balam* and various Spanish chronicles, but archaeologists had not undertaken to explore its ruins.

Native sources attributed an extremely important role to Mayapán during the concluding years of Maya history. Reportedly, it was here that the Itzá, under the supervision of the mighty Kukulcán, had founded a new capital after the abandonment of Chichén Itzá. Here, too, a ruling lord named Hunac Ceel was said to have established a dictatorship which subsequently brought a vast portion of Yucatán under his jurisdiction.

In his *Relación*, Landa gave the following account of the city's origin:

This Kukulcán established another city after arranging with the native lords of the country that he and they should live there and that all of their affairs and business should be brought there; and for this purpose they chose a very good situation, eight leagues further in the interior than Mérida is now, and fifteen or sixteen leagues from the sea. They surrounded it with a very broad stone wall, . . . leaving in it only two narrow gates. The wall was not very high and in the midst of this enclosure they built their temples, and the largest, which is like that of Chichén Itzá [El Castillo], they called Kukulcán, and they built another of a round form, with four doors, entirely different from all the others in that land. . . . In this enclosure they built houses for the lords only, dividing all the land among them, giving a town to each one, according to the antiquity of his lineage and his personal value. And Kukulcán gave a name to this city—not his own name as the Ah Itzás had done at Chichén Itzá, but he called it Mayapán, which means "the standard of the Maya." . . . Kukulcán lived with the lords in that city for several years; and leaving them in great peace and friendship, he returned by the same way to Mexico. . . .

In the *Books of Chilam Balam* we read how Yucatán was governed for almost two hundred years by a "triple alliance" consisting of the three most influential centers in the peninsula: Mayapán, Chichén Itzá, and Uxmal. The dates generally ascribed to this political union fall between A.D. 987 and 1185, although these vary somewhat according to discrepancies in conflicting versions of its history. Supposedly this "League of Mayapán," as it is called, brought about a high degree of political stability during its existence. Ostensibly the reins of government over the entire territory were held jointly by lords representing each of the League's three member cities. But frictions inevitably touched off intrigue and open revolt, resulting in a shattering upheaval which was to dissolve the League of Mayapán and provide the background for an obscure noble to seize singlehanded control of Yucatán.

Yet archaeological research has failed to bear out the details of these events. For one thing, there is substantial evidence that Uxmal was abandoned during most if not all of the period when the League of Mayapán supposedly existed. Moreover, Mayapán had emerged as an important center only *after* Chichén Itzá lost its position of eminence as the peninsula's leading city sometime around A.D. 1200. Thus the three cities supposedly comprising the ruling triumvirate did not flourish simultaneously, at least not during the entire two hundred years of the League's hegemony. Still, it is not impossible that such a confederation had once exercised a system of mutual control over Yucatán, and inaccurate recollections of its structure or confusion as to the dates involved have obscured its history.

Whatever the truth may prove to be, the League of Mayapán's dissolution brings us to a fascinating if equally hazy juncture—the famous "plot of Hunac Ceel." If native accounts of this event can be accepted literally, we encounter one of the most dramatic episodes in the whole sweeping panorama of Maya affairs. Regrettably, however, the references to Hunac Ceel in the *Books of Chilam Balam* are extremely vague, and there is disagreement among archaeologists over the date of his rise to power.

From what we can gather, this curious drama began at Chichén Itzá during the enactment of a sacrifice at the Sacred Cenote. For reasons which are not clear, Hunac Ceel, a powerful lord of Mayapán, was among the individuals cast into the well on this particular occasion; perhaps he offered himself voluntarily or had jumped into the water unexpectedly after the other victims drowned without delivering the divine prophecy so anxiously sought by the people waiting above. In any case, Hunac Ceel reappeared from the depths of the pool, claiming that he had personally spoken with the gods and received their prophecy. Evidently this heroic act ignited the admiration of the onlooking crowd, who brought Hunac Ceel up from the water and affirmed him as their ruler. Immediately after his ascendancy, Hunac Ceel selected Mayapán as the center of his authority, and using his family name he established a dynasty there known as the Cocom. Next he sought to eliminate the threat posed by the dissident lords of Chichén Itzá, especially its reigning chieftain—Chac Xib Chac.

Exactly how this was accomplished is again clouded by conflicting accounts, but an interesting reference in the *Books of Chilam Balam* would lead us to believe that Hunac Ceel exploited what amounted to a sexual intrigue to further his lordly ambitions. He declared war against Chichén Itzá when the untrustworthy Chac Xib Chac abducted the bride of an ally, Ah Ulil, the ruling chief of Izamal. Other sources differ as to the motives underlying the conflict, but whatever their excuse, Cocom legions overran Chichén Itzá and left the city so decimated that it was thereafter slowly abandoned. Next Hunac Ceel reportedly attacked his erstwhile friend, Ah Ulil, in order to eliminate any potential challenge to his authority from Izamal.

From this point on, Mayapán became the most powerful city in Yucatán. Its armies were swelled by professional soldiers recruited from Tabasco—fierce Mexican mercenaries known as the Ah Canul, whose devotion to the Cocoms was purchased by guarantees of prestige and the spoils of military victories. To insure the "loyalty" of Yucatán's other cities, their chiefs were forced to reside at Mayapán, where their policies and allegiances could be carefully watched. Surrounded by a walled city, defended by a private army, and with his potential enemies under close supervision, Hunac Ceel and his descendants maintained political control over much of the northern peninsula for roughly 250 years.

Despite a fairly effective centralized government at Mayapán, the Cocom's rule was preemptive and often abusive, even to supposedly favored chieftains. Resentment and intrigue—the inevitable fissures in a decaying regime—gradually began to shatter Cocom influence upon subordinate lords. Hostility toward the oppressive regime at Mayapán continued to grow until the partisans of one Ah Xupan, a member of the powerful Xiu family who ruled the territory around Uxmal, joined in a plot to overthrow the reigning Cocom lord. "This they did," wrote Landa, "killing at the same time all of his sons save one who was absent; they sacked his dwelling and possessed themselves of all his property . . . saying that thus they repaid themselves what had been stolen from them." Other accounts tell us in some detail how Mayapán was attacked and set afire by an army under the Xiu's command about the year 1441.*

---

* Because of ambiguities in native chronicles and the Short Count calendar, not all students agree with the preceding version of Hunac Ceel's rise to power, though it is the one most frequently recounted in literature on the subject. Some think the entire episode—Hunac Ceel's plunge in the *cenote* at Chichén Itzá, his treachery against Chac Xib Chac, and seizure of control in Yucatán—did not occur until over two centuries later, and that the Cocom dynasty at

Figure of an old man, Temple of the Chacmool, Chichén Itzá. (After Morris.)

Such was the brief outline of Mayapán's history as gleaned from the writings of Spanish and native chroniclers. It speaks of curious manifestations wholly foreign to older traditions: walled cities, professional warriors, political alignments, and a centralized government. But how much could be accepted as representative of actual occurrences? At best, the story's chronology was desultory and confusing, and its fragmentary details seemed to have been drawn largely from spurious legends rather than historical records.

Mayapán was actually founded by Hunac Ceel's ancestors during the period from A.D. 1263 to 1283. Accordingly, Hunac Ceel would have been Mayapán's last ruler, thus making him the victim of the Xiu rebellion of 1441.

Obviously Mayapán's enormous size, its unique layout, and prominent role in post-Conquest documents merited further study. With these facts in mind, a team of investigators from the Carnegie Institution set out in 1951 on a five-year project to excavate the city's principal buildings. Since the site proved to be even larger than previous estimates, it was a formidable undertaking; altogether Mayapán covered two and a half square miles, and the ruins of 3,600 structures were mapped within its boundaries. Yet out of the ensuing explorations there gradually emerged a remarkable set of circumstances not unlike those outlined in documentary sources.

Just as Landa had described it, the entire site was enclosed by a low stone wall breeched by narrow, easily defended gates, although a total of twelve entrances were found instead of only two as stated in the *Relación*. Within its central precincts stood the principal ceremonial structures dominated by a pyramid patterned after the Temple of Kukulcán at Chichén Itzá, with terraced sides and four stairways flanked by feathered serpent balustrades. Grouped around these temples were numerous rectangular buildings with colonnades and small interior rooms—perhaps the official residences of Cocom lords or the subordinate chiefs from neighboring cities who were required to live at Mayapán. Among the artifacts unearthed by excavators were finely worked flint arrowheads, which confirmed that the bow and arrow (previously unknown to the Maya) was used by Mayapán's armies, probably introduced from Mexico by the Ah Canul mercenaries. In addition, the majority of Mayapán's structures had unquestionably served as dwellings, and the entire city was highly urbanized. Frequently the houses, many with front porticos supported by columns, gave the impression of residential districts where nobles, craftsmen, and peasants lived in close proximity.

Especially interesting was the scarcity of major religious edifices at Mayapán. What few temples it did contain are unimpressive in size and reflect extremely poor workmanship; thick layers of stucco were used to disguise crude masonry, columns were badly assembled, and flat beam-and-mortar roofs all but replaced corbled vaults. In place of large-scale religious structures, there was an emphasis on small shrines or family oratorios incorporated into individual residences, a fact interpreted by archaeologists as a sign that religion had lost much of its importance. Aside from this degeneration in architecture, Mayapán's sculpture was unimaginative and poorly executed (often consisting of weak imitations of Mexican-inspired works at Chichén Itzá), and its ceramics could scarcely have been more prosaic, except for ornate funerary urns painted with garish colors.

Finally, there was positive proof of the city's destruction by fire-ridden violence about the middle of the fifteenth century. The roof timbers of many structures showed evidence of burning; in some instances masonry walls were blackened by fire, and there were signs of extensive looting, attributable perhaps to the havoc wrought by the Xiu insurrection as related in native chronicles.

A summary view of the findings at Mayapán reveals the chaotic spectacle of a once-brilliant civilization on the brink of disaster: a walled refuge garrisoned by paid troops, its supremacy maintained by force of arms, its inhabitants supported almost entirely by tributes, its art and architecture in severe decline, ruled by chiefs less in awe of their gods than the intoxication of military power, its governing councils filled with displaced lords of subjugated provinces—puppets in function but political hostages in reality. Elsewhere in Yucatán this unhealthy situation had a profound influence, climaxed by a widespread disintegration in art and architecture and the rise of warrior-oriented societies. A trend toward urbanized cities protected against attack is obvious at several ruins in Quintana Roo, notably Xelhá, Ichpaatún, and the spectacular seacoast site of Tulúm, all of which are surrounded by walls. Other cities dating from this period are known to have been enclosed by what Spanish chroniclers described as wooden palisades and watchtowers.

Grievous indeed were the mutations that carried the Maya so far from the stupendous attainments of their ancestors. Ultimately, the collapse of Classic civilization had left them all too susceptible to the corrosive effects of the Toltec-Itzá conquest, with its rampant militarism, political complexity, and sanguinary gods whose placation demanded endless human sacrifices. Although many of these elements became thoroughly intermixed with Maya culture, and feeble attempts were made—even at Mayapán itself—to revive certain older traditions, it was too late. The stage was already set for the violent end of Maya civilization.

Events in Yucatán after the downfall of Mayapán must again be inferred from post-Conquest narratives which provide us with only fragmentary information. We read how the one Cocom lord who survived the conflict (by virtue of being away on a trading expedition) led the remnants of his people to a new settlement known as Tibolón. Large numbers of Ah Canul, the Cocoms' mercenary guards, established themselves in the northwest corner of the peninsula. Some years before, a group of Itzá had journeyed southward into the Petén, where they founded the city of Tayasal at Lake Petén Itzá, and the victorious Xiu chieftains settled at Maní, a few miles south of Mayapán. Ironically, the word *Maní* signified "it is finished."

Within a short time thereafter the peninsula was divided into sixteen independent provinces, each ruled by petty chieftains with private armies under their command. No centralized authority had the power to unite these far-flung states, and it was not long before territorial disputes turned Yucatán into a series of antagonistic armed camps. Open warfare erupted throughout the area. Villages were raided for sacrificial victims and youths suitable for forced military conscription. Occasionally the raiders, striking at night, would set fire to outlying *milpas* in order to starve towns into submission. Ruling lords rose and fell in rapid succession, often displaced by betrayal or outright assassination. In one celebrated incident which occurred as late as 1536, Nachi Cocom, the great-grandson of Mayapán's last ruler, succeeded in luring two Xiu chieftains and their retinue to a banquet, whereupon Nachi Cocom's warriors unexpectedly attacked them and slaughtered the entire party.

Far to the south in the Guatemalan highlands the story was essentially the same. While the Maya in this region, who had maintained close ties to Mexico from the fifth century A.D. onward, appear to have been largely unaffected by the demise of Classic civilization in the lowlands, they were subjected to strong Toltec influences during the Postclassic period. Soon afterward the familiar pattern of militarism, the Quetzalcóatl cult, large-scale human sacrifice, and political expansion began to develop, and they eventually split into numerous antagonistic tribes ruled by chiefs who traced their ancestry directly to the Toltecs. Already the two most powerful groups—the Quiché and Cakchiquel—were locked in a bloody struggle for domination of the area. Violence and militarism quickly became a way of life here as it was in Yucatán, and many highland cities such as Utatlán, Iximché, Zaculeu, and Chutixtiox were situated on defensible hills surrounded by deep canyons and heavily fortified with ramparts, walls, and breastworks.

Everywhere art and architecture continued to disintegrate during this period, and the intellectual pursuits of earlier centuries were all but forgotten. No gifted leaders arose to redirect the tragic destiny that had overtaken the Maya; no one challenged the perverse demands of their gods or the egocentric schemes by which their rulers propelled them into constant warfare. Disunity, political intrigue, economic exhaustion, and moral decay had taken their toll, and the prophets of disaster went unheard.

It was now the spring of 1517. The ships of Hernández de Córdova were nearing Cape Catoche off the northeastern coast of Yucatán. Soon the Maya caught their first glimpse of the mysterious Spanish vessels, which appeared to them like "mountains rising out of the sea on clouds," remembering perhaps that the prophecies of Chilam Balam had forewarned of this event:

> *On that day, a cloud arises,*
> *On that day, a mountain rises,*
> *On that day, a strong man seizes the land,*
> *On that day, things fall to ruin. . . .*

Hastily a meeting was held among the Maya chieftains at Cape Catoche. Later they sent a delegation to meet with the emissaries of Charles V, Emperor of Spain, *the most powerful man of his day!*

Suddenly, then, Maya civilization came to an end, overwhelmed by an outside threat even more ominous than its own internal difficulties—the Spanish Conquest. We can only speculate on what course it might have taken had these events not occurred. As for its past accomplishments, they were quickly engulfed in obscurity, leaving us to marvel at splendid relics of long-forgotten ages, a tradition of art, architecture, science, and literature unequalled in pre-Columbian America. Indeed, Sylvanus Morley once characterized the Maya as "the Greeks of the New World," and numerous discoveries in recent years have overwhelmingly confirmed his analogy.

Along with the material remains of their achievements, the Maya have left us a bewildering paradox which has plagued students from the outset of their investigations: everywhere we encounter undeniable miracles shrouded by countless unsolved mysteries of crucial importance. Despite the giant strides which brought Maya research out of the limbo of nineteenth-century romanticism, archaeologists face an enormous challenge. Future disclosures may someday enable them to piece together the whole fascinating panorama of Maya history, but if this is ever to be accomplished, vast areas must still be explored, dozens of key sites excavated, the hieroglyphic inscriptions fully deciphered, and a huge accumulation of data analyzed, all requiring a tremendous outlay of time and money.

Nevertheless, scholars are meeting the challenge more vigorously than ever before. With the accelerated pace of new projects, important breakthroughs are taking place with increasing frequency, and certain previously insoluble problems are gradually yielding to modern research. Improved field techniques and methods of laboratory study are being applied to specific questions, along with the talents of highly trained specialists representing many scientific institutions and a variety of disciplines. Excavations are currently under way at a number of important sites—among them Yaxhá, Becán, Toniná, Yaxchilán, Cobá, Kohunlich, and Comalcalco—and significant studies dealing with every aspect of Maya civilization are constantly appearing in print.

Hardly a year passes without new expeditions setting off in search of further revelations into what has become a singularly intriguing chapter in American archaeology. And whatever the difficulties to be overcome, other scholar-explorers in the tradition of Stephens, Maudslay, Thompson, and Ruz will continue to probe Maya ruins until their secrets are known, for the lure of such things is irresistible.

14

BALANKANCHÉ: POSTSCRIPT TO A DEAD CIVILIZATION

 Regardless of the unresolved questions surrounding their history, we have seen that the Maya are not a "vanished race" as they are so often portrayed in popular literature. Today approximately 2,000,000 Indians of Maya descent still occupy the region, and next to the Quechua peoples of Peru and Bolivia, they constitute the largest surviving aboriginal culture anywhere in America.

Like their pre-Columbian ancestors, the contemporary Maya are divided into various tribes speaking related but often mutually unintelligible dialects, all of which presumably evolved from a common language. Among these groups the most populous are the Yucatec, who number in excess of 350,000 and inhabit Yucatán, Campeche, and Quintana Roo. Immediately to the southwest in Tabasco and eastern Chiapas live the Chol, Chontal, and Lacandón, and scattered throughout the uplands of central and southeastern Chiapas are the villages of the Tzotzil, Tzeltal, and Tojolabal. Guatemala's lofty highlands are populated by the Quiché, Cakchiquel, Tzutuhil, Chuh, Pokomam, Ixil, Chorti, Mam, and half a dozen smaller tribes; and two groups known as the Kekchi and Pokonchi occupy sections of central Guatemala, principally the Department of Alta Verapaz. Another Maya-speaking people—the Huastec—are found far to the north in the Mexican states of Veracruz and San Luis Potosí, where they apparently migrated centuries before the Conquest.

Modern Maya culture inevitably reflects the impact of prolonged contact with outside influences. Every major town has its Catholic church, public school, municipal buildings, stores, and even an occasional movie theater, gas station, or tavern. The government of each settlement or *municipio* is generally patterned after Spanish colonial models and is subject to the jurisdiction of national and state laws. Near populous centers such as Mérida, Guatemala City, or San Cristóbal de las Casas it is not unusual to find Maya houses (many painted with garish soft-drink signs) equipped with radios, electric lights, steam irons, upholstered furniture, and similar accouterments of contemporary life; and wherever roads have been opened through the countryside, trucks, automobiles, and buses are appearing in increasing numbers. Nowhere are the effects of acculturation more evident than in the marketplaces, which frequently display native goods—pottery, leatherwork, woven cloth, sandals, baskets, sisal hammocks, and the like—alongside a vast array of commercially made items ranging from cooking utensils, hardware, and canned foods to clothing, shoes, cheap perfume, and costume jewelry.

Yet despite more than four centuries of economic exploitation, religious indoctrination, and social upheaval, the Maya have maintained a remarkable ethnic cohesion. Many tribes still adhere tenaciously to certain aboriginal traditions—to the extent that ethnological studies of their culture have provided valuable insight into a wide spectrum of pre-Conquest practices. Especially in the more geographically remote villages, these links with the past pervade nearly every aspect of daily existence, and entering them one is acutely aware of suddenly being thrust into a realm of "living" archaeology.

Notwithstanding the efforts of missionaries, Maya religious beliefs incorporate a curious mixture of native and Christian elements, including a strong emphasis on magic, witchcraft, and the supernatural.

Activities such as planting crops, hunting, the treatment of illness, marriage, and childbirth are usually accompanied by ceremonies involving pagan deities, and several groups in the Guatemalan highlands determine important ritualistic events by means of the calendar employed in ancient times. Agricultural methods have remained essentially unchanged for thousands of years, with maize, beans, squash, chili peppers, and other venerable staples still being cultivated in *milpas*. Among most tribes traditional dress prevails over non-Indian clothing; native houses scarcely differ in design or construction from those that once surrounded the ceremonial centers, and crafts such as weaving, pottery making, basketry, and wood carving are carried on using age-old techniques.

Even in physical appearance the average Maya are quite similar to their ancestors: small, rather stocky, with copper to medium brown skin, straight black hair, and broad faces accentuated by pronounced noses, high cheek bones, and dark eyes. One often encounters Indians with the "hooked" nose, downturned lower lip, and almond-shaped eyes characteristic of profiles depicted by ancient artists, and Sylvanus Morley observed that "many of the modern Maya of Yucatán so closely resemble the figures on monuments and in paintings that they could have served as models for them."

A poignant example of how deeply the Maya venerate their plundered heritage was demonstrated by a remarkable event which took place in an underground cavern in Yucatán known as Balankanché. Situated barely four miles east of Chichén Itzá, this tunnellike cave had been explored by archaeologists and local Indians for years. But in 1960 an amateur speleologist and part-time guide at the Mayaland Hotel at Chichén Itzá—José Humberto Gomez—unexpectedly stumbled upon a previously overlooked passageway sealed with tightly cemented stones.

After breaking open the wall, Gomez squeezed through a narrow chamber leading into a maze of winding vaults. At the end of this tortuous corridor he found a large grotto, its ceiling covered with glistening stalactites. Near the center of the room these encrustations reached the floor and formed what seemed to be a gigantic pillar supporting the roof. No sooner had he entered the chamber than his flashlight revealed a breathtaking spectacle: scattered about were

Design from a ceramic vase, Northern Petén. (After Anton.)

dozens of pottery vessels, incense burners, miniature *metates* and *manos,* and similar offertory objects too numerous to distinguish in the darkness.

Aware of the significance of his discovery, Gomez notified Fernando Barbachano, the owner of the Mayaland Hotel, who in turn alerted officials in Mérida and the archaeologist E. Wyllys Andrews, director of the Tulane University-National Geographic Society expedition then excavating at Dzibilchaltún. When Gomez led investigators back to the cavern to view his findings, the sight confronting them far exceeded their expectations. Recalling his first impression of the grotto, Andrews wrote:

> The tiny tunnel suddenly opened into a small chamber facing a vertical wall of slippery rock which could be negotiated only by climbing a rope which Gomez had secured to a stalactite above. From

here going was easier, over piles of fallen rock and along flat passageways of muddy clay, until suddenly we emerged into a great domed chamber. The ceiling was coated with millions of tiny stalactites, the point of water on the tip of each winking back as the pencil rays of our headlamps cut through the blackness. Carved by nature in the great complex of stalactitic growth filling the center of the room was a deep niche which might have been the throne of some god. And we thought immediately of the cave's name: *Balankanché* in [Yucatec] means "Throne of the Balam" . . . a name given to the native priests in the last days before the Conquest. . . .

As the beams of our lights moved lower we saw that the pitted rock surfaces beneath the "throne" were literally covered with archaeological remains: brightly colored clay incensarios like nothing known before from the Maya area, beautifully carved stone cylinders showing women, warriors, and dancing figures with a wealth of detail, piles of pottery offerings—in short, an archaeological treasure trove.

While we were still standing with our mouths open, Humberto said, "This is only the first chamber." Before we had finished our inspection we saw three more groups of offerings, one even richer than the first. By morning when we staggered out of the cave, it was clear that we had seen one of the most striking and valuable discoveries in many years, and that immediate steps must be taken for its conservation. . . .

Accordingly, a joint effort by Tulane University, the National Geographic Society, and the Instituto Nacional de Antropología y Historia was launched to explore the cave. In spite of almost unbearable working conditions caused by excessive humidity and the lack of oxygen, a team of archaeologists, photographers, and artists spent five weeks excavating and studying its contents. Altogether over 600 artifacts were recovered, and some sections of the cavern had apparently been used as long ago as 1000 B.C. However, the most fascinating aspect of the discovery was the fact that the hidden grotto revealed by Gomez was actually a shrine to the Toltec rain god Tlaloc, the Mexican counterpart of the Maya deity Chac. Many of the objects in the vault bore Tlaloc's characteristic trademarks—exposed fangs, large ringed eyes, and a scroll-like device on the forehead—and the offerings had undoubtedly been placed in the cavern by the Toltecs sometime after their invasion of Chichén Itzá in the tenth century A.D.

Scarcely had work at the cave begun when a young Maya appeared on the scene. Introducing himself to Andrews as Romualdo Hoyil, he turned out to be an important *h-men* or native priest from the nearby village of Xkalakoop. Hoyil expressed eager interest in the newly discovered crypt, explaining how for generations his people had known of the existence of a secret *adoratorio* dedicated to the rain god, though no one had been able to locate it. After viewing the grotto and its offerings, he grew visibly excited and requested permission to conduct special religious ceremonies at the site without delay. "He then explained," Andrews wrote, "that the Chacs, gods of rain, whose sacred precincts had been violated, and the *balams*, guardians of the cave and the water sources, must be propitiated, not only to avoid retaliation on the individuals who had entered, but to insure against possible suffering on the part of the whole population. He insisted that the ceremonies begin the following day, and we, of course, agreed."

Soon after dawn the next morning the participants assembled at the cave. In addition to the scientific staff involved in the explorations, an expert in Yucatecan linguistics named Alfredo Barrera Vásquez, and Romualdo Hoyil, there were thirteen assistant priests who had been specially recruited for the occasion. Hoyil had taken particular care in collecting the necessary offertory items: thirteen hens, one turkey, thirteen black candles, two bottles of anise, thirteen jars of honey, plus copal incense, tobacco, corn, cloves, cumin, and other spices. The assistant priests were to be paid thirteen pesos apiece for their services, while Hoyil himself received fifty-two pesos. (Andrews pointed out the importance of the numbers thirteen and fifty-two in ancient Maya religion, especially fifty-two, which represented the cycle of years in the Calendar Round.) Hoyil announced that the ceremony would require twenty-four hours to complete, and no one would be allowed to leave until it was over. "We shuddered at the thought of twenty-four hours," recalled Andrews, "with twice the users of oxygen abetted by the smoke of incense, offerings, and tobacco. As it turned out our worst fears were short of reality."

Inside the grotto Hoyil instructed each of the priests to hold a candle and kneel in a circle around the huge stalactitic formation in the center of the room; everyone else was grouped together in the semidarkness behind them. On a makeshift altar two of the supplicants placed bowls of copal, tobacco, and maize, and when Hoyil was satisfied that the proper ritual code had been observed, the strange ceremony began. Slowly, in a low, solemn voice, the *h-men* chanted a curious prayer:

> *You then, my Lord! Thrice be honored, my Lord. You I humbly address—oh, my Lord. I am presenting my word to You then, my Lord, K'ulu Balam, greatly named by word, thrice be honored, my Lord, to You I give my word. So the warmth be cooled, my Lord, thrice be honored. . . .*

For hours the chanting droned on through a series of twenty-seven rites intended to placate the cave's guardian *balams* and the powerful rain god Chac. At the conclusion of each ritual the celebrants paused long enough to drink a thick sweet beverage made of corn gruel and honey served in gourds, then the incantations resumed. Everything about the scene—the sound of the half-sung prayers, the smoking incense, the sweat-soaked bodies of the priests illuminated by candlelight—was vividly reminiscent of ceremonies which must have occurred in the grotto centuries ago when the Toltecs had gathered there to worship Tlaloc.

During the last act of the ritual, seven small boys ranging from four to eight years old were brought in to serve as imitators of frogs and tree toads, the earthly messengers of Chac who announced the coming of rain. Since this was part of the well-known Cha-Chac ceremony widely practiced in Yucatán, the children had been trained to skillfully reproduce the sounds made by various species, and throughout the remainder of the night they accompanied the *h-men*'s chants with a chorus of high-pitched croaking and clicking, an eerie counterpoint to his monotonous prayers.

When the ceremony finally ended, everyone was given branches cut from a bush to use in "sweeping" evil spirits out of the cavern. As a final gesture the *h-men* symbolically "sealed" its entrance with a chant, ordering it closed to everyone for a period of forty-eight hours. To reenter before then, he warned, would risk the vengeance of its guardian spirits.

Outside the cave a feast prepared by members of Hoyil's village awaited the exhausted participants. For many hours the turkey and thirteen hens designated as sacrifices—which were killed, cleaned, and wrapped in plantain leaves—had been cooking in underground ovens called *pib,* and these were served along with special cakes made of corn dough and spices as part of the festivities. In the tradition of ancient Maya banquets, large quantities of *balché* brewed from fermented maize, *balché* bark, honey, and water were also consumed—its intoxicating properties well suited to bring men and gods into close contact.

And so the deities whose memory haunted the cave of Balan-kanché had been appeased. For perhaps a thousand years the grotto's secret had lain undisturbed, its existence only dimly recalled in folklore. Yet Romualdo Hoyil had honored the shrine as reverently as he would have done centuries ago, employing rituals he described as "intended for use in chambers hidden beyond the memory of man."

Elsewhere throughout the Maya realm similar acts of homage take place every day: ageless prayers are recited, copal incense is burned on crude altars, farmers seek the favor of earth gods before planting their *milpas,* and rituals are enacted in sacred shrines. Ironically, the Maya remain suspended between two contrasting worlds—ancient and modern—clinging stubbornly to threads linking them to remote depths of antiquity, to those unfathomed mysteries buried in the shattered, jungle-shrouded cities of their ancestors.

BIBLIOGRAPHY

 No attempt has been made to include all of the works consulted in the preparation of this book. Instead the references listed below are those I found particularly helpful and are intended to serve as a guide to further reading, with special emphasis on significant research during the last fifteen years.

Adams, Richard E.W. "Suggested Classic Period Occupational Specialization in the Southern Maya Lowlands," *Monographs and Papers in Maya Archaeology*, ed. by W.R. Bullard, Jr., *Papers of the Peabody Museum of Archaeology and Ethnology, Harvard University*, Vol. 61, 1970.

———. "The Collapse of Maya Civilization: A Review of Previous Theories," in *The Classic Maya Collapse*, ed. by T. Patrick Culbert, Albuquerque: University of New Mexico Press, 1973.

Andrews, E. Wyllys IV. "Dzibilchaltun: Lost City of the Maya," *National Geographic Magazine*, Vol. 115, No. 1, January, 1959.

———. "Excavations at Dzibilchaltún, Northwestern Yucatán, Mexico," *Proceedings of the American Philosophical Society*, Vol. 104, No. 2, 1960.

————. "Archaeology and Prehistory in the Northern Maya Lowlands," in *Handbook of Middle American Indians*, Vol. 2, ed. by Gordon R. Willey, Austin: University of Texas Press, 1965.

————. "Dzibilchaltún, A Northern Maya Metropolis," *Archaeology*, Vol. 21, No. 1, 1968.

————. "Balankanche—Throne of the Tiger Priest," *Explorers Journal*, Vol. 49, No. 4, 1971.

————. "The Development of Maya Civilization After Abandonment of the Southern Cities," in *The Classic Maya Collapse*, ed. by T. Patrick Culbert, Albuquerque: University of New Mexico Press, 1973.

Anton, Ferdinand. *Art of the Maya*, New York: G.P. Putnam's Sons, 1970.

Berlin, Heinrich. "El Glifo 'Emblema' en las Inscripciones Mayas," *Journal de la Société des Américanistes*, Vol. 47, 1958.

Blom, Frans. *The Conquest of Yucatan*, Boston: Houghton Mifflin Company, 1936.

————, and Oliver La Farge. *Tribes and Temples*, 2 vols. Middle American Research Series, No. 1, Tulane University, New Orleans, 1926.

Borhegyi, Stephan F. "Archaeological Synthesis of the Guatemalan Highlands," in *Handbook of Middle American Indians*, Vol. 2, ed. by Gordon R. Willey, Austin: University of Texas Press, 1965.

Bullard, William R., Jr. "Maya Settlement Patterns in Northeastern Peten, Guatemala," *American Antiquity*, Vol. 25, No. 3, 1960.

————. "Postclassic Culture in Central Peten and Adjacent British Honduras," in *The Classic Maya Collapse*, ed. by T. Patrick Culbert, Albuquerque: University of New Mexico Press, 1973.

Chamberlain, Robert S. "The Conquest and Colonization of Yucatán," *Carnegie Institution of Washington Publication*, No. 582, 1948.

Charnay, Désiré. *The Ancient Cities of the New World*, New York: Harper and Brothers, 1887.

Coe, Michael D. "La Victoria, An Early Site on the Pacific Coast of Guatemala," *Papers of the Peabody Museum of Archaeology and Ethnology, Harvard University*, Vol. 53, 1961.

————. *The Maya*, New York: Frederick A. Praeger, 1966.

————. *The Maya Scribe and His World*, New York: The Grolier Club, 1973.

Coe, William R. "A Summary of Excavation and Research at Tikal, Guatemala: 1956–61," *American Antiquity*, Vol. 27, No. 4, 1962.

———. "Tikal, Guatemala, and Emergent Maya Civilization," *Science*, Vol. 147, No. 3664, 1965.

———. "Tikal: Ten Years of Study of a Maya Ruin in the Lowlands of Guatemala," *Expedition*, Vol. 8, No. 1, 1965.

Covarrubias, Miguel. *Indian Art of Mexico and Central America*, New York: Alfred A. Knopf, 1957.

Duby, Gertrude, and Frans Blom. "The Lacandon," in *Handbook of Middle American Indians*, Vol. 7, ed. by Evon Z. Vogt, Austin: University of Texas Press, 1969.

Dutton, Bertha P. "Tula of the Toltecs," *El Palacio*, Vol. 62, 1955.

Ediger, Donald. *The Well of Sacrifice*, Garden City: Doubleday and Company, 1971.

Ekholm, Gordon F. "Transpacific Contacts," in *Prehistoric Man in the New World*, ed. by J.D. Jennings and E. Norbeck, Rice University Semicentennial Publications, Chicago: University of Chicago Press, 1964.

Gallenkamp, Charles. *Maya: The Riddle and Rediscovery of a Lost Civilization*, New York: David McKay Company, 1959.

Gann, T.W.F. *Maya Cities, A Record of Exploration and Adventure in Middle America*, London: Gerald Duckworth & Co., 1927.

Girard, Rafael. *Los Mayas Eternos*, Mexico, D.F.: Antigua Libreria Robredo, 1962.

Gordon, George B. "Prehistoric Ruins of Copán, Honduras," *Memoirs of the Peabody Museum of Archaeology and Ethnology, Harvard University*, Vol. 1, No. 1, 1896.

Haviland, William A. "Prehistoric Settlement at Tikal," *Expedition*, Vol. 7, No. 3, 1965.

———. "Ancient Lowland Maya Social Organization," *Middle American Research Institute Publication, Tulane University, Publication No. 26*, 1968.

———. "Tikal, Guatemala, and Mesoamerican Urbanism," *World Archaeology*, Vol. 2, No. 2, 1970.

Heine-Geldern, Robert. "The Problem of Transpacific Influences in Mesoamerica," in *Handbook of Middle American Indians*, Vol. 4, ed. by Gordon F. Ekholm and Gordon R. Willey, Austin: University of Texas Press, 1966.

Hurtado, Eusebio Dávalos. "Return to the Well of Sacrifice," *National Geographic Magazine*, Vol. 120, No. 4, October, 1961.

Kelley, David H. "Glyphic Evidence for a Dynastic Sequence at Quiriguá, Guatemala," *American Antiquity*, Vol. 27, No. 3, 1962.

————. "A History of the Decipherment of Maya Script," *Anthropological Linguistics*, Vol. 4, No. 8, 1962.

Kidder, Alfred V, Jesse D. Jennings, and Edwin M. Shook. "Excavations at Kaminaljuyú, Guatemala," *Carnegie Institution of Washington, Publication No. 561*, 1946.

Knorozov, Yuri V. "The Problem of the Study of the Maya Hieroglyphic Writing," *American Antiquity*, Vol. 23, No. 3, 1958.

Landa, Diego de. "Relación de las Cosas de Yucatán," translated and edited by Alfred M. Tozzer, *Papers of the Peabody Museum of Archaeology and Ethnology, Harvard University*, Vol. 18, 1941.

Littlehales, Bates. "Treasure Hunting in the Deep Past," *National Geographic Magazine*, Vol. 120, No. 4, October, 1961.

Lothrop, Samuel K. *Treasures of Ancient America: The Arts of the Pre-Columbian Civilizations from Mexico to Peru*, Geneva: Albert Skira, 1964.

MacNeish, Richard S. "The Origin of New World Civilization," *Scientific American*, Vol. 211, No. 5, 1964.

————. "The Food-gathering and Incipient Agriculture Stage of Prehistoric Middle America," in *Handbook of Middle American Indians*, Vol. 1, ed. by Robert C. West, Austin: University of Texas Press, 1964.

McQuown, Norman A. "The Classification of Maya Languages," *International Journal of American Linguistics*, Vol. 22, 1956.

Maler, Teobert. "Researches in the Central Portion of the Usumatsintla Valley: Report of Explorations for the Museum, 1898–1900," *Memoirs of the Peabody Museum of Archaeology and Ethnology, Harvard University*, Vol 2, Nos. 1 & 2, 1901–3.

————. "Explorations of the Upper Usumatsintla and Adjacent Regions," *Memoirs of the Peabody Museum of Archaeology and Ethnology, Harvard University*, Vol. 4, No. 1, 1908.

————. "Explorations in the Department of Petén: Tikal," *Memoirs of the Peabody Museum of Archaeology and Ethnology, Harvard University*, Vol. 5, No. 1, 1911.

Mangelsdorf, Paul C., Richard S. MacNeish, and Gordon R. Willey. "Origins of Agriculture in Middle America," in *Handbook of Middle American Indians*, Vol. 1, ed. by Robert C. West, Austin: University of Texas Press, 1964.

Marden, Luis. "Dzibilchaltun: Up From the Well of Time," *National Geographic Magazine*, Vol. 115, No. 1, January, 1959.

Marquina, Ignacio. *Arquitectura Prehispánica*, Mexico, D.F.: Instituo Nacional de Antropología y Historia, 1951.

Mason, J. Alden. "The American Collection of the University Museum: The Ancient Civilizations of Middle America," *Bulletin of the University of Pennsylvania Museum*, Vol. 10, Nos. 1 & 2, 1943.

Maudslay, Alfred P. *Archaeology: Biologia Centrali-Americana*, 5 vols. London: Porter and Dulau & Company, 1889–1902.

Morley, Sylvanus G. "The Inscriptions at Copán," *Carnegie Institution of Washington Publication No.* 219, 1920.

———. "The Inscriptions of Petén," 5 vols., *Carnegie Institution of Washington Publication No.* 437, 1938.

———. *The Ancient Maya*, Stanford: Stanford University Press, 1946.

———. *The Ancient Maya*, 3rd. edition, revised by George W. Brainerd, Stanford: Stanford University Press, 1956.

Morris, Earl H. *The Temple of the Warriors*, New York: Charles Scribner's Sons, 1931.

———, Jean Charlot, and Ann Axtell Morris. "The Temple of the Warriors at Chichén Itzá, Yucatán," *Carnegie Institution of Washington Publication No.* 406, 1931.

Pollock, Harry, E.D. "Architecture of the Maya Lowlands," in *Handbook of Middle American Indians*, Vol. 2, ed. by Gordon R. Willey, Austin: University of Texas Press, 1965.

———, Ralph L. Roys, Tatiana Proskouriakoff, and A. Ledyard Smith. "Mayapán, Yucatán, Mexico," *Carnegie Institution of Washington Publication No.* 619, 1962.

Proskouriakoff, Tatiana. "An Album of Maya Architecture," *Carnegie Institution of Washington Publication No.* 558, 1946.

———. "A Study of Classic Maya Sculpture," *Carnegie Institution of Washington Publication No.* 593, 1950.

———. "Historical Implications of a Pattern of Dates at Piedras Negras, Guatemala," *American Antiquity*, Vol. 25, No. 4, 1960.

———. "The Lords of the Maya Realm," *Expedition*, Vol. 4, No. 1, 1961.

———. "Sculpture and Major Arts of the Maya Lowlands," in *Handbook of Middle American Indians*, Vol. 2, ed. by Gordon R. Willey, Austin: University of Texas Press, 1965.

Rands, Robert L. "The Classic Collapse in the Southern Maya Lowlands," in *The Classic Maya Collapse*, ed. by T. Patrick Culbert, Albuquerque: University of New Mexico Press, 1973.

Recinos, Adrián, Delia Goetz, and Sylvanus G. Morley. *Popol Vuh: The Sacred Book of the Ancient Quiché Maya*, Norman: University of Oklahoma Press, 1950.

————, and Delia Goetz. *The Annals of the Cakchiquels*, Norman: University of Oklahoma Press, 1953.

Ricketson, Oliver G., and Edith B. Ricketson. "Uaxactún, Guatemala, Group E 1926–1937," *Carnegie Institution of Washington Publication No. 477*, 1937.

Rivet, Paul. *Maya Cities*, Paris: A. Guillot, 1954.

Roys, Ralph L. *The Ethno-Botany of the Maya*, Middle American Research Series, Publication No. 2, Tulane University, New Orleans, 1931.

————. "The Indian Background of Colonial Yucatan," *Carnegie Institution of Washington Publication No. 548*, 1943.

————. "Lowland Maya Native Society at Spanish Contact," in *Handbook of Middle American Indians*, Vol. 3, ed. by Gordon R. Willey, Austin: University of Texas Press, 1965.

————. *The Book of Chilam Balam of Chumayel*, Norman: University of Oklahoma Press, 1967.

Ruppert, Karl, J. Eric S. Thompson, and Tatiana Proskouriakoff. "Bonampak, Chiapas, Mexico," *Carnegie Institution of Washington Publication No. 602*, 1955.

Ruz Lhuillier, Alberto. "The Mystery of the Temple of the Inscriptions," *Archaeology*, Vol. 6, No. 1, 1953.

————. "Mystery of the Mayan Temple," translated by J. Alden Mason, *The Saturday Evening Post*, August 29, 1953.

Sabloff, Jeremy A., and Gordon R. Willey. "The Collapse of Maya Civilization in the Southern Lowlands: A Consideration of History and Process," *Southwestern Journal of Anthropology*, Vol. 23, No. 4, 1967.

Sahagún, Fray Bernardino de. *Florentine Codex: General History of the Things of New Spain*, 12 vols. Translated by Arthur J.O. Anderson and Charles E. Dibble, Santa Fe: School of American Research, 1950–69.

Sanders, William T. "The Cultural Ecology of the Lowland Maya: A Reevaluation," in *The Classic Maya Collapse*, ed. by T. Patrick Culbert, Albuquerque: University of New Mexico Press, 1973.

Satterthwaite, Linton. "Calendrics of the Maya Lowlands," in *Handbook of Middle American Indians*, Vol. 3, ed. by Gordon R. Willey, Austin: University of Texas Press, 1965.

————, and Elizabeth K. Ralph. "New Radiocarbon Dates and the Maya Correlation Problem," *American Antiquity*, Vol. 26, No. 2, 1960.

Saul, Frank P. "Disease in the Maya Area: The Pre-Columbian Evidence," in *The Classic Maya Collapse*, ed. by T. Patrick Culbert, Albuquerque: University of New Mexico Press, 1973.

Sharer, Robert J., and David W. Sedat. "Monument 1, El Porton, Guatemala and the Development of Maya Calendrical and Writing Systems," *Contributions of the University of California Archaeological Research Facility*, No. 18, August, 1973.

Shook, Edwin M. "Tikal Stela 29," *Expedition*, Vol. 2, No. 2, 1960.

————, and Alfred V. Kidder. "Mound E-III-3, Kaminaljuyú, Guatemala," *Carnegie Institution of Washington Publication No.* 596, 1952.

Smith, Robert E., and James C. Gifford. "Pottery of the Maya Lowlands," in *Handbook of Middle American Indians*, Vol. 2, ed. by Gordon R. Willey, Austin: University of Texas Press, 1965.

Soustelle, Jacques. *Mexico: Prehispanic Paintings* (Preface), New York: New York Graphic Society in cooperation with UNESCO, 1958.

————. *Arts of Ancient Mexico*, New York: The Viking Press, 1967.

Spinden, Herbert J. *Maya Art and Civilization*, Indian Hills, Colorado: The Falcon's Wing Press, 1957.

Stephens, John Lloyd. *Incidents of Travel in Central America, Chiapas, and Yucatan*, 2 vols. Edited by Richard L. Predmore, New Brunswick: Rutgers University Press, 1949.

————. *Incidents of Travel in Yucatan*, 2 vols. Edited by Victor W. von Hagen, Norman: University of Oklahoma Press, 1962.

Teeple, John E. "Maya Astronomy," *Carnegie Institution of Washington, Contributions to American Archaeology*, No. 2, 1930.

Thompson, Edward H. *People of the Serpent*, Boston: Houghton Mifflin Company, 1932.

Thompson, J. Eric S. *Maya Hieroglyphic Writing: An Introduction*, 2nd. edition, Norman: University of Oklahoma Press, 1960.

————. *A Catalog of Maya Hieroglyphs*, Norman: University of Oklahoma Press, 1962.

————. "Archaeological Synthesis of the Southern Maya Lowlands," in

Handbook of Middle American Indians, Vol. 2, ed. by Gordon R. Willey, Austin: University of Texas Press, 1965.

―――. "Maya Hieroglyphic Writing," in *Handbook of Middle American Indians*, Vol. 3, ed. by Gordon R. Willey, Austin: University of Texas Press, 1965.

―――. *The Rise and Fall of Maya Civilization*, Norman: University of Oklahoma Press, 1954.

―――. *Maya History and Religion*, Norman: University of Oklahoma Press, 1970.

―――. "A Commentary on the Dresden Codex," *Memoirs of the American Philosophical Society*, Vol. 93, 1972.

Tozzer, Alfred M. *A Comparative Study of the Mayas and the Lacandones*, New York: Macmillan & Company, 1907.

Vogt, Evon Z. "Some Aspects of Zinacantan Settlement Patterns and Ceremonial Organization," *Estudios de Cultura Maya*, Vol. 1, 1961.

―――. "Some Implications of Zinacantan Social Structure for the Study of the Ancient Maya," *Actas y Memorias del XXXV Congreso Internacional de Americanistas*, Vol. 1, 1964.

Von Hagen, Victor W. *Maya Explorer: John Lloyd Stephens and the Lost Cities of Central America and Yucatán*, Norman: University of Oklahoma Press, 1947.

Von Winning, Hasso. *Pre-Columbian Art of Mexico and Central America*, New York: Harry N. Abrams, 1968.

Wauchope, Robert. "Modern Maya Houses: A Study of Their Archaeological Significance," *Carnegie Institution of Washington Publication No.* 502, 1938.

―――. *Lost Tribes & Sunken Continents: Myth and Method in the Study of American Indians*, Chicago: University of Chicago Press, 1962.

―――. "Southern Mesoamerica," in *Prehistoric Man in the New World*, ed. by J.D. Jennings and E. Norbeck, Rice University Semicentennial Publications, Chicago: University of Chicago Press, 1964.

―――. *They Found the Buried Cities*, Chicago: University of Chicago Press, 1965.

Webb, Malcolm C. "The Peten Maya Decline Viewed in the Perspective of State Formation," in *The Classic Maya Collapse*, ed. by T. Patrick Culbert, Albuquerque: University of New Mexico Press, 1973.

Willey, Gordon R. "The Structure of Ancient Maya Society: Evidence from the Southern Lowlands," *American Anthropologist*, Vol. 58, No. 5, 1956.

———. *An Introduction to American Archaeology*, Vol. 1, *North and Middle America*, Englewood Cliffs: Prentice-Hall, 1966.

———, and William R. Bullard. "Prehistoric Settlement Patterns in the Maya Lowlands," in *Handbook of Middle American Indians*, Vol. 2, ed. by Gordon R. Willey, Austin: University of Texas Press, 1965.

———, and Demitri B. Shimkin. "The Maya Collapse: A Summary View," in *The Classic Maya Collapse*, ed. by T. Patrick Culbert, Albuquerque: University of New Mexico Press, 1973.

———, and A. Ledyard Smith. "New Discoveries at Altar de Sacrificios, Guatemala," *Archaeology*, Vol. 16, No. 2, 1963.

———, and A. Ledyard Smith. "The Ruins of Altar de Sacrificios, Department of Petén, Guatemala: An Introduction," *Papers of the Peabody Museum of Archaeology and Ethnology, Harvard University*, Vol. 62, No. 1, 1969.

INDEX

Abaj Takalik, 66, 67
Acosta, J. R., 157
Adultery, punishment of, 121
Adams, Richard E. W., 125
Afterlife, belief in, 128
Agriculture: contemporary Maya practice of, 191; crops, 26, 29, 123-24, 141; development in America, 56; in Maya Formative period, 59; *milpa* system as cause of Maya decline, 139-41; techniques and tools, 122-23
Ah Canul mercenaries, 182, 184, 186
Ah Kinchil (sun god), 102
Ah Puch (god of death), 102, 104 (illus.)
Ah Ulil (Izamal chieftain), 182
Ah Xupan (Xiu lord), 182

Aké, 38
Altar de Sacrificios, 58, 145, 147
Alvarado, Pedro de, 4
Amebic dysentery, 8
Andrews, E. Wyllys, 151-52, 192-94
Animals, domesticated, 124
Annals of the Cakchiquels, 12
Aqueducts, 79
Architecture: astronomical observatories, 37, 79, 152; building materials, 80; corbeled arch, 27, 29, 62, 80, 82 (illus.), 184; features of, in Classic period, 67, 78-80; in Formative period, 57-58, 61-62; habitations, 57-58, 121, 124; interiors, 78-79; in late Classic period, 146; preparation of land for, 80; substructures, 80; stylistic disintegra-

illustrations for *Incidents of Travel in Central America, Chiapas and Yucatan*, 37; Palenque expedition, 32–35, 89; Quiriguá discovered, 31–32; Uxmal explorations, 35–38
Ceiba tree in Maya cosmology, 103
Ceramics. *See* Pottery and ceramics
Ceremonial events, 105
Chac (rain god), 66, 76, 102, 103, 104, (illus.); abode in Sacred Cenote, 164; contemporary veneration of, 194–96. *See also* Tlaloc
Chac Xib Chac (chieftain of Chichén Itzá), 181–82
Chacmools, 154, 157
Charles V of Spain, 8, 187
Charnay, Désiré, 156–57
Chenes district, 150–52
Chi, Gaspar Antonio, 15, 121
Chiapas, Mexico, contemporary Maya in, 189
Chichén Itzá, 5, 37, 48, 84, 149, 151; architecture of, 152–54 (*see also* El Caracol, El Castillo, Temple of the Jaguars, of Kukulcán, of Chacmool); Ball Court, 37, 152; center of "New Empire," 163, 164; decline of, 179, 181–82; in League of Mayapán, 180; Mercado, 115, 152; Mexican influences, 160–61; name, meaning of, 169–70; Sacred Cenote (*see* Sacred Cenote); sculptural motifs in, 154, 157, 161; Toltec-Itzá colonization and influences, 160–63; Tomb of the High Priest, 166–68
Chicomecóatl (maize goddess), 163
Chilam Balam, Books of, 12, 17, 51, 154, 160, 179, 180, 181, 187
Childbearing, 105; death of mother in, 128; patron goddess of, 102, 117
Chol tribe, 189
Chontal tribe, 161

Chorti tribe, 190
Christian missionary activity among Maya, 5–6, 8–10, 90
Chronology of Maya history: Goodman-Martínez-Thompson system, 52–53; Spinden system, 53; table of, 54. *See also* Calendar and calendrics
Chuh tribe, 190
Chutixtiox, defenses of, 187
Cimatán, as commercial center, 115
Cities: ball courts, 79; baths, 79; bridges, 79; collapse of, in central area, 138–49; collapse of, in Yucatán, 151–52, 186–87; in Late Classic period, 145; layout of, 76, 122, 150; water and drainage systems, 79, 122
Classic period: flowering of, 69–70; Late Classic, 144–46; "Old Empire" theory, 149–50; regional uniformity of, 70; in southern highlands, 67–69; in Yucatán, 151
Climate. *See* Environmental conditions
Cloth and clothing: cotton used for, 58, 85; feathers used for, 85; of modern Maya, 191; patron goddess of weaving (Ix Chel), 102; of peasant class, 122
Cobá, 80, 188
Cocom dynasty of Mayapán, 14, 181–82, 186
Codices. *See* Maya literature: Codices
Coe, Michael D., *The Maya,* 161
Cogolludo, Diego López de, *Historia de Yucatán,* 15
Colors, symbolism of, 98, 103
Columbus, Christopher, 3
Comalcalco, 188
Commerce and trade, 107, 114–15; centers of, 115, 163; marketplaces, 115, 190